Gender, Identifications, and Identities

Gender, Identifications, and Identities considers the increasing visibility of sexual and gender diversity and reflects on how this is felt within psychoanalysis.

The international contributors focus on identifications, gender, and identity, including gender and sexuality in psychic development, as well as the link between identifications, body, and gender. The book also considers how gender fluidity can be a challenge for approaching the coexistence of different states of the self, as well as transference–countertransference experiences and implications, working through and implications for theory and technique. It offers an opportunity to air conflicting psychoanalytic views and rethink established concepts.

Gender, Identifications, and Identities will be key reading for psychoanalysts and psychotherapists in practice and in training. It will also be of interest to academics of psychoanalytic studies and gender studies.

Frances Thomson-Salo, Ph.D., is a training adult and child psychoanalyst and the European co-chair of the IPA Sexual and Gender Diversity Studies Committee.

Luca Bruno, Ph.D., is a psychologist and psychoanalyst in Milan. He is a member of the Italian Psychoanalytical Society and the IPA European Committee on Sexual and Gender Diversity Studies.

Eva Reichelt is a psychiatrist and psychoanalyst in Berlin. She is a member of the German Psychoanalytical Association and the IPA European Committee on Sexual and Gender Diversity Studies.

IPA Sexual and Gender Diversity Series
Series Editor: Leticia Glocer Fiorini

Gender, Identifications, and Identities

Dialogues at the Edges

Edited by Frances Thomson-Salo, Luca Bruno, and Eva Reichelt

Routledge
Taylor & Francis Group

LONDON AND NEW YORK

First published 2026
by Routledge
4 Park Square, Milton Park, Abingdon, Oxon OX14 4RN

and by Routledge
605 Third Avenue, New York, NY 10158

Routledge is an imprint of the Taylor & Francis Group, an informa business

British Library Cataloguing-in-Publication Data
A catalogue record for this book is available from the British Library

ISBN: 978-1-032-87778-5 (hbk)
ISBN: 978-1-032-87781-5 (pbk)
ISBN: 978-1-003-53444-0 (ebk)

DOI: 10.4324/9781003534440

Typeset in Palatino
by KnowledgeWorks Global Ltd.

Contents

Acknowledgements

Material from *Blutbuch* by Kim de l'Horizon is included here by the kind permission of DuMont Buchverlag. Kim de l'Horizon, "Blutbuch" © DuMont Buchverlag, Cologne.

Contributors and editors

Dana Amir, Ph.D., is a clinical psychologist, supervising and training *analyst,* Israel Psychoanalytic Society, full professor, vice dean for research and head of the interdisciplinary doctoral program in psychoanalysis at Haifa University, editor in chief of *Maarag.* She is the author of six poetry books, two memoirs in prose and four psychoanalytic non-fiction books. She is the winner of many literary as well as academic prizes, including five international psychoanalytic awards.

Laura Balottin is a clinical psychologist, child and adolescent psychotherapist, and psychoanalyst of the Italian Psychoanalytic Society, and works in Milano. After receiving her Ph.D. in clinical psychology, she carried out research and taught General and Developmental Psychopathology in the master's degree course in Clinical Psychodynamic Psychology at the University of Padua.

Tiziana Bastianini is a supervising and training psychoanalyst, Italian Psychoanalytic Society, and was President of the Psychoanalytic Centre of Rome. She has extensive experience in psychiatric contexts for the care of psychotic patients, director for the Lazio Region of various training projects about the contribution of psychoanalysis to the care of serious patients.

Simonetta Bonfiglio is a psychologist, psychoanalyst, and a full member of the SPI and the IPA, and an IPA child and adolescent psychoanalyst and is trained as a group psychoanalyst. She is President of the Centro Milanese di Psicoanalisi, a trainer and supervisor in public institutions. She has published works on adolescence, body issues, countertransference, and family bonds.

Davide Bruno, M.D., Ph.D., is a psychiatrist at the Azienda Socio-Sanitaria Fatebenefratelli-Sacco in Milan and candidate of the Italian Society of Psychoanalysis. His interests include transcultural psychiatry, gender studies, and new forms of addiction. He has written for "Pensiero Scientifico editore" the book "Al di là della 180. Storie di migrati e psichiatria pubblica".

Luca Bruno, Ph.D., is a psychologist and psychotherapist, a member of SPI. He was a member of the IPA Sexual and Gender Diversity Studies Committee and has authored scientific publications on psychopathology, particularly on melancholy, narcissism, and perversion. He is interested in psychodiagnostics and is the current president of the Italian Rorschach Association.

Leticia Glocer Fiorini, M.D., is a training and supervising analyst, Argentine Psychoanalytic Association, current chair of the IPA Sexual and Gender Diversity Studies Committee. Professor of Gender Studies at the University of Buenos Aires, past APA President, past Chair of the IPA Publications Committee and the APA. Her paper, "The feminine position: a heterogeneous construction" was awarded the Celes Cárcamo prize.

Siri Erika Gullestad, Dr. philos., is a professor emeritus of clinical psychology, University of Oslo, and training and supervising analyst, former Head of Department, Department of Psychology, and former president of the Norwegian Psychoanalytic Association. In 2019, Gullestad received the Mary Sigourney Award. Currently, she is Chair of the IPA Research Committee.

Vittorio Lingiardi, M.D., is a full professor of Dynamic Psychology, Sapienza University of Rome, and a member of the International Journal of Psychoanalysis Editorial Board. His many publications include co-authoring the Psychoanalytic Diagnostic Manual with Nancy McWilliams. He was awarded the IPA Sigourney Award for "pioneering work in psychodynamic diagnosis and LGBTQ+ issues".

Paul E. Lynch, M.D. is a psychiatrist and psychoanalyst in private practice in Boston, and on the faculty of the Boston Psychoanalytic Society and Institute. During psychoanalytic training, he received the American Psychoanalytic Association's Karl A. Menninger Award and co-edited with Alessandra Lemma (2015), *Sexualities, Contemporary Psychoanalytic Perspectives* (Routledge).

Mauro Manica is a psychiatrist, a training psychoanalyst of the Italian Psychoanalytic Society, honorary member of the Italian Association of Analytical Psychology. In addition to various contributions in scientific journals, he has published several volumes on the psychoanalysis of serious pathologies, on analytical theory and technique. He received the IPA Tycho Award in 2009. He was editor of the *Rivista di psicoanalisi*.

Luisa Marino-Coe is a psychoanalyst, member of the Italian Psychoanalytic Society, and currently Chair of the Psychoanalyst Emigrating and Relocating Committee. She was formerly editor of the Italian Psychoanalytic Annual, co-authored *Reading Italian Psychoanalysis (Borgogno,*

Luchetti, Marino-Coe, 2016, Routledge), and won the American Board & Academy of Psychoanalysis Prize for best Edited book in 2016.

Paola Marion is a training and supervising analyst, Italian Psychoanalytic Society and child psychoanalyst. Past Chair of the IPA Outreach Committee for Europe and past Editor of the Rivista di Psicoanalisi, and her most recent book is *Il disagio del desiderio. Sessualità e fecondazione al tempo delle biotecnologi* (2017, Donzelli, *Sexuality and procreation in the Age of Biotechnology. Desire and its Discontents*, 2022, Routledge).

Eva Reichelt is a psychiatrist and psychoanalyst in Berlin, a member of the German Psychoanalytical Association and a member of the IPA European Committee on Sexual and Gender Diversity Studies.

Anat Schumann is a clinical psychologist, training psychoanalyst of the Israel Psychoanalytic Society. She teaches in various psychoanalytic and psychotherapy programs, including the training institute of the IPS. She received the 27th Frances Tustin International Prize (2024) for her paper "Encountering Otherness – On the Ability (and Inability) for Psychic Movement Within Sexual States of Mind".

Frances Thomson-Salo, Ph.D., is a training adult and child psychoanalyst, European co-chair of the IPA Sexual and Gender Diversity Studies Committee, Fellow of the International Journal of Psychoanalysis College, former Committee on Women and Psychoanalysis Chair, and Associate Professor, Department of Psychiatry, University of Melbourne, taught on the Masters of Mental Health Sciences for 20 years. She has written/edited 18 books, including *Engaging infants: Embodied Communication in short-term infant-parent therapy* (2018) and *Infant observation: Creating transformative relationships* (2014).

https://orcid.org/0000-0002-6577-5275

Series preface
IPA Sexual and Gender Diversity Studies Committee

With this volume we continue the *Sexual and Gender Diversity Series* project, edited by the IPA's Sexual & Gender Diversity Studies Committee. The aim of the series' project is to explore, expand, and update psychoanalytic thoughts focusing on today's sexual and gender migrations. This objective is part of the Committee's mandate to present debates and controversies in the psychoanalytic field in order to better understand contemporary changes on subjectivities.

This applies to the review of epistemological, theoretical, and clinical tools in the psychoanalytical field focusing on changes which demand continuing to develop new concepts and to reconsider others. By confronting them, we might find agreements and disagreements which should be worked through in an open dialogue. In this frame, our perspective is to grasp a contemporary and present point of view on these topics. At the same time, there are crucial axes of psychoanalysis from Freud's onwards that should be maintained.

There is a complex fabric which includes different psychoanalytic theories, different clinical approaches, and different cultures in the same or diverse latitudes. Certainly, the necessary intersection between psychic reality with otherness and culture runs throughout this proposal.

All these facts lead to set out relevant ideas and themes that were and are discussed by several psychoanalytic theories as well as by gender and post-gender theories. This approach inevitably includes the clarification of the logical and epistemic perspectives from which different proposals are read today. Listening to other viewpoints inevitably guides us to a better listening of our patients, especially of what is new and original, meaning a space of freedom both to analysts and to patients.

In this context, concordances can be found, but also divergences that should be sustained in tension in the perspective of exploring which are the effects of the crucial changes that are part of current societies. Indeed, this implies an extra work for the reader to illuminate these contradictions in a fruitful way. In this way, our purpose has been to go beyond a unique, uniform line of thought in order to sustain differences which each reader might process creatively, and surpass as well.

The S&GDS Committee's objective is to share these ideas with the psychoanalytic community and with professionals of other disciplines with the aim of generating a productive interchange between the text and the reader. We assume the challenge of displaying these debates that involve significant contributions to think about nowadays construction of subjectivity.

Lastly, our special acknowledgement to the authors for their outstanding contributions as well as to the Psychoanalytic International Association for their support to undertake this project.

Leticia Glocer Fiorini
Series Editor

Introduction

Luca Bruno, Eva Reichelt, and Frances Thomson-Salo

The International Psychoanalytic Association (IPA) set up the Sexuality and Gender Diversity Studies (SGDS) committee in 2017 under the Presidency of Stefano Bolognini to explore and create a place within organised psychoanalysis in which the many questions and complexities surrounding sexual and gender diversity could be studied. It has done this through the creation of study groups, the organising of scientific meetings on relevant topics, and publications. Leticia Glocer Fiorini (Buenos Aires) is currently the overall Chair and Frances Thomson-Salo (United Kingdom and Australia) is the co-chair of the European subcommittee which consisted of Luca Bruno (Italy), Eva Reichelt (Germany), Konstantinos Argyropoulos (Athens) as an IPSO member, and two consultants, Dana Amir (Israel) and Nicolas Evzonas (Paris).

Many of the papers in this book were presented at the Study Day, "Experiencing Gender Diversity in Psychoanalysis and beyond", in September 2023 in Milan, organised by the SGDS European subcommittee, together with the Italian Psychoanalytic Society. Those papers have been integrated with other papers presented by committee members and colleagues at Study days and European Psychoanalytical Federation conferences.

We are currently facing a significant cultural transformation in the broader West, in which the topic of *gender* can be seen to have taken the limelight. Psychoanalysis, due to the effective strength of a tradition that both created and improved several theories on sexualities, currently needs to develop theories of gender. Currently, *gender identity*, subject as it is to conflictual tensions, can be viewed as at a crossroad between nature, culture, and an individual's innate constitutional urges. Gender identity can be viewed as a key dimension of core identity, the path to integration of gender identity can be slow, conflicted and uncertain, with gender identity organised by exquisitely subjective aspects, by the complex intertwining of unconscious identifications relating to the relationship between mind and body, as well as by social and cultural elements, and gender roles acquired during one's personal history.

Gender variance is currently an important issue; it is positive that it is finally being explored and elaborated in the psychoanalytic milieu. People with sexual and gender variance are a heterogeneous group. For example, partially identifying with the term, genderqueer, can mean several things, including a person who identifies as both genders, as neither gender, nor with a different gender identity altogether – a unique personal composite, not limited by a binary. Many psychoanalytic colleagues in different countries seem to show a concerning lack of thinking about gender variance. Confusing ideas on these subjects may still appear, full of fear and prejudice. Likewise, the confusion-based overlapping between sex, gender, and affectional and erotic orientation is still widespread. The issues connected with gender variance currently represent an area for analytic investigation, as they are still largely obscure nowadays and deserve in-depth study.

Both the *prejudice* and ideas that are affected by conscious or latent homo–bi–trans-phobic positions can heavily influence mental well-being. Ingrained homo-, bi-, or trans-phobia can be regarded as a traumatic area, as the experiences it contributes to are produced by the outcomes of transgenerational trauma. Not only the serious expressions of violence (whether individual or social) but also the dilution or deprivation of rights for LGBTIQA+ people are the serious, sometimes tragic, consequences of homo- and trans-phobia. The IPA Committee acknowledges the harm caused by some forms of the so-called reparative psychotherapy to such people.

People with sexual and gender variance are increasingly seeking psychological help. The analysis of gender identity should be based first and foremost on a patient's statements, with the analyst offering a listening ear and providing help to individual existences, which, even as they may have some features in common with each other, experience a condition that should be wholly understood in its uniqueness.

The *regulatory ideals* connected with cisgender or heterosexual identity and a binary view of sexuality usually hinder resolution of the stigma towards people with gender nonconformity. Analysts usually move within a delicate border zone and may take an aprioristic stance, if they fail to suspend judgement and if they forget that psychoanalytic theories are not facts and should not be translated into medical or pedagogical indications. The dangers of regulations focused on binarism and cisgender identities, as well as rigid or defensive adoption of theories currently available to psychoanalysts, the lack of specific exploration of what happens in the therapeutic relationship, and the countertransference risk contributing to serious breakdowns and interruptions of an analysis.

Analysts, possibly in a more intense and conflictual way than how they work with heterosexual cisgender patients, find themselves revisiting their own childhood sexual orientation, their own psychic bisexuality, and their ability to integrate those male and female identifications conflicting with the binary aspects of biological sex and gender. They must carefully consider (albeit inevitably always under the double shadow of uncertainty and incompleteness) *their countertransference*, as it may contain unresolved identity conflicts and unprocessed anxieties about bodies and sexuality.

Transgender patients, as well as ones with *fluid gender identities,* may not only not show psychopathological aspects but may not even ask for a sex change by means of hormonal treatments and surgeries. Based on both clinical experience and the scientific studies on sexual identity, there is no evidence to pathologise any expression of gender. Many people with gender nonconformity remain well in touch with reality and do not deny the biological dimension of their sexuality. They seek an appropriate correspondence between their gender identity and their bodies instead. They look for unity and coherence as they deal with the inescapable aspects of pain and acknowledge and manage their limits, without distorting or avoiding deep aspects of their own identity and their way of loving because of that.

If Freud (1925) considered female sexuality to be the "dark continent", nowadays the multiple expressions of the identities connected with gender and sexuality make up a territory that is still poorly mapped, as well as some regions of the mind that are unexplored, unknown, or that we may risk ignoring, not least because of the fear that they may evoke in us. *Hic sunt leones?*

Such people almost never ask for psychoanalysis because of distress about their identity. Analysts get to identity issues step by step, by exercising significant tact and caution. Negative capability, waiting, suspension in uncertainty, and respectful listening are the cornerstone elements here. The issues of identity and the unconscious identification processes are importantly and complexly intertwined with body representations. The bodies of transgender and gender fluid patients are inhabited by *phantasms,* by some sexualised parts which are not completely rejected, but neither are they completely acknowledged. Such patients can be helped as they face conflicted parts of their sexuality, to approach psychic bisexuality again, thus representing and reintegrating the gender dysphoric aspects of their physicality into the self, as they begin to forgive parents, carers, and others who did not understand a patient's earlier struggles to understand him or herself with the result they inhibited, repressed and castrated vital and creatively expressive parts of themselves.

As psychoanalysts, we need to offer a safe space for listening to and acknowledging the pain and conflict that many of these patients experience as they search for their identity. What they feel is often conflicted, fragile, and uncertain, and essentially involves the very human desire to "be what and who we are" (and indeed, was this not the original goal of analysis, by any chance?), also where the body is concerned.

The situations that psychoanalysts are dealing with require them to identify some activities that may be significantly complex and conflictual in nature. These include the sexual sphere of any analyst, the *"sexual"* that Laplanche emphasises in its multiplicity, and which is built on both the infantile and the unconscious. And also, a particular way to listen to the body which interfaces with the anxieties connected to the passivity that Freud placed in the concept of "biological bedrock", itself a limit beyond which analysis often fails to enter in its exploratory and elaborative work, are particularly and massively stressed.

In the perspective appealing to a geography of spaces, there is an intermediate space between "inside" and "outside" that separates and unites them, an area that Winnicott calls "transitional". It is indeed an interstitial space, devoted to games, fantasy, creativity, and illusion. We rely on it to help our patients develop skills in symbolisation and internalisation that can prevail over the symptomatic recourse to acting out, while allowing them to carry out the integration between some unknown parts of the self.

As psychoanalysts, *the ethical focus* should be only on helping patients to connect with their wider knowledge of the self, while looking for their deepest and truest personalities, as well as their wish to live a sufficiently gratifying life, without forgetting the capacity to tolerate unavoidable human unhappiness. We hope that the scientific contributions here may help readers extend their experience involving thought and affection when applied to such delicate and complex psychological topics. Psychoanalysis also concerns a continuous process elaborating both mourning and disillusion. As many authors, such as Meltzer and Bion, have pointed out, such processes are more possible with an analyst's negative capacity, being able to tolerate the unknown and uncertainty, without hurrying and looking for explanations.

Metapsychology should always be attentive to interactions and relationships and adapted for this. Such an approach should never let theories prevail over both the associations created by patients and analysts, and the deep emotional experience taking place in sessions. We need a careful exploration of the unconscious dynamics of the two people in the consulting room and what happens between them. Having done this, it will then perhaps be possible to follow what should be the specific tension of psychoanalysis: the drive to know the motions of the unconscious and of deep emotional truths, while respecting both liberties and differences.

Reference

Freud, S. (1925). Some psychical consequences of the anatomical distinction between the sexes. *S.E.* 19: 241–258.

Part I
Gender and sexuality in psychic development

Introduction

Simonetta Bonfiglio

Today, the exploration of the origins of sexuality, its development and possible outcomes in the construction of identity and the subjectivation pathway, challenge and raise many questions for contemporary psychoanalysis (although we could say psychoanalyses). These topics were the subject of reflection, examination and discussion at a conference held in Milan on 9 September 2023 and the papers given on that occasion are included in this book. It was an intense meeting, like taking a walk in the enigmatic woods of sexuality and identities, dealing with the "mysterious leap" between mind and body, and wandering in the lands of the nature–culture dilemma. It was a walk with roadblocks and difficult parts, which belong to a broader ongoing debate in the psychoanalytic-scientific landscape.

Leticia Glocer Fiorini, Paul Lynch and Paola Marion address the issues of sexual development, gender identity and primary identifications and illustrate their main points, delving into the archaic times of origins and revisiting the Oedipus complex. Each of them takes original pathways, reaching important convergences. In particular, the three authors agree on the need for an expansion of theoretical resources for understanding and listening to patients who question the binary model with their requests and call for research that, by expanding the theoretical frontiers, can go hand in hand with an exploration of uncharted lands that require new tools to be explored. Glocer Fiorini clearly highlights the fears that are stirred by this challenge and forcefully argues how important it is to increase the capacity for observation and listening, without fear of losing the cornerstones of psychoanalytic theory – and we would say without fear of losing our own identity. It is a key and sensitive aspect, upon which Lynch and Marion also agree.

In 2002, in a book with the provocative title *La fin du divan?* (The End of the Couch?), Cahn pointed out – in the light of emerging complexities in treating borderline cases – the need and freedom for transformations that would respond to the call for help and the challenge of "continuing to be a psychoanalyst, by psychoanalytically ceasing to be one."

Change is inevitable in a living organism. Like a living language, psychoanalysis seeks and finds new words, uses new insights to represent

DOI: 10.4324/9781003534440-2

new organisations and new psychic emergencies. It is not possible, argues Glocer Fiorini, "to think new things with the same theoretical categories" that were useful earlier. In these chapters, we see some awareness of the potential tensions and defences that the necessary search for new ways and paradigms inevitably arouse. "Ramparts to be breached" (Glocer Fiorini) and "facets of bedrock" (Lynch) are mentioned. We may associate these images with the dangers of an earthquake shaking and destroying the theoretical cornerstones upon which we rely. Even for psychoanalysis, change and entering uncharted territory can appear catastrophic.

Perhaps it is no coincidence that the word "courage" is used several times. Bion opened a seminar in Italy by saying: "I am curious to hear what I will say today." A thought-provoking expression, a challenge, an invitation to approach the experience of knowledge and to explore new places by being open to curiosity when getting in contact with the unknown and tolerating perturbations without the assumption of knowing or sticking with knowledge defensively. These three authors and others make the same appeal. The former refer to the profound changes of contemporary times: the mutations in the construction of sexual subjectivity (Glocer Fiorini), the anthropological changes leading to new postmodern identities (Marion) and the changes in sexuality and the influence of family, culture and environment on the conscious and unconscious experience of gender and sexualities (Lynch).

Some 20 years ago, at the beginning of the new millennium, the Italian journal *Psyche* outlined new challenges, unprecedented scenarios of psychism, new dynamics, links and transformations in the subject, the family structure and society to be addressed, pointing to potential discontinuity with respect to the past. The journal issues were as follows: "Nuove identità" (*New Identities*) (2002), "Corpi e controcorpi" (*Bodies and Counterbodies*) (2003) and "Mutazioni antropologiche" (*Anthropological Mutations*) (2008). Thus, a new path was opened, and we have since taken it, pushing the horizon further. Marion mentions this when she recalls Axel Honnneth's interview on the new postmodern subject, characterised by multiple co-existing facets of identity, "fluidification" of psychic life and openness to ambiguity and multiplicity. The cover of "Anthropological Mutations" featured a work by Louise Bourgeois, an artist who explored male-female intersections and the fluidity of transitions, still an enigmatic theme.

Work is in progress, warns Paola Marion, and Tiziana Bastianini emphasises in quoting Freud how important it is not to take any *a priori* position, as a reminder of a necessary state of mind to address the task, implicitly indicating how difficult it is to authentically maintain an attitude open to research. Beyond our conscious will, we must deal with unconscious and uncanny aspects, which we must be able to monitor. Exchange and dialogue in the group we belong to and in the wider community are essential tools.

The topic we are dealing with is so delicate that Alessandra Lemma (2022) went so far as to speak of "moral panic that can unnecessarily interfere with thinking, just as being open and 'liberal' can lead us to gloss over the complexity of the issues" and "to silence suffering" (Marion). The risks of finding ourselves navigating between Scylla and Charybdis are thus outlined, with the danger of getting stranded or shipwrecked without even being able to get out to sea. Ethical, moral and theoretical issues as well as human and world views are all present and implicitly pervade the chapters.

In this respect, it is important to bear in mind just to what extent every psychoanalytic theory rests on an implicit conception of human nature. In the 1990s, Strenger (1997, 1989) initiated a debate about how analysts are inevitably affected by not only a cognitive but also profound attitude towards the human, in terms of clinical practice and theory formulation. This attitude, implicit in nature, is introjected by the patient "or enters the 'analytical field'," as Mauro Manica reminds us.

The way we look at the world has consequences for the way we relate to the world. In our professional identity, endorsing a theoretical model is necessarily also driven by inclinations that arise from within ourselves and our relationship with ourselves and the world, based on our orientation or our defence mechanisms, as well as our generational place in the culture of the time. It is part of our ethical responsibility, as psychoanalysts, to explore and acknowledge it. This issue, or rather the awareness of this dimension, runs beneath the surface in the three papers and is developed by referring to the indispensable work "on our countertransference and self-analysis… in order to avoid falling into moralism or a search for aetiopathogenesis" (Marion).

This is the backdrop to the chapters here, looking for the conditions and meanings of sexual and identity choices that "often appear so extreme and alien" (Marion). Glocer Fiorini has been working in this field for many years as a groundbreaking pioneer who forcefully advocates the need for an approach that, by overcoming the normative rigidity and implicit fixity of gender identifications in the Oedipus complex, leads to the paradigm of "complexity, multiplicity and heterogeneity" which sheds light on the authentic and specific functioning of the psyche.

Marion, in turn, takes up Glocer Fiorini's expression – "sexual and gender migrations" – to highlight a new geography of neo-sexualities, which are not necessarily part of an assessment of perversion. Sexual difference "is not erased, but must be included in a complex network, with different meanings across time and cultures" (Glocer Fiorini). Lynch urges us to overcome our "professional, traditional biases," which are often conveyed and confirmed by the terminology in use and justifies the appeal to replace the Oedipus complex with the concept of triangulation. Re-thinking the model, the idea of sexuality and perversion, to better understand the new postmodern subject is advocated by all.

By revisiting Freud, Glocer Fiorini thinks of an "expanded, trans-familial Oedipal model" that, while considering the intra-familiar, goes beyond it and considers cultural and transgenerational messages and their impact in transmission to the child. Relevant "enigmatic signifiers" (Laplanche), concerning sexuality and the gender assigned at birth, are central themes for understanding development. Marion addresses them as she considers the original unconscious projections between child and environment and the inescapable psychic decoding that the child must make, considering how "elusive and impenetrable" they are for the work of representation. Something can never be represented. Lynch in turn emphasises the impact of the unconscious, the enigmatic messages conveyed in early interactions, using Target and Fonagy's model of attachment and mentalisation with the interplay between physical caregiving and the caregiver's affective mirroring. It is a developmental model of "body and mind in a relational context" that leads to the "recognition of variety in Oedipal configurations" as being "clinically relevant."

For many decades, contemporary psychoanalysis has delved ever deeper into the terrain of the pre-oedipal, unrepressed unconscious, unthought experience, original experience, pre-natal and early interactions. It is the place of an experience that, although not yet or never represented, leaves an imprint on the body and development of the subject. Research has increased our knowledge about the development and vicissitudes of the self and has led to extensions and spin-offs in the clinical approach. The book edited by Bastianini, Ferruta, Guerrini Degl'Innocenti (2021), *Ascoltare con tutti i sensi* (Listening with all the senses) explores new ways of listening between "unconsciouses" to foster vital transformations.

Returning to the three authors, we observe extensive evidence of their consideration of the original and pre-oedipal experiences that range from the role and dynamics of primary identifications and the possible outcome in new forms of identity to the impact and meanings of the crisis, starting with the body, in adolescence – a second birth – where old experiences are revived with new and disruptive meanings.

Starting with the maternal and paternal functions, which can be performed independently of the gender of the parents, Glocer Fiorini uses the paradigm of "difference" to analyse the events of primary and secondary identifications. She emphasises the power of the "cultural imperative," which is intertwined with the parents' conscious and unconscious desires and expectations. "The child is identified" by desires and illusions transmitted by the parents. Gender assignment contains ongoing cultural changes, and intrapsychic identification occurs within complexity. What is the destiny of these early identifications? Pre-oedipal identifications leave a trace that re-emerges in adolescence: in the adventure of subjectivation and identity response, the adolescent will respond to new sensations, new drive demands where a blend of desire and gender identifications can express a circulation of enigmatic and "nonaligned" messages. It is during adolescence that the issue of gender, identity and the object of desire comes to the fore, in a combination of past and present, subjective and social imagery.

For Lynch, the clearest and most obvious understanding of normative, behaviourally binding messages, the censures from family and society are "dangers" that de-legitimise desires, cause anxiety and shame and inhibit sexual desires in intimate relationships. Lynch believes that the transition to oedipal development opens up fantasies, desire for triangular competition and object relations. This author focuses mainly on homosexual desires and the fallout of unconscious homophobic internalisations. Glocer Fiorini highlights the link between desire and gender and the consequences of dynamic psychic entanglements and movements: "Gender mandates bind desire; desire transcends gender mandates." The destiny of subjective becoming will be shaped by intrapsychic and interpsychic dynamics: the more flexible the gender identification, the freer the desire will be to flow and vice versa. Rigidity will hinder desire and the psychic freedom of subjectivation.

What is the price of suffering we should consider? As Marion points out, a task as a psychoanalyst in the face of patients suffering is to help them to bring to light the unconscious factors and their significance. An issue nowadays is an increasing call for help from adolescents, who are overwhelmed by powerful identity crises and dissociative states between sex and gender, often associated with transgender expectations or choices. This is a complex field that challenges both theories and assessment, strongly stirs countertransference and involves ethical stance and responsibility, which are considerably activated when we are faced with people who present destiny-related potential and risks.

In describing the clinical cases of two adolescents aged 16 and 17, Marion highlights the weight of primary identifications and archaic processes for understanding and exemplifies several outcomes in relation to different histories and organisations. For Matilde/Luz, grappling with the reactivation of conflicts and the rejection of their new sexed body, a potential space for initiating subjectivation and questioning themselves opens. For Gaia/Alex, the urgency and necessity of transition arises as the only "compensatory solution to a breakdown or to the aftermath of psychosis."

The authors outline a postmodern subject who is potentially open to a variety of different outcomes and identity transitions. It is interesting to emphasise the use of the term ambiguity in a positive sense (Glocer Fiorini, Marion) to indicate the strength and maturity of the subject capable of accessing the multiplicity and fluidity of the self. Racamier (1992) develops this concept originally, writing about "the eulogy of ambiguity" which he defines as "one of the most valuable virtues of the psyche... a quality that the psyche could not do without harmlessly, and without which our knowledge would not progress." He also quotes a dictionary definition: "Ambiguity is that which brings together two opposite qualities, and which simultaneously participates in two different natures."

These different qualities are not in contrast: "They come together, they do not clash...there is no dilemma, no conflict, the ambiguous is by nature of the order of the undecidable." And finally, "ambiguity is not confusion, which blurs everything and asserts nothing." Racamier's words are enlightening and very relevant to our reflections.

The balance between fluidity and stability is delicate and always at risk. The psyche also needs stability. Glocer Fiorini uses the metaphor of the anchor to represent her thought of "subjective identity in motion" and to indicate the protection required so that psychic life is not overwhelmed and disorganised. The identifying anchor is not "fixed and immovable." It keeps the boat safe and mobile at the same time, one can up anchor to sail to a different place.

At the end of the conference, I felt that the verb "to conclude" did not match the wealth of new perspectives, hypotheses and questions encountered in the dialogue between speakers and participants. A space for research and new challenges had opened. I would like to quote Marion's patient, who when confronted with the mysteries of her changing body: "I'd like to know what's wrong with my body. Maybe my body is telling me things I can't understand, and I'll understand them when the time is right." Her quest and her interrogation point to our research in progress.

References

Bastianini, T., Ferruta, A., & Guerrini Degl'Innocenti, B. (2021). *Ascoltare con tutti i sensi*. Roma: Giovanni Fioriti Ed.

Cahn, R. (2002). *La fin du divan?* Paris: Edition Odile Jacob.

Lemma, A. (2022). *Verso una pratica psicoanalitica basata sull'etica con gli individui transgender*, Lecture at the Centro Milanese di Psicoanalisi.

Racamier, P. C. (1992). *Le génie des origines. Psychanalyse et psychoses*. Paris: Edition Payot.

Strenger, C. (1989). The classic and the romantic vision in psychoanalysis. *International Journal of Psychoanalysis*, 70, 593–609.

Strenger, C. (1997). Further remarks on the classic and the romantic vision in psychoanalysis: Klein M., Winnicott D. and the ethic. *Psychoanalysis and Contemporary Thought*, 20, 207–243.

Journals

Nuove Identità (2002). *Rivista di cultura psicoanalitica*, X (1), Roma: Il Saggiatore.

Corpi e Controcorpi (2003). *Rivista di cultura psicoanalitica*, XI (1), Roma: Il Saggiatore.

Mutazioni antropologiche (2008). *Rivista di cultura psicoanalitica*, XVI (2), Roma: Il Saggiatore.

1 Sexuality and gender in development

Facets of bedrock and beyond*

Paul Lynch

I briefly review some aspects of psychoanalytic theories of gender and sexuality, particularly as they relate to psychosexual development. I will review some of the fluctuations in what has been and what may now be considered bedrock. Considering both body and mind in the development of psychosexuality, I will also consider influences from family, culture and the social environment on one's conscious and unconscious experience of gender and sexuality. This includes the developmental effects of pervasive binary idealisations of bifurcated masculinity and femininity, to maintain coherence in the social construction of gender ideals.

Much has changed in the realm of sexuality and gender since Freud's time, and yet, many of Freud's original body-focused terms persist in our common parlance – anal obsession, oral fixation, etc. As psychoanalytic theory evolved from the body and drive to the increasingly more abstract concepts of object relations, ego- and self-psychology, and interpersonal and relational psychoanalysis, the language of the body, of infantile sexuality and of drive theory continued in psychoanalytic discourse, mostly unintegrated with the newer theories. The role of the body and biology in concepts of both gender and sexuality has competed with the role of the mind and social influences.

While some believe there was a simpler time when psychoanalytic theories about psychosexual development and gender were straightforward and clear, that is a fallacy. Theories of sexuality, the very heart of psychoanalysis, have been fragmented from the start. We've never had a comprehensive explanation of the developmental path from infantile sexuality to latency, the Oedipus complex and adult sexuality.

Freud (1905) knew this, and he didn't. He fluctuated in his Three Essays on the Theory of Sexuality between establishing such theoretical pathways and disrupting them, often diverging diametrically from his text in his

* Parts of this chapter are reworked from the published article, Lynch, P. E. (2022), Sexuality and Gender in Development: Facets of Bedrock and Beyond. In: McCann, D. (Ed.), *Same-Sex Couples and Other Identities: Psychoanalytic Perspectives.* Routledge.

DOI: 10.4324/9781003534440-3

footnotes. Consider, for example, the basic connection between the sexual instinct and the sexual object. Freud said, "We are thus warned to loosen the bond that exists in our thought between instinct and object. It seems probable that the sexual instinct is in the first instance independent of its object; nor is its origin likely to be due to its object's attractions." In loosening this bond between instinct and object, Freud disrupted the existing theories of sexuality. However, Freud apparently did not entirely appreciate the full force and effect of this concept of a sexual instinct fully independent of the sexual object, and as Davidson (1987) puts it, "Freud's mental habits never quite caught up with his conceptual articulations." Thus, rather than marking out a clear path from infantile erogenous zone sexuality to adult whole-object relations, Freud widened and blurred the developmental path by breaking the link between aim (drive) and object – even if at other times it appears that he still thought of them as inter-dependent.

Freud emphasised that we are born with a constitution which varies from one to another in its biological or physiological components and that our constitution interacts with our various accidental experiences arising in the family and environment. Since neither constitution nor experience alone can predict a sexual outcome, we are hard pressed to outline any individual's path, even in retrospect, due to the number of variables involved in the interaction of constitution and experience. Lacking reliable knowledge of what guides any one individual on the path from infantile sexuality to adult sexuality, psychoanalysts nonetheless retain Freud's idea that adult sexuality only makes sense as an iteration of earlier experience. Ironically, it does seem obvious when we think about adult sexuality to trust that it is built on the residual effects of childhood experience, even though those building blocks are mostly obscure.

The contributions of many who followed Freud shifted the focus away from his roots of psychosexuality in physiology and the organs of the body. For example, Fairbairn's shift from "pleasure seeking" to "object seeking" diminished the bodily sexuality of the seeking. Melanie Klein's shift from pleasure and unpleasure to the good or bad breast also moved the primary emphasis of psychosexual development from the body and the drive to the object, and to the realm of fantasy. That "today's sexuality is not Freud's sexuality" is a sign that our discipline is still evolving. More recent work by Fonagy (2008) and Target (2007) brings together bodily drives with object relations, by theorising sexuality as an important component of object relations.

Roots of sexuality in body, mind and relationship

A mother most often tends to a child's physical and sensual needs without conscious awareness of sexuality, and at times, we psychoanalysts do much the same with our patients, despite the sexual foundations of psychoanalysis. Mary Target built on work that she and Peter Fonagy have done over many years in the realm of attachment between mother and child and laid out a developmental model of sexuality that holds together body and mind in a relational context. Essential to Target and Fonagy's model of development is the way that affective self-understanding develops out of primary object relationships in the processes of mother's mentalisation of the infant's affective states and her affective mirroring of them. As the infant's mind develops in the context of the caregivers' mentalisation, it is influenced by unconscious messages, or what Laplanche (1995) called "enigmatic signifiers" conveyed (unconsciously) as the earliest communication of the caregivers' unconscious feelings about sexuality and gender.

Target (2007) proposes a common failure of mirroring in relation to infantile sexual excitement. The infant experiencing sexual tension in the presence of a sensitive and responsive parent would generally not be offered a congruent, metabolised representation of his or her sexual excitement or pleasure, even though other feelings may be reflected in a mostly attuned way. Without mirroring, sexual excitement is poorly reflected or integrated in the growing child's sense of his social self. Target postulates that the unresolved, unmentalised and obscure state of childhood sexual feelings may provide the impetus in adolescence and adulthood to search for a partner outside the family with whom to express, share and potentially contain sexual excitement.

In the infant and caregiver milieu, which Laplanche calls the "Fundamental Anthropological Situation," most sexual communications are not conscious for the adults themselves – let alone for the infant who lacks the ability to understand the sexual dimensions that are unconsciously present during the acts of ordinary care. Because we are sense-making beings, Scarfone (2019) notes that we will always try to translate the obscure sexual elements, but "for lack of any possible 'code' regarding the Sexual, the child's interaction with the adult in this domain is necessarily clouded with enigmas." What we hear from adult patients then "comes cloaked under layers of translations, retranslations, displacements, sublimations, [and] fixated in character traits and symptoms."

Our innate sexuality is shaped by our experience – but mostly outside of our awareness, and therefore, it can repeatedly be experienced as both authentic and alien. It surprises us – feeling found, feeling new and exciting – with enigmas of the past repeatedly translated in the light of current experience. However, enigmatic signifiers of gender and sexuality are also affected by restrictive forces and cultural codes, what Evzonas (2020) has called "the normative unconscious at the root of repressions." He proposes a model of enigmatic messages to be translated, which considers an intersectional approach encompassing gender, ethnicity, social classifications, religion, etc. – considering power relations and cultural patterns of oppression.

Sexuality in the "Oedipal" mind

Once "Oedipal" development is in motion, we have a situation that involves desires that are not primarily physical, which now prominently involve fantasy – a fantasy that a small child could take the place of an adult as lover or mate of another adult and could be victorious in competition for the coveted position as the desired or chosen one. Oedipal development in 2025 is not necessarily about being male or heterosexual. However, essential elements of the myth, including desire, jealousy, fantasy and triangular competition, remain essential to our thinking about maturational development and the beginnings of more object-focused and less narcissistic relations. The dynamics of maturation, growth and change that we associate with the term "Oedipal" remain indispensable in clinical work, even though original bedrock assumptions about binary gender and compulsory heterosexual object choice have not stood the test of time in contemporary psychoanalytic thought. Recognition of variety in oedipal configurations is clinically relevant. Among others, Isay (1987) has written about the painful sequelae of empathic failure when families fail to recognise or engage with a homosexual child's affections for a same-sex parent. When the family can tolerate and play along with the "Oedipal" drama of romance, competition and aggression, as they typically do when daddy's little girl wants to marry daddy, then they assist the child to work out the disparities between wishful fantasies and reality. However, maturation and growth may be impeded if the family is not empathically attuned to the child's struggles or if they respond punitively to signals of sexuality or aggression (as they might, for example, if they suspect that their little boy has a special attraction to daddy).

From enigmatic signifiers to explicit dangers

As a child grows, psychosexual development gradually shifts from less enigmatic to more explicit forces – for example, the celebration of childhood behavioural expressions that conform to expected (heterosexual) norms, and the admonition of desires and behaviours deemed outside the norm. As censures from society compound those within the family, the young person who holds "de-legitimised" desires understands that it is dangerous to express oneself freely.

The danger in the environment is something that Freud warned about, yet regarding anti-homosexual bias in his cultural milieu, he often ignored what he knew about it. Freud (1923) told us that the ego serves three masters and is "consequently menaced by three dangers: from the external world, from the libido of the id, and from the severity of the super-ego. Three kinds of anxiety correspond to these three dangers since anxiety is the expression of a retreat from danger." Gulati and Pauley's (2019) reconsideration of Freud's "Leonardo Da Vinci and a Memory of His Childhood" demonstrates beautifully how Freud failed in writing this "pathography" to consider the dangers to Leonardo from his environment, including dangers well-known to Freud, and failed to consider the adaptive skills of Leonardo's psyche to cope with those dangers. Although Freud wrote in other places that homosexuality cannot be classified as an illness, Gulati and Pauley show that regarding Leonardo, he failed to fully comprehend the concept of a healthy homosexual. In another example of knowing and not knowing, Freud (1912) showed that excessive opposition to an adolescent's sexual object choices could lead to the sequestration of sexual pleasure and potency from loving intimacy. He described this Madonna/Whore phenomenon in detail about heterosexual men but failed to see how well suited his schema was for understanding the problems of love, sex and shame that some gay men struggle with.

If the family or the environment strongly opposes the youth's choice of new objects, it impedes the enjoyment of sensuality within affectionate, intimate relationships. For gay men who have trouble integrating intimacy with sex, I have emphasised the need for exploration of the shame and anxiety that results from the failure of the family or the social environment to sanction a homosexual boy's erotic desires. Excessive anxiety and shame over the danger of unacceptable desires leads to the sequestration of sexual desires from intimate relations and relegates the sexual to fantastic expression with unfamiliar or denigrated others (in anonymity, with strangers, etc.). While some clinicians still avoid the origins of such phenomena, or even dismiss sex without attachment as simple "perversion," I have found that appreciation and attention to the shame that underlies the disconnection is more useful to help patients work through it.

Gender: anatomy is destiny?

As with sexuality, psychoanalytic conceptions of gender began with a focus on the body and were troubled in later iterations by various emphases on social and environmental forces. Freud first used his famous phrase, "Anatomy is destiny," in 1912 to acknowledge the proximity and overlap of sexual organs with excremental organs, to emphasise the animalistic nature of sex. In 1924, he used it again in reference to the morphological smallness of the little girl's clitoris, as compared to the larger penis of a playfellow. He said this causes her to perceive that a wrong was done to her and is "a ground for inferiority." The errors of Freud's ways about understanding women have been well exposed and examined for decades. Yet, the base of Freud's point, that biology or anatomy affects psychic development and self-perception, was a cornerstone of early psychoanalytic theorising about gender and gender identity development, and it remains compelling for many today.

Second-generation psychoanalysts, including Karen Horney and Clara Thompson, argued that culture played a larger role than anatomy in determining who felt inferior rather than privileged, by determining which traits were regarded as valued and masculine, such as agency, strength and independence. They exposed gender as a cultural creation whereby social meanings were assigned to biological differences.

Despite the compelling arguments for social influence as a primary determinant of gendered personality, connections between biology and gender identity held their ground. Indeed, many of the developmental theorists who sought to understand female development from the perspective of the girl returned to anatomy. Concepts like core gender identity and primary femininity were introduced. Several prominent papers were published by female analysts about female genital anxiety, which focused significantly on the qualities of the girl's vagina. Bernstein (2003) wrote that a girl's fear of access to the genitals, fear of diffusivity and fear of penetration, "complicates the formation of ego boundaries and a firm sense of self." For Mayer (1995), conflicts about primary femininity were rooted not in the phallic castration complex or penis envy, but rather in fantasies of danger to the female genital.

Social construction and regulation of gender

I am certainly not being thorough, but I hope that I am conveying the way in which the material body has played and continues to play a role in what is thought about gender. This is the case despite persuasive postmodern arguments that the body is just a surface on which is inscribed a series of culturally determined meanings.

Butler (1990) argues that there is no essence of gender to be expressed and gender is nothing without its performative acts. There is no original masculine or feminine to be expressed or imitated. Rather than expressing something innate or inborn, gender is nothing more than a series of social significations inscribed on and performed by a body. In this schema, gender characteristics and gender acts are "the way in which a body shows or produces its cultural signification." Because "there is no preexisting identity by which an act or attribute might be measured; there would be no true or false, real or distorted acts of gender, and the postulation of a true gender identity would be revealed as a regulatory function." Butler's ideas are helpful in thinking both about the individual's use of binary gender traits for settling on a coherent identity and about the tensions in our current culture which denigrate outliers for the benefit of simplified, coherent norms. Butler shows that the differentiation of the gender binary is a process whereby the culture regulates and controls the boundaries, thereby creating "Others," and expelling or excreting people or traits which threaten to destabilise coherence. We end up with dirty or polluting people at the margins, who must be defined as "not us," not normal, and expelled from the inner world of our "normal" subjectivity. In this regard, Butler shows the social construction of gender to be a limiting and regulatory process. Here, we see some of the cover for violence, uncivil attempts to rid an individual or a society of its unwanted elements.

For the individual, these constricted processes of identification show themselves in a form that Butler refers to as "melancholy gender." In the process of incorporating identifications within the male or female binary, non-conforming identifications are repudiated. However, gendered identifications and desires that are not allowed into consciousness cannot be consciously repudiated or mourned. For example, under the forces of compulsory heterosexuality, one cannot admit knowledge of an early desire for a same-sex parent. Such desire is not consciously lost and mourned during development in our culture, but as Butler puts it, it is "foreclosed," as if it never existed. It requires vigilance to keep the knowledge or affective memory of its actual existence at bay, and thus, repetitive repudiation reifies that which is repudiated. Therefore, masculinity or femininity is haunted by that which it has repudiated outside of awareness – a melancholic identification is maintained with that which has been foreclosed. This process is easiest to see in clinical work when the repudiation is especially strong – in characters of extreme gender stereotypes, rigidly and desperately reaffirming their gendered identifications by aggressive repudiation of characteristics of the perceived "opposite sex."

Gender in foreground and background

Construction of gender in a field of many variables becomes a very personal project, and one in which we are all burdened by infantile ideals of masculinity and femininity that are ingrained in our social order. What Kaplan (1997) calls "The Perverse Strategy" is a defensive manoeuvre that involves a deception of self to protect against anxiety and painful knowledge about shame-filled identities and desires – particularly about our failures at gender purity. In her book about female perversions, she shows how socially normalised gender stereotypes are both the crucibles of the classic perversions, and central to all human behaviour. Kaplan shows that the manifest experience of gender stereotypes is used to foreground in consciousness a coherent and shameless gendered identity, as a deception to protect against anxiety about latent, shamed and disavowed aspects of oneself (often perceived as belonging to the opposite sex). One familiar example of the perverse strategy was described by Joan Riviere (1929) in Womanliness as Masquerade – where she wrote, "women who wish for masculinity may put on a mask of womanliness to avert anxiety and the retribution feared from men." Idealised femininity is performed then to deceive both performer and observer about the true motivations underlying the behaviour and to keep at bay anxieties over impure gender identities, to remain coherent gender-wise and keep oneself in the realm of the normal.

Kaplan states, "the fetishistic strategy is ubiquitous. It infiltrates every living situation." "A vivid foreground should be suspected of obscuring a background that is potentially threatening." As in Butler's melancholic gender, what cannot be conscious cannot be valued or mourned, and aspects of gender identities and same-sex attractions that are "foreclosed" by gender idealisations and heterosexist strictures are repeatedly renunciated in the performance of perverse strategies. With different styles, both Butler and Kaplan show that civil structures aim to maintain sexual and gender coherence and conformity. Their work shows how non-conforming identities and behaviours are boxed into categories and extruded from "normal," to protect the bourgeois family, its gender idealisations and the social order it represents. Yet, along the way, we all fail to meet idealised conventions of gender and sexuality, and repeated renunciations of non-conforming aspects of ourselves via perverse strategies attempt to protect us from the truth of non-conformity.

In managing anxiety, the foregrounding of a vivid presence works well because it is also enlivening. We would not want to be reminded at every moment that our new suit, colourful dress, athletic achievements or sexual adventures are distractions from our primitive fear of annihilation, ridicule or exclusion. Yet, they are all enacted within the foreground/background strategy, employing gender stereotypes to animate our lives with emotions that feel good.

Yanof (2000) has shown that gender is imbued with layered meanings that can be employed creatively in changeable compromise formations. In contrast to Freud's static gender of anatomic destiny, her work affirms the functional benefits and uses of dynamically changeable gender identity. It also asserts that gender is constantly being reorganised under the influences of biology, object relations and social construction and that gender animates conflicts outside the domain of gender and in turn is impacted by non-gendered conflicts as well.

Gender: anatomy as destination?

For a few decades at least, psychoanalysis was moving steadily towards the recognition that much of our gender bifurcating was fetishistic and defensive and that all people were capable of multiple identifications without diffusion or fragmentation of self. Treating caricatures of gender stereotypes as defensive compromises, we came to value fluidity and the ability to both empathise and identify across the binaries of sex and gender. We came to think that openness and psychic penetrability are good for men, just as strength and agency are good for women.

Many of us were challenged by certain trans subjectivities that seemed to be resisting the sharing of characteristics across genders. While liberated women and metrosexual men were enjoying new freedom to blur and blend gender norms, some transsexuals seemed to argue for the necessity of the binary, for the segregation of gender characteristics, and even for the essentialist, biological distinctions that others worked so hard to undo.

Here was an irony: Gender transitioning was scorned as an unacceptably radical transgression by conservative gender watchdogs, yet it was perceived as a conservative turn towards biological essentialism by progressive advocates of fluidity and flexibility. In some cases, trans folks appeared to value gender stereotyping and hoped to embody and perform a gender idealisation. Of course, there are as many trans subjectivities as there are trans people, and they shouldn't be lumped together – I simply want to acknowledge this body-based challenge to our hard-won progressive idealisations of fluidity and flexibility. Instead of having easy answers, we are now challenged to renew our commitment to listen to individual and unanticipated unique subjectivities.

Many psychoanalytic theoreticians have attempted in recent decades to bring some of the previously marginalised sexual and gender minorities into the mainstream fold. González (2015) wrote, "Psychoanalysis today posits an exceedingly complex relationship between gender, sexuality, the body, and the social, one that tends towards agnosticism on its resolution and highlights the enigmatic." However, recent publications have shown that not all psychoanalysts are comfortable with the enigmatic, and some still show a predisposition for diagnosing pathological aetiologies and regulating behaviour.

The editors of the *International Journal of Psychoanalysis*, under the heading of *"Psychoanalytic Controversies,"* recently asked whether we can even think psychoanalytically about transgenderism (2021). Bell's answer to the question is to raise alarm about our current social order, in which he asserts children are infected through "social contagion" with sudden and urgent needs to get hormone blockers or genital surgeries, and to accuse our current culture of preventing thoughtfulness about such actions. In contrast, Saketopoulou sees no need for analysts to add affective charge to these matters and suggests that we lower the temperature of our discussions and instead focus on what we learn from patients. Evzonas and Laufer (2019) name psychoanalytic theory and treatment, along with family and social forces, as potentially contributing elements of violence to the complex dynamics of gender subjectivity. In this setting of anxiety about the actions of transitioning, and with the tendency of clinicians to diagnose and regulate away our own discomforts, the ability of the clinician to recognise and examine countertransference is central to good therapeutic work.

Along with interrogating our individual prejudices, we must also be vigilant about examining our professional, traditional biases. We are all, individually and collectively, at risk of behaving like Freud in knowing and not knowing – in claiming theories that fail to affect our clinical behaviour. We must wonder, for example, why we hang on to terminology that is not precise. Why do we stick with "Oedipus complex" rather than "Triangulation" or some other word or words with fewer idiosyncratic and variable connotations? Are we unwittingly holding on to some of the heterosexist histories of "the Oedipal," even though we acknowledge that maturation into triangular relations is important for all genders and sexual orientations? When we use non-specific traditional terminology, we may perpetuate biases that we have theoretically eschewed. Here is an opportunity for us to learn from Freud's shortcomings – to avoid knowing and not knowing, and instead to have the courage of our convictions to scrutinise our application of theory as actively as we evolve the theories themselves.

References

Bernstein, D. (2003). *The Gender Conundrum*. Taylorfrancis.com.

Butler, J. (1990). *Gender Trouble: Feminism and the Subversion of Identity*. Routledge.

Davidson, A. I. (1987). How to do the history of psychoanalysis: A reading of Freud's 'Three Essays on the Theory of Sexuality.' *Critical Inquiry*, 13(2): 252–277. JSTOR, http://www.jstor.org/stable/1343491

Evzonas, N. (2020). Gender and "race" enigmatic signifiers. How the social colonizes the unconscious. *Psychoanalytic Inquiry*, 40(8): 636–656.

Evzonas, N. & Laufer, L. (2019). The therapist's transition. *The Psychoanalytic Review*, 106(5): 385–416. https://doi.org/10.1521/prev.2019.106.5.385

Fonagy, P. (2008) A genuinely developmental theory of sexual enjoyment and its implications for psychoanalytic technique. *Journal of the American Psychoanalytic Association*, 56(1): 11–36. https://doi.org/10.1177/0003065107313025

Freud, S. (1905). *Three Essays on the Theory of Sexuality*. S. E. Vol. 7. Hogarth Press. pp. 123–246.

Freud, S. (1912). *On the Universal Tendency to Debasement in the Sphere of Love*. S. E. Vol. 11. 177–190.

Freud, S. (1923). The Ego and the Id. S. E. Vol. 19. 1–66.

Freud, S. (1924). The Dissolution of the Oedipus Complex. S. E. Vol. 18. 171–180.

González, J. A. (2015). *The Bonds of Love, Revisited*. Routledge.

Gulati, R. & Pauley, D. (2019). The half embrace of psychic bisexuality. *Journal of the American Psychoanalytic Association*, 67(1): 97–121.

Isay, R. A. (1987). Fathers and their homosexually inclined sons in childhood. *Psychoanalytic Study of the Child*. Taylor & Francis.

Kaplan, L. J. (1997). Clinical manifestations of the perverse strategy. *Psychoanalysis & Psychotherapy*, 14(1): 79–89.

Laplanche, J. (1995). Seduction, persecution, revelation. *International Journal of Psycho-Analysis*, 76: 663–682.

Mayer, E. L. (1995). The phallic castration complex and primary femininity: Paired developmental lines toward female gender identity. *Journal of the American Psychoanalytic Association*, 43(1): 17–38.

Riviere, J. (1929). Womanliness as a masquerade. *International Journal of Psycho-Analysis*, 9: 303–313.

Scarfone, D. (2019). The Sexual and psychical reality. International Journal of Psycho-Analysis, 100:148–155.

Target, M. (2007). Is our sexuality our own? A developmental model of sexuality based on early affect mirroring. *British Journal of Psychotherapy*, 23(4): 517–530.

Yanof, J. A. (2000) Barbie and the tree of life: the multiple functions of gender in development. *Journal of the American Psychoanalytic Association*, 48(4): 1439–1465. https://doi.org/10.1177/00030651000480042701

2 Neosexualities and gender identity

Is there a psychic place where they originate?

Paola Marion

Introduction

I offer a reflection on the formation of the representation of one's own body. The construction of the feeling of one's own bodily self involves the other goal of the early phases of development, to be a starting point for the possible paths of subjectivation to which it may give rise. The processes of assignment and recognition that designate the infant's gender do not correspond to an objective knowledge according to anatomical sexual signs, but are conditioned by the parent–child interactions, by unconscious fantasies, and by the internal world of the caregivers, and require us to distinguish between the *anatomical*, *subjective*, and *fantasy* body. In this scenario, the primary identifications, supported by perceptions and sensory states, play a specific role in forming the bodily ego which will later have to deal with the secondary identifications: we can speculate that the transitions from the former to the latter represent the perimeter within which the game is played out between the body of the ideal ego and the comparison with the given body, the discovery of sexuality, and the recognition of gender difference in relation to one's anatomical body.

We know that psychoanalysis develops in a specific historical and cultural context and is not indifferent to the *Zeitgeist* and its relationship to the societal discourse takes shape and manifests itself in behaviours, difficulties, and discontents, calling into question the link between external and internal reality, between "what is called reality and fantasy," as Winnicott puts it (1988). The enquiry into how the two poles relate to each other constitutes one of the most difficult challenges for psychoanalysis. It is a challenge we find ourselves facing today when we investigate the question of identity and the problems connected to it, which seem to represent the hallmark that characterises the anthropology of the present time. Baumann (2003, 13–14) claimed that:

> (...) the identity reveals itself uniquely as something to be invented rather than discovered ... this precarious and perennially incomplete status of identity is a truth .... Today this truth is harder to hide than it was at the start of the modern era.

DOI: 10.4324/9781003534440-4

The author of the concept of "liquid identity" correctly grasped and described an epochal shift, or rather the revelation of a change we have witnessed in the second part of the "short century," and even more so in the first part of this century, and which has given centre stage to the problems, investigations, and questions about who we are and how we want to define ourselves. Quoting Baumann again, "the popular hero," becomes "the freely floating individual with no encumbrances," whereas "'being fixed', inflexibly 'identified', with no possibility of rethinking, becomes more and more unpopular" (31).

Axel Honneth (2002, 26) offers a brilliant reflection on these themes, setting the psychoanalytic paradigm against the problems posed by postmodern identity and underlining how the image of the individual that is being asserted is that of a subject characterised by an inner multiplication of identities. The postmodern personality is characterised by an extreme fluidification (*Verflüssigung*) of psychic life in which different sides of the personality and many periods from one's history live together as multiple possible identities. Ambiguity becomes a prevailing category, and the maturity of the subject is measured by the capacity for welcoming multiplicity and fluidity, thereby taking over "the place that had been occupied in early psychoanalysis by the concept of ego strength." This thesis is shared by Glocer Fiorini (2017), according to whom the postmodern subject is in contact with a type of "fragmentation" very different from the splitting of the Freudian subject, one that would be equivalent to "de-subjectivation." This concept was also taken up by Saketopoulou (2022, 31) who maintains that the "fragmentation" of the Ego represents a form of "undoing," "untying meanings and laying bare the enigma." On the other hand, the entry of biotechnology and virtual reality has profoundly changed the relationship between our fantasies, needs, and desires, and the circumstances and ways in which they are realised. Our way of being in relation to others has also changed, expressing itself in ever more "disembodied" forms. The expression and fulfilment of everyone's desires through more and more refined technical procedures may, for some people, lead to confirmation of the idea that the problem is irreducibly "planted" in the body, or that the solution can be found via virtual devices, instead of within human relationships (Marion, 2017), risking, as Lorena Preta (2023, 3) writes, the imposition of reality "with its evidence and urgency, leaving no critical spaces, or hardly any … and no connection to the underlying world of fantasy."

It is within this scenario that as psychoanalysts we are called upon to reflect on the topic of sexual and gender identity, with the new forms, including transgender, that they assume in individuals, in young people. We need to attend to the questions that this raises, together with the situations of suffering and discontent that it can create. How are we to think psychoanalytically about these phenomena, which do not let themselves be summed up in a single definition and may be the expression of highly diverse psychological situations? How are we to think about the sense of incongruity between one's assigned sex and the conviction of one's own gender identity? Where can we find the roots of the disconnect that patients bring us or take refuge in, and which sometimes feels so painful? For us, "thinking psychoanalytically" about these topics (Blass, 2020; Heenen-Wolff, 2021) represents a difficult challenge and a complex task, a challenge and task that also involve the adequacy of our conceptual instruments, the question of whether they can help us to address problematic areas like these. These concerns prompt reflection about the problems and doubts that navigating these seas requires us to tolerate, about the questioning it demands from us, interrogating our psychoanalytic theories and the help they may or may not be able to offer with such thorny issues. This is about working on our countertransference and the self-analysis that is required to avoid falling into moralism or a search for aetiopathogenesis and instead direct our attention to the search for meaning and the function of choices that, to us, often appear so extreme and alien.

Gender and transgender identities

The question of gender and the reflection on these themes leads the discussion onto troubled territory. This is not the place for me to run through its history and the stages of a journey through what look more like jagged outcrops than a unified landscape (Marion, 2017, 2023), a route that has often diverged from psychoanalytic thought, at least in its most traditional form. The phenomena associated with problems in the area of gender identity express the wish to assert paths of subjectivation that are not circumscribed by the binary choice and should be considered as "a normal variant of human expression" (Lingiardi et al., 2023), an "atypical" expression of identity lived in a way that does not match one's physical characteristics. In fact, as Marchand, Pelladeau, and Pommier (2019, 150) write, transgender identity is a concept that expresses "a different relationship of the subject to his gender identity, their sexed body, and to the difference between the sexes." The prefix "trans" evokes a movement from one condition to another and, as in Ovid's *Metamorphoses*, we can imagine ourselves as being in continual mutation, seeking to register ourselves as other than we were originally.

In this panorama, the binary schema is thrown into crisis. Glocer Fiorini (2017) speaks of "nomadic sexualities and genders" to indicate a spectrum of subjectivities that would not find a place in the classical male–female duality and would come to constitute the sphere of the "neosexualities," giving new meanings to the term introduced by McDougall in 1982. Nevertheless, given the time that has elapsed since McDougall's text was written, almost two generations, the sphere of the "impossible" to which she referred, the "neosexuality" she spoke of has expanded and taken on meanings, characteristics, and colours that were not on the horizon then (Marion, 2023). Writing about "Sexual and gender migrations," Glocer Fiorini (2017) uses the term "neosexualities" to refer to all those expressions of sexuality and gender that diverge from the binary and heterosexual model without implying any reference to perversion. Thus, defining the new geography of "neosexuality" today brings together those features, especially the issue of "fluidity," which, as I wrote at the start, have contributed to the appreciable change of panorama. This climate, in which we are immersed, and of which we can be aware, becomes a potent element capable of influencing the image we have of ourselves and the other, our way of living relationships, and the ways in which distress is expressed and the forms it takes. The subjective appropriation of our own being and hence the construction of our identity go beyond reference to a given dual system in terms of both gender and sexual orientations and all the expressions of sexuality and gender that diverge from the binary model and heterosexuality are asserted as "creative differences" (Ehrensaft, 2014). There is growing recognition that the *gender question* and the possible modifications of the body connected to it refer, as Alessandra Lemma (2023, 52) writes, to "a new way of thinking about the mind-body relationship," to the fantasies and meanings that accompany each of our paths of identification. So, we are witnessing a change of perspective in which the theme of sexuality migrates into the theme of identity and is superimposed onto it, and feelings of incongruity between anatomical sex and the way one feels in one's own body raise questions about the relationship between gender and sexuality in its various permutations.

As psychoanalysts, we think that the contribution we can make to the understanding of these phenomena and the suffering that accompanies them involves exploring unconscious factors and their impact on the process of self-representation that each of us constructs. Given the complexity of the subject and the still provisional nature of what we know about it, as well as our awareness that there are many ways of looking at it and multiple paths into these phenomena, I would like the reflections I offer to be considered only as thoughts in progress and suggest that a collective discussion will be indispensable in fostering a growth and broadening of the way we think about it.

The body and the gaze

Anatomy represents a starting point. It suggests that what is perceived as given is a fact, although not objective in the proper sense of the adjective: this is what speaks about us, and from the beginning, it is interwoven with the other's fantasies and unconscious expectations. The parents' first question about their unborn baby is their baby's gender and, based on the answer, they begin to compose a private story about the baby even before they see him or her. This is something the subject does not know, something that precedes them and it concerns the way they begin to take shape in the other's mind, to be imagined by the other. We recognise how the path towards the construction of gender identity not only starts in the earliest periods of development, but also at a time that is completely alien to the subject themselves and it will only be encountered later by the subject. It refers to an unconscious world of fantasy that involves the other and goes on to occupy and mark the subject's subsequent evolutions and feeling of self.

The genesis of the path along which gender identity is constructed is in that region of the *caregiver*–infant relationship that involves the primitive preverbal area where corporeality predominates through physical and sensory exchanges. Progress towards the establishment of the psyche in the body is both a delicate and a complex process (Winnicott, 1958, 1988); it accompanies the experience of being in one's own body, the process of setting up a primary experience of identity, and reflects "the unconscious transmission of gestures, posture, mannerisms, rhythms, all of which that contain affectively laden representations of self-in-interaction-with-the-other" (Lemma, 2023, 61). The processes of assignment and recognition that designate the newborn's gender are not responses to an objective knowledge based on anatomical signs of sex, but are conditioned by the interactions between the parents and the child and by the parents' unconscious fantasies about femininity and masculinity (Chiland, 2008; Carratelli & Massaro, 2016): what the parent sees as they look at and interact with their little child is influenced by their own internal world, by the quality of the relationships that inhabit it, by their relationship with their inner parents, and by their own identificatory journeys. These considerations require us to distinguish between an *anatomical, objective, spatialised body* founded on the view and perception of sex difference from outside and a *fantasied body*, which is by contrast a matter of how the body is psychically represented and the experience we have of it, which is not immediately and easily figurable (Gibeault, 1993).

The relationship between gender identity and sexuality is well articulated by Laplanche (2007), who shows us how gender precedes sex but is organised by it. And not only because the definition of gender derives, or should derive, from the anatomical sex, but above all because it is hard to think that the question of gender assignment is not infused with the *"sexual"* of the other. Indeed, as Laplanche (2007, 215) writes:

> It is therefore ... above all what is *le sexual* in the parents that makes noise in the assignment. I say, 'mainly *le sexual*' ... because in the presence of the child, the adults ultimately come to reactivate their infantile sexuality above all.

This is a *sexual* concerned with the other's unconscious, one that cannot be recognised as such early on because of the infant's immaturity, and only acquires meaning later, *a posteriori, nachträglich*, involving the presence of the parental fantasies, the other's gaze, the "enigmatic messages" that are sent. These fantasies, gaze, and messages infuse and condition the biological reality and act as "a psychic imprint" (Green, 1973). The *"sexual"* represents a dimension beyond sexuality, influences the psychic processes, takes shape, and expresses itself in the experience we have of ourselves and of ourselves with others, and denotes a pleasure which – notes Balsamo (2022) – applies to an infinitely plastic body capable of usurping the place reserved for sexuality and genitality. As is described in the film *The Danish Girl*, at the end of her story Lili feels free in her female body, like the scarf that flutters lightly in the sky, and recounts the fantasy that has accompanied her on her dramatic journey: "*I was a baby in my mother's arms. She looked down at me and she called me Lili.*" This is an image of a primitive mother, a single, omnipotent parent who in her contact with the baby transmits not only a *recognition* and a *designation* (and hence a psychological and social representation) but also – and, I would say, above all – a *pleasure*, the meaning of which cannot be recognised as such in this phase.

Problems of identity involve a complex range of expressions which are not all solved by the request for a gender transition. The crisis of gender identity unleashed by the irruption of puberty, which includes the outcomes of pre-existing conflicts, is different from feelings of incongruity which, at least as the subject describes them, seem to have their roots in primal situations and accompany the subject on its life path. We cannot rule out the possibility of the two situations existing concurrently and, as Nicolò and Accetti (2023) argue, we must distinguish between patients who express a dissociation between sex and gender which involves archaic processes associated with the establishment of the psyche in the body; patients who come into conflict with the image of a monstrous child who is inhabiting them and from whom they want to escape, resorting to omnipotent fantasies of being able to change the reality of the body; and patients for whom the transgender choice represents a compensatory solution to a breakdown or to the aftermath of a psychosis.

Two brief clinical vignettes

This would seem to be the scenario that characterises the situation of Gaia/Alex (aged 17, F to M)[1] who insistently claims to feel, and always to have felt, male. He asks to be called Alex. The sessions are poor in stories and associations. He isolates himself in social contexts, does not participate at school, and is often absent, locked indoors, declares that he does not feel seen by other people. The fantasy is that, in his words, "after transitioning I'll be able to feel good in my new body and will make myself be seen." He goes through an arduous transfer from the adolescent service to the adult service at the hospital that is treating him, accompanied by confirmation of the diagnosis of gender incongruity against a background of severe depression, and also by his starting to use hormones and so begins the process that will lead him to transition. Everything that Alex ascribes to his female identity, such as the gynaecology appointment required by the protocols, terrifies him. Despite gestures that would seem to indicate an openness to the analyst, acknowledging for example that a break in treatment seemed "eternal," the patient denies and undervalues the relationship. When the analyst tries to connect the profound feelings of "weariness" that Alex experiences to the very demanding process he is dealing with, to "feeling on a knife edge" between two conditions, and to depressive episodes provoked by the process of bodily transformation, the patient denies and rejects the analyst's words. The patient's condition is well expressed by an image that comes up when he is talking about a cartoon he has drawn. These are half-human, half-robot figures with no eyes or mouth. Then, he tells the analyst about another image he has thought of and wants to draw: a little boy walking along a dark corridor with a hand over one eye. He is accompanied by a brother who is holding his hand and closing the other eye. The image seems a good representation of the patient's refusal: on the one hand not wanting to see what awaits him from the psychic, emotional viewpoint, but also feeling, or fearing, that he is not being seen. Alex refuses to listen to the internal resonances and meanings that the various phases of the process arouse: on the contrary, any hint of them irritates him or makes him angry. The introduction of hormone therapy, together with an antidepressant and the news that he can start to think about the operation, make him feel better and prompt him to ask for an immediate reduction in the number of sessions, leading to the analysis being suspended.

By contrast, in the case of Matilde/Luz (aged 16, F to M),[2] the theme of gender identity is situated against a different background and seems to express a problem connected to passing through adolescence and mourning for bisexuality. What is at stake here is the body, the bedrock, and equally at stake are the themes connected to the integration of one's own sexed body. He asks to be called by an indefinite name (and yet uses a masculine pronoun), because he is aware that gender is an epiphenomenon in his malaise, and he seems able to keep "balancing on the brink" while he looks for an identity that is not yet clear to him. He tries to hide his body in shapeless clothing and his hair is cut short in a masculine manner, but he keeps his fingernails long and feminine, displaying them to his therapist, just as he tells her when he is having a period. He talks about a girl who was also a trans male for a time and has now gone back to being female, and he adds with reference to transition, "But I don't know much about my gender identity. I use masculine words for myself because there's no neuter in Italian, but I feel neuter, and that's fine. Now I have other problems: that I should start accepting my body for what it is, that's the real problem." He tells the therapist that he wants to get a tattoo under his breast. He's been thinking that the breast is the part of the body that makes him feel female, the part that scares him. And then he says, "If one day I wanted to transition, the tattoo will mean I'll always have a reminder that I was female." Unlike Alex, and thanks to the analytic path he is on, Luz seems able to attain a deep and painful awareness of how choosing an ambiguous identity expresses the sense of confusion he experiences in relation to her body: "I'd like to know what's wrong with my body. Maybe my body is telling me things I can't understand, and I'll understand them when the time is right."

A hypothesis about the psychic place where gender identity originates

The idea one has or wants to have of one's own gender, the gender one wants to belong to, and how this is entwined with the definition of one's own sexual identity, represents a strong feeling that inhabits the subject and gives form to expressions of self and one's sexuality. How is this "representation of the body in the mind" formed? Where does this construction, which brings together unconscious fantasies of self and other, enigmatic messages, come from? I am following lines of thought from two very different authors in quite different times who nevertheless seem to offer some conceptual hypotheses with which to approach and reflect on these types of phenomena. They are hypotheses that reprise well-known observations but develop them, adding precision to ideas about psychic processes that could be the basis for one outcome or another.

The first author to whom I refer is Heenen-Wolff (2021), who in a recent study advances a "metapsychological" hypothesis about the "genesis of the sexual ego." Hers is a long and complex work from which I shall only take some points that seem illuminating in relation to certain stages of psychic development. This author dwells especially on the role played by the primary identifications[3] which, unlike the secondary ones, do not yet consist of object cathexes in relation to a person, an object relation, and apply instead to the mechanism of oral incorporation. The author starts from Freud's idea of the "bodily Ego" (Freud, 1923), whose primary formation precedes the recognition of one's anatomical sex. This is a direct and immediate identification, something more ancient than and prior to any object investment. Heenen-Wolff turns her attention specifically to the weight of the primary identifications, supported by perceptions, both on the formation of the bodily ego and on the earlies stages of development. Within this frame, she concentrates on the mirror stage (Lacan, 1976; Winnicott, 1971), considering it a vital crux during which self-awareness is constructed and of which the maternal or parental gaze acts as the precursor. The other's gaze, how the newborn infant is looked at, anticipates what will come into play in the mirror phase during which, by way of its own reflected image, the baby starts to have a first idea or sensation of self-awareness. Nevertheless, that idea or awareness passes via an adult who points to the baby's image in the mirror and confirms it. This is a movement in which the adult's role, the ways they look at the baby, the affective qualities of the environment, and the messages conveyed by recognition or misrecognition have a central place. According to Heenen-Wolff (2021, 470), it is in these first transitional phases that the first identifications occur, which are not yet identifications *with* the other but "*by*" the other, and they activate the development of a "primary ideal Ego," an "image *reflected*

– glorified – by the mirror/the caregiver's gaze." In the relational context, the ideal ego acquires "an additional quality" (Heenen-Wolff, 2021, 470), corresponding not only to the image that the subject feels is desirable for him/herself, but also to the image that the subject imagines to be desirable for the other person. Over the course of development, where things go well enough, the child gradually takes account of the need to come to terms with the ideal image of themselves, which has to do with their own narcissism: they are confronted with the need to mourn the ideal ego to move on to the ego-ideal. When there are problems connected to gender, at the point when one's anatomical body and gender differences are recognised, it is not the ideal ego that has to deal with the anatomical body, the signs of gender, and the acknowledgement of any non-correspondence between the ideal image and the given body, but the body that must adapt itself to the ideal which, I add, for the subject, represents an unquestionable source of pleasure. The transgender person would retroactively regard their own body as the "wrong," alien body, "rejects on" with the aim of maintaining the ideal self-image, in the various forms that everyone imagines for themselves. To sum up, "this 'gendering', as a result of the corresponding (more or less contradictory) cathexes, precedes the discovery of gender difference and the identification with one's own anatomical sex" (473). In this reconstruction, I would emphasise both the image of the ideal body as a source of pleasure which on an unconscious level prompts, accompanies, and supports the subject in their "transitions," and the prevalence of the visual (the mirror phase), "a scopic economy" which represents a nucleus and character-forming experience of gender. Luz, for example, expresses this dramatically when he says to his therapist that what terrifies him is that, even after transitioning, he will look at himself "in the mirror" and still see himself as a woman.

The reflections on the imitative processes by Gaddini (1969, 166) at an earlier time seem to go in a similar direction, concentrating on the role of "imitation" over the course of development. The mechanism of imitation, which precedes both introjection and identification, is in the sensory area. In the psychic model of imitation, "the object is in the service of the Self," as we are clearly reminded by the words of Lili, the protagonist of *The Danish Girl*. Gaddini stresses that "the primitive imitative perception seems conducive to fantasies of fusion *by modifying one's own body* [my emphasis] and to imitations in the desire to be the object" (164). In these cases, the knowledge of and relationship with the other would come about through the sensations of one's own body, linked to omnipotent unconscious fantasies.

If, drawing on the observations of these two authors I have cited, and as the words of Lili from *The Danish Girl* suggest, we therefore hypothesise the formation within us of a "bodily Ego" based on a process of primary, immediate identifications. We could say that primary and secondary identifications, the shifts from one to the other, represent the perimeter within which the game is played out between the body of the ideal ego and the comparison with the given body, the discovery of sexuality, and the recognition of gender difference in relation to one's own anatomical body. Here, the theme of infantile polymorphous sexuality makes its reappearance and the *sexual*, which expresses that supplementary pleasure linked to the drive, and denotes "a component which cannot evolve in a maturational sense ... but will always remain excessive and deviant" (Conrotto, 2002, 9).

To conclude, there is no doubt that, in contradiction to Freud, anatomy is no longer destiny. It nevertheless remains a "foundation stone," and destiny appears to us instead as the result of complex interactions between the way anatomy is recorded and signified by means of the other's gaze, and via one's own and others' unconscious phantasmatic world; these shape the perception of the given body and the expressions of sexuality. I believe we can affirm that today destiny is declined in the plural, destinies, to indicate the multiplicity of solutions that individuals feel authorised to choose for themselves, solutions that mirror all the variables in play along all our paths of subjectivation, and the way each of us modulates the dream of our own identity. In Rilke's (1921–1926) words, we can say that "we are born, so to speak, provisionally, it doesn't matter where. It is only gradually that we compose within ourselves our true place of origin so that we may be born there retrospectively, in *après-coup*."

Notes

1 This is a case brought in supervision, I am grateful to the therapist for her permission to use the material.
2 This is a case brought in supervision, I am grateful to the therapist for her permission to use the material.
3 As Laplanche and Pontalis (1967) put it, primary identification indicates a "primitive mode of the constitution of the subject on the model of the other person – a mode not dependent upon any prior establishment of a relationship in which the object can at first lay claim to an autonomous existence. Primary identification is closely bound up with the relation known as oral incorporation." For Freud, it represents the "original form of the emotional tie with an object" and precedes the difference between the subject and the other person, and any object cathexis.

References

Balsamo M. (2022). Il sessuale della psicoanalisi. *Frontiere della psicoanalisi: il disagio del sessuale*, 1: 2022.

Baumann Z. (2003). *Intervista sull'identità*. Roma: Laterza.

Blass R. (2020). Introduction to "Can we think psychoanalytically about transgenderism?" *International Journal of Psychoanalysis*, 101 (5): 1014–1018.

Carratelli T. & Massaro V. (2016). Il bambino rosa: alla ricerca della leggerezza dell'essere. Note teorico-cliniche. *Richard e Piggle*, 4: 356–372.

Chiland C. (2008). *Sex Makes the World Go Round*. London: Karnac.

Conrotto F. (2002). Introduction to the Italian Edition of Widlöcher D. In: *Sexualité infantile et attachment*. Paris: PUF. (Ital. trans. By Franco Conrotto, *Sessualità infantile e attaccamento*. Milano, Franco Angeli)

Ehrensaft D. (2014). Listening and learning from gender-nonconforming children. *Psychoanalytic Study of the Child*, 68: 28–50.

Freud S. (1923). L'Io e l'Es. In: *OSF, IX*. Torino: Boringhieri.

Gaddini E. (1969). Sull'imitazione. In: *Scritti (1953–1985)*. Milano: Cortina, 1989.

Gibeault A. (1993). Riflessioni a partire dal libro di Jacqueline Cosnier *Destins de la fémininité*. In: Breen D. *(a cura di) L'enigma dell'identità di genere*. Roma, Borla, 2000. In: Breen D. (ed.) *The Gender Conundrum: Contemporary Psychoanalytic Perspectives on Femininity and Masculinity*. London: Routledge.

Glocer Fiorini L. (2017). *Sexual Difference in Debate. Bodies, Desires, and Fictions*. London: Karnac.

Green A. (1973). Le genre neutre. In: *Narcissisme de vie, Narcissisme de mort*. Paris, Les Éditions de Minuit. Tr.it: *Il genere neutro*. In: *Narcisismo di vita, narcisismo di morte*. Roma: Borla, 1985.

Heenen-Wolff S. (2021). Gender and transgender: a metapsychological contribution to the genesis of the sexual ego. *International Journal of Psychoanalysis*, 102 (3): 464–478.

Honneth A. (2002). Teoria delle relazioni oggettuali e identità postmoderna. Sulla presunta obsolescenza della psicoanalisi. *Psiche*, 1, 13–29.

Lacan J. (1976). *Scritti. Volume 1*. Torino: Einaudi.

Laplanche J., Pontalis J-B. (1967). *Vocabulaire de la psychanalyse*. Paris: PUF.

Laplanche J. (2007). *Sexuale*. La sessualità allargata nel senso freudiano 2000–2006. *(edizione italiana a cura di* Alberto Luchetti). La Biblioteca, Bari: Laterza.

Lemma A. (2023). *Transgender Identities. A Contemporary Introduction*. London, Routledge. Tr. It.: *Le identità transgender. Un'introduzione contemporanea*. Milano: Franco Angeli, 2023.

Lingiardi V. et al. (2023). *Consulenza psicologica e psicoterapia con persone lesbiche, gay, bisessuali, transgender, non binarie*. Milano: Cortina.

McDougall J. (1982). *Teatri dell'Io. Illusione e verità sulla scena psicoanalitica*. Milano: Cortina.

Marchand J-B, Pelladeau E. & Pommier F. (2019). Transexualism and transgenderism: Unraveling sex and gender, and abstractions of the sexed body. *International Journal of Psychoanalysis*, 100 (2): 206–228.

Marion P. (2017). *Il disagio del desiderio. Sessualità e procreazione nel tempo delle biotecnologie*. Roma: Donzelli. Tr. English: *Sexuality and Procreation in the Age of Bioechnology. Desire and its Discontents*. London: Routledge. 2022.

Marion P. (2023). "Il teatro dell'impossibile": una o più sessualità? In: Paolo Cotrufo, Rosaria Tuccillo (eds.) *La sessualità umana perversa, polimorfa, pervasiva*. Milano: Franco Angeli.

Nicolò A. & Accetti L. (2023), *The Transgender Illusion: The Enigma of Identity*, lavoro presentato alla Conferenza FEP, Cannes, Marzo, 2023.

Preta L. (2023). La fantasia di autogenerazione tra diniego, illusione, speranza. IX Colloquio di Venezia "Diniego, illusione, speranza", 7–8 ottobre, 2023.

Rilke R.M. (1921–1926), *Lettere milanesi*. Milano: Mondadori.

Saketopoulou A. (2022), *Il richiamo del soverchiamento: consenso, rischio e la ritraduzione dell'enigma*. Frontiere della psicoanalisi: il disagio del sessuale, 1, 73–104.

Winnicott D.W. (1971). *Playing and Reality*. London, Tavistock Publications.

Winnicott D.W. (1958). *Collected Papers*. Tr.it.: *Dalla Pediatria alla Psicoanalisi*. Firenze: Martinelli, 1975.

Winnicott D.W. (1988). *Human Nature*. Tr.it.: *Sulla natura umana*. Milano: Cortina, 1989.

3 An approach to contemporary subjectivities

Identifications, gender, and sexual difference*

Leticia Glocer Fiorini

This chapter aims to discuss a key issue in psychoanalysis such as gender identifications and identity in a world that shows significant changes regarding contemporary subjectivities. We are facing *mutations* (Green, 1982). This means that we should work with unexpected changes, random transformations, and not only gradual transitions with reference to the construction of subjectivity. We can add that these mutations encompass intersubjective relations as well as trans-subjective signifiers at play in current cultures. I am going to focus on gender identifications that link with a controversial issue in the psychoanalytic domain: identity.

The point of departure of my proposal involves the significant increase of consultations from different age groups related to sexual and gender diversity, new family configurations as well as advances in assisted fertilisation, gamete donation, and uterus surrogacy, among other changes that can be observed in contemporary subjectivities. Undoubtedly, the feminine and masculine positions are deeply involved and open important debates. I will approach these points in this new *epoque* with the aim of rethinking crucial issues such as the Oedipus complex, the itineraries of desire, identifications, and the notion of identity. Undoubtedly, our conceptions about bodies are included in these developments.

I have been working on these issues for several decades (Glocer Fiorini, 1994, 1998) and find the possibility of sharing and debating ideas between psychoanalytic developments in Europe, Latin America, and North America of great interest, including the theoretical variants that exist in each of these regions. These are notions that challenge psychoanalysis and psychoanalysts, and the point is how to keep crucial axes of psychoanalysis, and at the same time expand theoretical and epistemological resources to better understand changes that are observed in current subjectivities and that can expand our clinical approach.

* An earlier version was presented at the EPF Panel, Florence, March 2024, and based on my books: *Deconstructing the Feminine* (Routledge) and *Sexual Difference in Debate* (Karnac/ Routledge).

DOI: 10.4324/9781003534440-5

I will choose several points that are topics of debate in the psychoanalytic field and that have an impact on how people, couples, and families with unconventional sexuality or gender are analysed, adding possible effects on their children. I will focus on how identifications are constructed when parents do not embody sexual difference, either because of their anatomy, their sexual orientation or their assumed gender (transsexual, transgender parents).

1   I start from the assumption that the classical Oedipus complex (Freud, 1923, 1924) does not cover current subjectivities due to its normative heterosexual resolution which includes the implicit fixedness of gender identifications. These resolutions do not take into account the Oedipal complexity. For my part, I have approached this question from the *paradigm of complexity* (Morin, 1990), based on a complex epistemology regarding multiplicity and heterogeneity, just as the psyche functions. Complexity means that it is not only about the sum of determinations at play but about how they are related to each other; that is, in a psychic space of interfaces and intersections, where concordances and oppositions coexist. Let us remember Winnicott's (1959) transitional space where something new happens in the mother/child relationship: a new space different from each of them considered separately.

   According to the Freudian positive Oedipus complex, gender identifications should fall into one of two pigeonholes, masculine or feminine. However, Freud himself had detected that there was a limit here. He therefore proposed another approach: the complete Oedipus complex, which opens wider perspectives, since it encompasses the multiplicity of identifications, crossed fantasies, and plural desires that coexist in the psyche. But even so, the Oedipus complex is reduced to the intrafamilial triad, mother/father/child, certainly linked to the parents' Oedipal resolution. In addition, this proposal also implies a binary heterosexual, "normal", resolution of the complex.

2   From this obstacle, I took the concept of an *expanded, trans familial Oedipus complex*, with the perspective that not everything takes place in the father/mother/child triad (Glocer Fiorini, 2017/2015). *An open Oedipus, porous* in its internal–external exchanges, taking as a metaphor Deleuze's proposal (Deleuze & Guattari, 1972) of exchange vacuoles between the internal and the external world. This means that it is necessary to go beyond the narrative and embodiments of the intrafamilial Oedipus although it also exists as a fact in our clinical approach. And here I emphasise an important point related to significant messages and signifiers that are transmitted from culture, parents, and transgenerational messages. That is why I include Laplanche's notion of *enigmatic signifier* (Laplanche, 1999), as well as Castoriadis-Aulagnier's (1975) concept of *identificatory project*, both bringing enigmas and meanings to decode that the infant will have to decipher as far as possible. These enigmas concern both

sexuality and gender assigned at birth. This psychic work may take a lifetime, with conflict, as Pontalis (1973) pointed out.

In this context, I have proposed to think of the Oedipus in terms of *functions* (Glocer Fiorini, 2014, 2017). This means that the trans-familial Oedipus no longer refers only to the embodied triad mother/father/ child but that we must add the necessity of thinking of it in terms of functions. What we usually call maternal function is a reference to the functions of care, affection, and support attributed to mothers, just as the so-called paternal function which "introduces the law" is attributed to fathers (although aiming to be a metaphor) who perform a symbolic function. That is to say that these functions acquire representation, in a natural and normative way, embodied in mothers and fathers according to their sex and gender. However, nowadays this is becoming more complex. While they are useful concepts, at this point they are insufficient. Lacan (1972–1973) had already suggested that these functions could be performed by substitutes of mothers and fathers (grandparents, uncles, and aunts, among others). However, if these functions are implemented by persons whose anatomical sex and/or gender does not correspond to the culturally accepted parents, what could happen to their children? This a frequent question for psychoanalysis and psychoanalysts. For some authors, these children will become "perverse" or psychotic because they would not supposedly access to sexual difference. The risk is that this position leads us to a dead end. On the contrary, our question is: Is it possible to think novelty with the same theoretical categories? *In my experience, access to difference in a symbolic sense does not depend on the sexual orientation or gender variants of their parents.* I will refer to this point below revising the concept of "difference".

3 Following this line of thoughts, I will approach the question of *identifications*. These have a strong imaginary support, but also symbolic resolutions based on secondary identifications that arise from the Oedipal resolution, thought as an open, trans-familial Oedipus. Besides, here we refer not only to identifications in general but particularly to *gender identifications*, which act since every child is assigned to a gender, masculine or feminine or another possibility. The child is identified. I stress that gender identifications respond to the field of ideals (the ideal ego-ego ideal axis is at stake). So, how are identifications with a couple of parents of the same sex/gender generated? Is there a real impossibility that theory cannot cover? Or we should explore and rethink theory more deeply? As mentioned, identifications go beyond real parents: discursive, cultural factors are also involved.

4 I aim to show current questions and debates without offering answers *à la carte*. This leads us to another question that generates confrontations: *Is gender a psychoanalytic concept?* We know that there are psychoanalytic theories that do not recognise it as such. There are differences between regions: it is not the same in North America, Latin America, or Europe,

including the internal differences between societies and theories within each country and region. So let us also focus on this debate on *gender identifications* and another concept linked to them: *gender identity*.

I start from the premise that Freudian theory on sexual difference in the context of the Oedipus complex is a theory of gender; there is an implicit vision about gender that needs to be reviewed. Freud develops his view on the construction of subjectivity (identifications and desires at play) based on the structure of the nuclear family and focused on the perspective of a heterosexual resolution for boys and girls. This proposal derived from many objections from a clinical and theoretical point of view that also involve epistemology, metatheories, and private/ implicit theories that every psychoanalyst has regarding sexual difference. Likewise, we remember criticisms regarding the girl's Oedipus complex (Freud, 1925) to which I cannot refer here, but which remain to this day (Glocer Fiorini, 2020/2001). It is therefore essential to consider that norms change, classic family structures change, the paths of desire expand and branch on and on, and genders migrate. Again, this means thinking of an expanded Oedipus complex.

On the other hand, we must *distinguish between social gender and subjective gender* (Glocer Fiorini, 2017/2015). The latter is the one assigned at birth in most known societies and is a cultural imperative that is crossed by the parents' desires and expectations, whether they are of the same or different sex/gender. *It is at the base of gender identifications* and is crossed by transgenerational and discursive/cultural changes. This imperative is undergoing transformations both in everyday life and current laws. Thus, gender assignment becomes intrapsychic within a greater complexity, and children will have to decipher the riddle of their own assigned gender through the expectations, desires and illusions that their parents inevitably transfer to them.

It is important to add that *between gender identifications and desire there are complex and contradictory relationships*; enigmatic messages circulate between these categories. Gender mandates constrain and limit the paths of desire, and at the same time, desire always tries to overflow gender mandates. It is in this interplay that subjectivity is constructed. I would like to emphasise that to the extent that gender identifications are flexible and in movement, desire will circulate in better conditions for each subject. At the same time, how itineraries of desire circulate will determine less rigidity of gender identifications. That is why I had proposed many years ago the notion of *"going in and out of gender"* as a metaphor that alludes to the construction of subjectivity and the possibility of thinking with greater freedom in subjective becoming, beyond mandatory strict dichotomies (phallic–castrated, masculine–feminine), which are insufficient to encompass the complexity of the psyche (Glocer Fiorini, 2020/2001, 2022). We also know that gender binarism inevitably embodies power relations, which need to be deconstructed. This implies being able to think about gender identifications in a context of greater mobilities.

5   Now, some brief words on the concept of *identity*, connected with the previous point. If identity is understood as "equal to oneself", it cannot be a psychoanalytic concept. But if we speak of *subjective identity*, we will be able to think of it not as a frozen identity always equal to itself, but of a subjective identity, in becoming. The concept of identity is linked to identifications. There should be necessary identificatory anchors that prevent psychic life from becoming disorganised. And, at the same time, these anchors can change during a person's life, meaning that they are not fixed and unmovable.

6   If we now return to *identifications*, we must think that there are *pre-oedipal gender identifications* since the newborn is assigned to one of two genders or to a "third box" according to some legislations. As I pointed out above, children will have to decipher this assignment in their own subjective construction. *In other words, gender is present in subjectivity, even if someone thinks that it is not a psychoanalytical concept.* And this generates in each person different types of conflicts. It should be added that the assignment of gender at birth implies that it is impossible to deny this notion for psychoanalysis, since children differentiate gender before their access to sexual difference, as Laplanche (1980) rightly pointed out. So, there is a pre-oedipal recognition of gender: "I am a boy or a girl or this assignment is uncertain". This complexity/plurality of identifications that Freud already pointed out when speaking of the complete Oedipus complex contributes to the heterogeneity of psychic identifications and involves the field of desire. This leads us to analyse each case without standardised adaptive solutions.

7   In short, how can we think about current subjectivities, and I add subjectivity in general, within the framework of changing itineraries of sexuality and gender? In my opinion, it can only be approached through the notion of "difference"; meaning, how do we think about the symbolic access to "difference", regardless of sexual orientation or gender variants that each person assumes, consciously or unconsciously?

Then, if we return to Freud, recalling his notions of fantasy, of multiple identifications, as well as contradictory and heterogeneous desires, we can think beyond a binary division of the psyche. I highlight the proposals of Castoriadis (1986), Morin (1990), and Trías (1991) and their interdisciplinary contributions that allow us to think about Freudian work from a multicentric, plural, and complex perspective. And especially to think in terms of interfaces, of "lines of flight" between binary polarities (Deleuze & Guattari, 1980), focusing on what emerges in the intersections of variables, and not in oppositional terms. *This implies rethinking the notion of difference beyond sexual difference, although including it in a complex network.*

Even reproduction, which was always the predominant plot, ceases to be unfailingly linked to the male–female union. This affects the notion of gender identification, which has always been subject to dualistic frameworks. Added to this point is the fact that while the egg–sperm union marks a biological difference, advances in cloning may be moving faster than our ability to imagine new forms of reproduction, such as cloning from stem cells. These developments force us to think within the paradigm of complexity (Morin, 1990) and go beyond the classical binary sexual difference; these are notions that demand to be deconstructed. As referred to previously, these thoughts do not erase sexual difference: the proposal is to include it within a complex network and to recognise its different significations according to time and culture (Laqueur, 1990).

Within the framework of these developments, I had proposed *to think of "difference" as a symbolic operation, a category that marks distinction*, as Heidegger (1988) pointed out. And that this symbolic motion involves different levels of differences:

a *gender difference* (based on identifications including gender identifications)
b *anatomical difference* always subjected to interpretations
c *psychosexual difference* within the field of desire (including infantile sexual theories) and also
d linguistic and discursive differences that can be analysed in the patient discourse.

Gender identifications as well as itineraries of desire are never only masculine or feminine. Patients' imaginary narratives on "difference" therefore lead us to pay attention to notions that are usually naturalised within the norms in force. In my view, we can think of them as constituting a kind of *bastion or bulwark*, using the notion proposed by Baranger and Baranger (1961–1962). A bastion that needs to be deconstructed both by patients and analysts, since everything I have developed also applies to ourselves as analysts. Transference and countertransference are at stake, as well as beliefs, ideologies, and implicit or explicit theories of each analyst.

In this line of thought, I stress that the recognition of sexual difference is only one aspect of the broad domain of symbolic difference, to which I add that sexual difference always responds to an interpretation of culture, as already pointed out. In this sense, let us recall the infantile sexual theories, an interpretation of the male child in the face of sexual difference; a difference that he interprets as castration. This imaginary narrative reveals that he interprets difference with the elements possessed by a small child centred in the narcissistic threat to his most precious organ (false interpretation, as Freud [1908] pointed out). Many conclusions can be drawn from here about adult sexual theories and psychoanalytic sexual theories.

Finally, *difference itself is an enigma, it is the unknown, it is an opaque category*. And we, children and adults, psychoanalysts or not, in the frame of different cultures tend to provide meanings to the enigma, to the question of why we are different. Access to the category of symbolic difference implies for each subject crossing a way out from extreme narcissism and this means that finally, *access to difference is the recognition of otherness*, of what is radically other with respect to the self. This is a symbolic operation that goes beyond sexual object choice or gender identification. *From this symbolic access, which exceeds classical dualisms, we can think of a broader notion of difference and rethink the notions of identification and identity, which are always in the process of becoming.* This proposal recognises the different levels of differences already mentioned but including them within the encompassing category of "difference" as a symbolic operation. This exceeds the classical binarism although including it as part of a totality that is more than the sum of its parts. Clinical approach to current unconventional subjectivities demands that we include the coexistence of these different levels of difference(s).

8   To conclude, the access to symbolic difference understood as a symbolic operation requires a function that is usually called *paternal function* or *paternal law.* In several publications, I proposed calling it the *third-party symbolic function* to avoid the inevitable androcentric connotations of that denomination (Glocer Fiorini, 2013). That is, although we all know that it is a function that can be performed by the mother, a grandparent or another significant other, the mere fact of calling it "paternal" naturalises something that should be deeply discussed. It is not that the mother internalises a function called "paternal" or the "father's law", but that she has her own symbolic reserves to perform this function (Benjamin, 1988). Therefore, it is not the same to speak of the paternal function as the third-party symbolic function. In my opinion, this is a key element in relation to the analysts' position, their theories, private and official, their beliefs and ideology. Thus, my proposal is to consider the third-party function as a deconstruction of the paternal law and its androcentric connotations. In this context, we can say that identifications, as well as desires, represent the multiplicity of the phantasmatic life but that both are normalised in a dualistic way. "Normalisation" tends to erase that symbolic difference goes beyond strict dichotomies and seeks for the recognition of otherness.

References

Baranger, M. & Baranger, W. (1961–1962). La situación analítica como campo dinámico. *Revista Uruguaya de Psicoanálisis, IV*(1): 3–54.

Benjamin, J. (1988). *The Bonds of Love: Psychoanalysis, Feminism and the Problem of Domination.* New York: Pantheon.

Castoriadis, C. (1986). *El psicoanálisis, proyecto y elucidación.* Buenos Aires: Nueva Visión, 1992.

Castoriadis-Aulagnier, P. (1975). *The Violence of Interpretation: From Pictogram to Statement.* Hove: Brunner/Routledge, 2001.

Deleuze, G. & Guattari, F. (1972). *El antiEdipo.* Barcelona: Barral Ed, 1973.

Deleuze, G. & Guattari, F. (1980). *Mil mesetas.* Valencia: Pre-Textos, 1994.

Freud, S. (1908). On the sexual theories of children. *S. E., 9*: 207–226.

Freud, S. (1923). The ego and the id. *S. E.*, *19*: 3–66.

Freud, S. (1924). The dissolution of the Oedipus complex. *S. E.*, *19*: 171–179.

Freud, S. (1925). Some psychical consequences of the anatomical distinction between the sexes. *S. E.*, *19*: 243–258.

Glocer Fiorini, L. (1998). The feminine in psychoanalysis: A complex construction. *Journal of Clinical Psychoanalysis*, *7*: 421–439. [In Spanish [1994]: La posición femenina. Una construcción heterogénea. *Revista de Psicoanálisis*, 51(3): 587–603].

Glocer Fiorini, L. (2013). Deconstruyendo el concepto de función paterna. Un paradigma interpelado. *Revista de Psicoanálisis*, *LXX*(4): 671–681.

Glocer Fiorini, L. (2014). Repensando o complexo de Édipo. *Revista Brasileira de Psicanálise*, *48*(4): 47–57.

Glocer Fiorini, L. (2017). *Sexual Difference in Debate. Bodies, Desires, and Fictions*. London: Karnac. In: Spanish: *La diferencia sexual en debate. Cuerpos, deseos ficciones*. Buenos Aires: Lugar Editorial, 2015.

Glocer Fiorini, L. (2020). *Deconstructing the Feminine. Subjectivities in Transition*. London: Routledge. (In Spanish: *Lo femenino y el pensamiento complejo*. Buenos Aires: Lugar Editorial. Primera edición, 2001).

Glocer Fiorini, L. (2022). The analyst's attempts to classify and their effects on countertransference. *Psychoanalytic Review*, *109*(3): 257–276.

Green, A. (1982). El género neutro. In: J.-B. Pontalis et al. *Bisexualidad y diferencia de los sexos*. Buenos Aires: Ed. del 80 [*Bisexualité et différence des sexes*]. Paris: Gallimard, 2000.

Heidegger, M. (1988). *Identidad y diferencia*. Barcelona, España: Anthropos.

Lacan, J. (1972–1973). *The Seminar, Book XX: Encore*. London: Norton, 2000.

Laplanche, J. (1980). *Problématiques II: Castration-symbolisations*. Paris: PUF.

Laplanche, J. (1999). *Entre seducción e inspiración: El hombre*. Buenos Aires: Amorrortu, 2001.

Laqueur, T. (1990). *Making Sex: Body and Gender from the Greeks to Freud*. Cambridge, MA: Harvard University Press.

Morin, E. (1990). *Introducción al pensamiento complejo*. Barcelona: Gedisa, 1995.

Pontalis, J-B. (1973). El inasible a medias. In: *Bisexualidad y diferencia de los sexos*. Buenos Aires: Ed. del 80, 1982 [*Bisexualité et différence des sexes*]. Paris: Gallimard.

Trías, E. (1991). *Lógica del límite*. Barcelona: Destino.

Winnicott, D. (1959). The fate of the transitional object. In: *Psycho-Analytic Explorations*. London: Karnac, 1989.

Part II

Identifications, body, and gender

Introduction

Siri Erika Gullestad

Historical perspective

In our present-day societies, and within psychoanalysis, the debate about sex and gender has become hot and polarised. Problems previously found in clinical work have now moved to the courts and politics. However, as historians have argued, attempts to define sex and gender have been a recurrent theme in medical history, a basic question being whether sex and gender are dichotomies or spectrums. Medicine has always been preoccupied with bodies and identities it has categorised as "abnormal", from homosexuality to trans identity (Slagstad, 2021). In the late 19th century, however, psychiatrists developed a diagnostic framework for so-called "abnormal sexuality" that previously had been a moral and religious concern. The German psychiatrist Richard von Krafft-Ebing created a taxonomy for what he saw as sexual "perversions", published in *Psychopathia sexualis* in 1896. Krafft-Ebing saw homosexuality as a *degenerative disorder* and spoke about the *delusional* idea of sex transformation, or the feeling of belonging to the "other" sex. On the other hand, however, there were sexual reformists psychiatrists, like Magnus Hirschfeld, who established the *Institut für Sexualwissenschaft* in Berlin in 1919. This institute became a place where sexual minorities could come together. Hirschfeld placed sex and sexuality on a spectrum, and homosexuality was *part of human variation*: "the human being is not man or woman but man *and* woman" (quoted from Slagstad, 2021, 2). Under the supervision of Hirschfeld, doctors performed the first sex-reassignment surgeries on trans people. The institute and its enormous library were burnt by Hitler's gangs in the early 1930s. Certainly, a demonstration of "the political nature of sex" (Slagstad, 2021, 1).

Psychoanalysis

What about psychoanalysis? To be sure, the attitude of open inquiry towards human sexuality that we find in Freud's (1905) work has not dominated psychoanalysis since. When during the seventies the American Psychiatric Association removed homosexuality as a diagnosis, psychoanalysts

DOI: 10.4324/9781003534440-7

protested and tried to reverse the decision (Fonagy & Allison, 2015). The American psychoanalyst, Ralph Roughton, has documented how standard psychoanalytic practice for long implied efforts to change gay people's sexual orientation (Roughton, 2000, 2001) – a successful analytic outcome was synonymous with attaining a heterosexual orientation.

The current controversial discussion about transgender reminds us about the pathologising discourse of homosexuality in the past. For example, psychoanalytic authors have regarded transgender as indices of underlying *narcissistic disturbance* (Chiland 2000; Oppenheimer 1991, 1992; Quinodoz 1998; Stein 1995), as *perversion* (Argentieri 2009; Limentani 1979; Socarides 1970), and as *difficulties in separating* (Coates 1990, 2006; Coates and Moore 1998) or *disidentifying from the mother* (Stoller 1985) (all cited from Saketopoulou, 2014). Or trans is seen as a *defence against castration* and as a *refusal of the classical distinction between man and woman*. What is promising, as I see it, is that the different positions within psychoanalysis, e.g., concerning how to define sex and gender, are now being openly debated. An example: The *Psychoanalytic Controversy* section in *IJP* recently reported a long discussion between David Bell and Avgi Saketopolou. Here, the moderator maintains that "however much someone feels he's a girl, the *fact* is that he's a boy" (Blass, Bell, & Saketopoulou, 2021, 975, my italics), a binary definition contrasting major medical institutions' broader, more complex spectrum definitions of gender. On the other hand, in 2017, the IPA established a *Sexual and Gender Diversity Studies committee* with the aim of investigating and exploring the many questions and complexities that surround sexual and gender diversity. In 2019, the American Psychoanalytic Association issued a formal apology to the LGBTQ+ community for its previous views and discriminatory actions (Knafo & Lo Bosco, 2020). And in 2022, the psychoanalyst, Jack Drescher, received the prestigious Sigourney Award for his pioneering work and critical psychoanalytic re-thinking of gender and sexuality on a scientific basis (Drescher, 2020). Importantly, Drescher contributed to the recent revision of ICD-11 that helped end decades of diagnostic pathologising of sexual and gender identities.

On this background, the present book originating in the work of the *Sexual and Gender Diversity Studies committee* is a precious gift to our field! When reading this section on *Identifications, body, and gender*, I was reminded of Freud's discussion of what characterises a scientific theory, i.e., what is the difference between a speculative theory and a theory erected on empirical interpretation (Freud, 1914). Theoretical ideas, says Freud, are not the foundation of science – "That foundation is observation alone". Ideas are not at the bottom, but "the top of the whole structure, and they can be replaced and discarded without damaging it" (Freud, 1914, 77). This formulation implies that the starting point for psychoanalytic concepts is clinical observation. Furthermore, psychoanalytic science knows its concepts are tentative and imperfect and in continuous development towards greater precision – psychoanalysis is prepared to replace existing concepts with new ones, if necessary.

The chapters in this book are characterised by the kind of attitude Freud describes – an attitude of open inquiry towards the new sexual landscape of today. To be sure, the way we think about sex and gender has radically changed in the past few decades, a main reason being that young people challenge norms that offer only two options: male and female, straight or gay. Many are identifying as *queer* or *pansexual*, queer as an umbrella term for diverse non-heterosexual identities (Knafo & Lo Bosco, 2020). Among this growing profusion of sexual and gender identities, many analysts are left perplexed (Drescher, 2020). And while progress has been made in the study of gay and lesbian sexual behaviour, bisexuality and transgender sexuality for long remained "the stepchildren of psychoanalytic understanding" (Blechner, 2015, 203). My own concern has been that we in the psychoanalytic field will not be able to meet the challenge presented by gender diversity, but that we rather will hold on to a biological binary model of sex and a dogmatic understanding of sexual development. In short, my worry has been that we will pathologise transgender, like psychoanalysts too often did with homosexuality in the past (Fonagy & Allison, 2015; Roughton, 2000, 2001).

In line with Freud, Tiziana Bastianini in her chapter *Body, Sexuality, Gender: between identifying project and desire* reminds us that clinical work should be the primary source for theoretical exploration, so as not to risk abstract speculation – an easy ground for the establishment of ideologies and prejudices. Furthermore, from a research point of view, I would like to emphasise the importance of systematic studies, e.g., of how non-binary identities develop. In his chapter, *Gender identities and identifications in a changing world,* as stated by Lingiardi, a qualitative study of interviews inviting young adults identified as non-binary to narrate the history of their development. The study makes us listen to the young people's voices, to their own subjective experiences, and allows us to become sensitised to their exploration, uncertainty, deconstruction, and need for mirroring. Gender incongruence calls us to the deepest respect for subjectivities, as stated by Lingiardi, which in the current age are sometimes sacrificed in the name of identity politics, with easy media traction. For sure, transgender identity may be binary, often from a very early age, resulting in need for gender affirmative treatment; the non-binary adolescents, however, may understand themselves as subjectivities "beyond the genders". Whereas the psychoanalyst, Robert Stoller, looked for the individual's "core gender identity", careful listening to the new subjectivities invites new metaphors for describing gender, like "soft assembly" (Harris, 2005), "self-theorization" (Saketopoulou & Pellegrini, 2023) or what Bastianini in her chapter calls an "autopoietic dimension".

New observations may imply critically revising existing theoretical concepts. For example, Lingiardi creatively suggests that we revisit the

Oedipal "complex" as Oedipal "complexity", arguing that the latter, emphasising "the third" within the parental couple as well as the "position within generations", may apply irrespective of parents' anatomical characteristics. Such revision allows us to meet the new family constellations of our present Western societies, like growing up with same-gender parents, with an attitude of open inquiry rather than prejudice.

As psychoanalysts we should attend empathically also to voices expressing gender transformations through literature and photography. Lingiardi, as well Luca Bruno in his chapter *Trans-identifications,* call attention to Paul Preciado's texts. Strongly critical of a psychoanalysis that, according to Preciado, often represents a medical gaze, Preciado articulates the need for questioning the binary epistemology and the naturalisation of genders by affirming that there is an irreducible multiplicity of sexes, genders, and sexualities: "Sexuality is a political theatre in which desire – not anatomy – writes the script" (Preciado, 2019). Certainly, psychoanalysis needs to be in dialogue with our current culture! However, the conceptual opening of identity as subjectively perceived, no longer imposed by biology, but affirmed by desire, is in no way an easy process on the concrete, lived level. To be sure, processes of identification and change may also contain pain, anxiety, and mourning.

All chapters refer to Freud's radical theory of *psychosexuality,* a driving force referring to pleasure seeking which must be distinguished from sexuality as a reproductive function. Pleasure seeking takes manifold forms and has different non-genital expressions in all of us. Bisexual and homosexual desires as well as rude, obscene, and polymorphously perverse fantasies are part of human eroticism – our sexuality is often experienced as an "otherness" (Gullestad, 2020). Indeed, Freud (1905, 160) sees the so-called perverse as part of normal sexuality:

> No healthy person, it appears, can fail to make some addition that might be called perverse to the normal sexual aim; and the universality of this finding is in itself enough to show how inappropriate it is to use the term perversion as a term of reproach.

Hence Freud has a neutral stance on the value of sexual practice (Moss 2014; Scarfone, 2014). Rather, it is lack of tolerance for the perverse that leads to neurosis: "Thus symptoms are formed in part at the cost of abnormal sexuality; neuroses are, so to say, the negative of perversions" (Freud 1905, 165). The roads of desire are multifarious! Stein speaks about "the normative abnormality of sexuality" (Stein, 2008, 47).

Pointing to our "psychological bisexuality" Freud emphasised that speaking of "masculine" and "feminine" ways of behaving is "only giving way to anatomy or convention" (Freud, 1933, 114). Anat Schumann, in *Reclaiming Psychic Bisexuality: Revisiting Winnicott's "The Split-off Male and Female Elements to be Found Clinically in Men and Women"* (1966), explores the dialectic interplay between "masculine" and "feminine" as a creative psychic movement relating to the "bisexual subjectivity" in both men and women. Psychoanalysis does not describe what a woman is, Freud says, but sets out enquiring how she comes into being, "how a woman develops out of a child with a bisexual disposition" (ibid., 16). In her feminist manifesto, *The second sex*, published sixteen years after Freud's essay, the writer and philosopher Simone de Beauvoir (1949), referring to Freud, famously stated that one is not *born* as a woman, rather one *becomes* a woman. The body cannot be described exclusively in biological terms, to be a body is to live in a body in a specific culture. As elaborated by the present book, culture implies emphasising human relatedness, how we are exposed to others' gaze – and our deep need and desire for recognition and psychic validation by other people. Many transgender individuals report the pain of being misrecognised by their families.

The present polarised political debate about transgender seems to bear witness to what has been called a kind of binary terror – panic unleashed when people are faced with the blurring of boundaries (male/female; active/passive) that have been integral to a culture's social fabric. With our concept of countertransference, psychoanalysts are in a unique position to understand such anxieties. Confronted with transgender, we need to abandon illusions of understanding in favour of a humble, inquiring attitude.

I want to congratulate the editors of the present book for inviting contributions that demonstrate a respectful, attentive listening to the broadened field of subjectivities we encounter today, conveying new ways of articulating and of living sexuality and gender.

References

De Beauvoir, S. (1949). *Le deuxième sexe*. Paris: Gallimard.

Blass, R., Bell, D. & Saketopoulou, A. (2021). Can we think psychoanalytically about transgenderism? An expanded live Zoom debate with Avgi Saketopoulou, moderated by Rachel Blass. *International Journal of Psychoanalysis*, 102 (5): 968–1000.

Blechner, M. (2015). Bigenderism and bisexuality. *Contemporary Psychoanalysis*, 51 (3): 503–522.

Drescher, J. (2020). From bisexuality to intersexuality: rethinking gender categories. In L. Hertzmann & J. Newbigin, (eds.) *Sexuality and gender now. Moving beyond heteronormativity*. New York: Routledge, 167–188.

Fonagy, P. & Allison, (2015). A scientific theory of homosexuality. In: A. Lemma, & P. Lynch, P. (eds.) *Sexualities. Contemporary psychoanalytic perspectives*. London: Routledge.

Freud, S. (1905). Three Essays on the Theory of Sexuality. *S. E.*, Vol. 7, 123–245.

Freud, S. (1914). *On Narcissism: An Introduction. S. E.*, 14, 67–102.

Freud, S. (1933). Femininity. New introductory lectures. Analysis terminable and interminable. *SE*, 22, 112–135.

Gullestad, S. E. (2020). The otherness of sexuality: Exploring the conflicted nature of drive, desire and object choice. *International Journal of Psychoanalysis*, 101(1): 64–83.

Harris, A. (2005). *Gender as soft assembly*. Hillsdale, NJ: The Analytic Press.

Knafo, D. & Lo Bosco, R. (2020). *The new sexual landscape and contemporary psychoanalysis*. London: Confer Books.

Moss, D. (2014). "Introduction: "The sexual aberrations" – Where do we stand today?" *The Psychoanalytic Quarterly* 83: 241–247.

Preciado P. B. (2019). *An apartment on Uranus: Chronicles of the Crossing*. MIT Press, Semiotext(e).

Roughton, R. (2000). Sometimes a desire is just a desire: Gay men and their analysts. *Gender and Psychoanalysis* 5: 259–273.

Roughton, R. E. (2001). Four men in treatment: an evolving perspective on homosexuality and bisexuality, 1965 to 2000. *Journal of the American Psychoanalytic Association* 49: 1187–1217.

Saketopoulou, A. (2014). Mourning the body as bedrock: Developmental considerations in treating transsexual patients analytically. *Journal of the American Psychoanalytic Association* 62 (5): 773–806.

Saketopoulou, A. & Pellegrini, A. (2023). *Gender Without Identity*. New York, Uit Books.

Scarfone, D. 2014. "The Three Essays and the Meaning of the Infantile Sexual in Psychoanalysis." *The Psychoanalytic Quarterly* 83: 327–344.

Slagstad, K. (2021). The Political Nature of Sex –Transgender in the History of Medicine. *New England Journal of Medicine*. Doctoral dissertation, University of Oslo, Norway.

Stein, R. (2008). The Otherness of Sexuality: Excess. *Journal of the American Psychoanalytic Association* 56: 43–71.

4 Body, sexuality, gender

Between identificatory project and desire

Tiziana Bastianini

Freud (1914) wrote "Every vested interest is alien to me". This comment underlines the spirit in which I intend in these brief reflections to address a complex issue such as the one that has emerged over the last twenty years in the scientific community, including the psychoanalytic community, concerning the relationship between sexuality and gender. His statement, in my view, represents the Freudian psychoanalytic spirit that has ceaselessly confronted us throughout time, with the awareness of the *provisional dimension* of any "clinical–theoretical truth" based on conjectures that may prove inadequate to explain from time to time the "new phenomena" observed. Such a perspective highlights the fallout on the epistemological and more generally theoretical level, of a focus on the complexity of the nodes of possible relations between observed phenomena. We think of human beings as living organisms, rich in relations with outcomes that are not immediately foreseeable, autopoietic systems (Maturana & Varela, 1985) capable of generating their own organisation by themselves in relation to an environment with which they dialogue in terms of identifications, collisions, fluctuations, and collusions. A psyche that can reveal to us the complexity of the levels at play, beyond the usual patterns, *in a conceptualisation that is more open to meaning and history*: to encounter, finally, *the unexpected*.

In this perspective, our considerations may provide an opportunity to resume and/or continue a reflection on the themes of the sexual, of gender, in their complex current articulations. Here, I refer to the psychic pluralisation of the sexed subject, which, starting from the problem posed by sexual differences (in their intricate historical genealogy, just bear in mind the other voice of the feminine), has gradually extended its ramifications through research into themes such as gender, sexual orientation, and sex. The question of the human and its constitution in original bonds runs across numerous disciplines, and the theme of gender in dialogue with the gendered dimension of existence represents one of its most significant junctions. Although we are aware that the paradox of gender does not represent something unique to be found at the nuclear level of the individual, it nevertheless constitutes a specific experience of identity that can create psychic friction. I am thinking of the multiple and heterogeneous origin of

DOI: 10.4324/9781003534440-8

infantile sexuality, which only later will be organised into the adult genital assumption. If extended sexuality in the Freudian sense (see Laplanche's *Sexual*, 2019) – first and foremost infantile psychosexuality, unconscious and embodied, beyond the difference between the sexes, hence not a mere biological dimension – is the paradigm of research and exploration that can transform any function or place of the body into an erogenous zone according to the drive of the subject's unconscious creativity; likewise, we become increasingly aware that this drive represents that territory of exposure to the adult that nourishes and protects at the origin of life and simultaneously activates desire and pleasure and thus exposes us to total dependence. It is a desire that decentralises and exposes us to the other whose gaze, recognition, and love, we have a primary need. Thinking about the theme of recognition makes us aware of how much we cannot separate the biological from the cultural dimension, between the embodied and the symbolic bodies; moreover, it helps us understand how the other we refer to is a complex other that is not necessarily enclosed in the dyad, *being at the same time another object and a subject* carrying a history, bonds and a future horizon that makes her/him the interlocutor in a complex chain of investments, identifications, and desires which only fortuitously and temporarily becomes enclosed in the dyad. We are born within psychic matrices, immersed from conception in the universe of the deep investments of those who generated us. The subject's psychic space takes shape in the experience of the place occupied in the other's mind and in the images of the self that the other can and will be able to mirror back. Every human subject, even before birth, is called upon to take up some places in the chain of desire or need of another, or sometimes of several others: "We constitute ourselves on their dreams of unrealised desires" (Kaës et al., 1993; Kaës, 2004).

I believe it is fundamental in this perspective to continue to question ourselves around the body, gender, desire, and the bond that unites and at the same time separates us from the other outside of us, the other in us, the other of the other, in order to carry out the deconstruction of the elements that impede the singular and unique trajectories of development through forms of subjective appropriation, creating suffering in each human being in search of the psychic uniqueness, at the basis of the sense of self, which lies at the origin of life beyond the difference of sexes and genders. If relatedness is a constitutive event of the subject's self, inscribed in the dialectic of recognition, this relatedness is the matrix against the background of which the subject's autopoietic dimension takes shape, capable of bringing its unconscious creativity into play, *even in a profound dialogue with the generations that preceded it*. If, following Freud, we continue to think that the drive has a bodily source linked to sensory, sensorimotor experiences, until it becomes an imaginary source that invests the body in its multiple dimensions in constant connection with the object, it is to this dialogue that we refer to identify the coordinates of the process of the formation of individuality. This process is plastic and constantly involves forming and dissolving forms that reveal a profound logic of feeling. If gender appears to be the element that upsets thought, as Freud reminds us, the pair in male–female opposition is the most rebellious and enigmatic one. Numerous reasons inscribed in the primacy of the other can be condensed in it. Other, whose assignment at the origin of life makes us that boy or girl, the product of the desire and fantasies of the couple that conceived and generated him or her. This process, passing through the identificatory vector must be able to reach, in each subject, a necessary quality of subjective appropriation of gender in dialogue with sex *with respect to attributions and identificatory junctions*: an inner dialogue capable of containing aporias, contradictions, and latency, until reaching those integrative possibilities that the individual psyche allows.

We ask then: What comes first, gender or sex? What does bodily care convey within the primary attachment relationship? What affects of pleasure/disappointment, fantasies are present in the maternal, paternal psyche in thinking about the gender and sex of their son/daughter? In what form does their unconscious sexed desire come into play in this hypothetical assignment? Gender, although originally assigned, must subsequently be placed on the side of the ego or subject and not on the side of the object and object choice. I am reminded of the words of a young man grappling with his own painful tribulations and identity transitions. At some point, he put it this way: "I am a woman because that is how I feel and recognise myself, in a biologically male body. Who will fall in love with this bizarre being? And will I fall in love with a man as a woman can or as if caught in a homosexual current?" The question arises: With whom is the young man identified when he attempts to be the subject of his own love desire, or when he aspires to be its object? Is this perhaps the precariousness and complexity of the binary logic to which some theorists dealing with these issues refer? Perhaps, we can imagine a kaleidoscope of perspectives in which desire and identification need not be thought of as mutually exclusive, perhaps, we need to conceive of "even a way to describe how heterosexuality becomes the locus of homosexual passion, or to describe how homosexuality becomes the secret passage to heterosexual passion?" (Butler, 2004).

What is the price we pay as we become what we are? What are the conditions of growth that allow an individual to exist as an expression of "I am, I am alive, I am myself", Winnicott (1975) wondered? In her reflection, Butler (2004) emphasised the psychic and social costs of the exclusion that the subject puts in place in the expression of parts of themselves, under the pressure of environmental expectations, to gain an acceptable, intelligible identity, worthy of recognition. If, in part, the constitution of the subject passes through the mourning of possessing what is different from oneself, this process can take place in different ways from the plurality and multiplicity of identificatory processes. Psychic bisexuality, after all, was a central issue for Freud (1920, 524) in line with the studies of biology and embryology of his time:

> Psychoanalysis places itself on the same plane as biology in that it as-
> sumes an original bisexuality of the human (as well as the animal) in-
> dividual. It cannot, however, elucidate the profound essence of what
> is called 'masculine' and 'feminine' in everyday language or in biol-
> ogy, and must limit itself to assuming these two concepts as the basis
> of its work. If it attempts a further reduction, masculinity dissolves
> into activity and femininity into passivity, which is too little.

Again in 1930, he added "The theory of bisexuality still has numerous obscure points, and we cannot but feel strongly embarrassed in psychoa-nalysis that we have not yet succeeded in finding its links with the theory of drives". In this perspective, Malobou's (2022) thoughts on the living and its logics, on the need to think in epigenetic terms of our history, seem to me fruitful. A continuous cross-reference between physical factors and en-vironmental and social influences, and then:

> (…) how can we not see at work, in the constitution of phenotypic in-
> dividuality, the formation of a singularity… and place epigenesis, the
> development of every living being in the entre-deux of biology and
> history? It is surprising to note that the work of epigenetics is often
> described metaphorically by scientists as an improvisation, a practical
> or artistic elaboration, a creative spontaneity, as if it referred back to
> the register of interpretative freedom.

Once again, psychoanalysis is called upon to question the conflicting and increasingly complex relationship in the evolution of the human spe-cies of the numerous implications inherent to the nature–culture binomial, without simplifications of any kind. We need to cultivate a reflection that makes hypotheses and thoughts dialogue dialectically and circulate in a complex way, starting with our clinical work – a constitutive feature of psychoanalysis – with which we are confronted daily. What I wish to em-phasise is the complexity of the relationships between sexuality, gender identity, and the bonds of love between human beings, articulated in their various forms. After all, we intend to explore this aspect of life. Expanded sexuality (Laplanche, 2019) is the great psychoanalytic discovery and, in this perspective, in order to keep our theorising alive we must continue to ask ourselves whether it is possible to outline a model of the sexual, an expanded metapsychology that can take into account an infantile sexual-ity with its own libidinal polysemy, permanently housed in the adult and in constant dialogue with the dimensions of primary love, of the other as referent, both in a dyadic and triadic sense.

Laplanche (2019) states that gender is plural. It is usually double, with masculine and feminine, but not by nature. It is often plural, as in the history of languages, and in social evolution. Sex is dual. It is so because of sexual reproduction. Just as the pleasure of play resides in the possibility of maintaining a dialectical tension between reality and fantasy and loses its enjoyment when one of the polarities collapses because of a profound split in the psyche, in the same way infantile sexuality with its creative force and the equally fundamental drive inherent in the search for the object, will be equally indispensable in order to maintain one's own sense of existence intact. The initial disposition of the issue is, therefore, the necessary cross-reference between body and relation that modulates itself as a constitutive necessity of the presence of others in the making of a subject. Once again, it is the presence of the other conceived early on in both a dyadic and triadic sense. In this respect, Butler's (2004) discussion with the hypotheses put forward by Benjamin is very interesting and I refer to the issues concerning pre-oedipal identifications in constant dialogue with oedipal identifications, the way they can be integrated or kept separate in the psyche and can be an obstacle to bonds, and to the male–female dialogue, as with the male and female aspects present in each psyche. Boys and girls struggle from the earliest moments of life to maintain an identification with both sexes in the need/desire to have both mother and father as safe and recognising objects. In harmonious situations, identifications with both parents allow the child to assimilate the characteristics of each without identity limits; identification with the opposite sex can coexist with identification with one's own sex. It is in the later oedipal events that, while recognising one's own gender, everyone should be able to express the masculine and feminine aspects of the self. This integration of identifications can be the premise that allows one to understand both the other and the self.

In the same way, I think it is important to revisit the theme of the creation of a triangular space, starting from the primary scene, as a fundamental organiser of the internal and external relations inherent in the possible interweaving of the subject's sexuality and creativity. We know from research on childhood and from psychoanalytic clinical work, that in the child's mind, there is a kind of primary triangle, in which the infant is in relation to the couple bond that the parents share. This sharing of the couple bond, both in duality and triangularity, can find its matrix in the mode of the affective pattern of being and relating. In this perspective, infants – from their experience of encountering their mother, father, and any significant person in the developmental environment – build a pattern of the characteristics shared in the encounter with the peculiarities and specificities of that environment. These patterns of being with and doing together represent the first matrices of what constitutes "being and doing as a couple", that is, that they can be invested as a psychic "object". They represent the form beforehand of what will become the *"couple object"*, at the centre of the oedipal configuration and organiser of the latter (Roussillon, 2014). This mode of relating to the couple object prefigures the various possibilities that the child's psyche can play in terms of presence, exclusion from and in the couple in relation to the elements at play, whether they are oedipal or pre-oedipal, that is, identifying with difference and/or similarity to the point of being able to reach that psychic acquisition that characterises the oedipal vicissitudes: "to be alone in the presence of the couple" (Roussillon, 2014).

Of course, these trajectories are profoundly influenced by the evolutionary vicissitudes of the subject, they may allow for a feeling of self that is constituted of representations of different nature including those related to gender. What is important to emphasise in this perspective is that for each individual the representation of the self with his/her own gender coexists with a representation of the self of the opposite gender. A person capable of integrating these aspects and maintaining a fluidity and flexibility towards each part of the self could, therefore, feel that he or she harbours a female or a male ego, without thereby feeling the perception of self as belonging to one or the other sex compromised (Winnicott, 1966). The traumatic scenario, on the contrary, would rigidly fix the identifying polarities without any dialectic between multiplicity and identity. In short, the psyche would lack the capacity to contain integration, cohesion, and identity in dialectical relation with multiplicity and difference (Bastianini, 2017).

We continue to question the metamorphosis of the sexual in relation to desire and the forms it takes in this historical phase. The expression of desire traces trajectories in which sexual investment, gender, and orientation become divided, pluralised. Moreover, we are increasingly aware that the pleasure to which we link the sexual can depend both on arousal, which sometimes turns out to be too "enigmatic", and on pleasure related to the lowering of tension. It is relevant, from my point of view, to keep in mind that the "the sexual and its discontent", or its metamorphoses, seem to move along apparently opposing polarities: on the one hand, in contemporary clinical work, we observe the fall of desire that often leads to a disinvestment of the erotic dimension and young men and women are increasingly afraid of the intimacy that connects them to one another. On the other hand, we observe the expression of a desire that, in the search for pleasure, pursues trajectories that break down and pluralise the subject in a whirling dimension, in which the importance of the object through which pleasure is obtained is attenuated, to the point of disappearing. Sometimes, the defensive search for a sense of just one's own existence that can sustain itself on sexual experiences alone becomes a priority.

Love was a religion even in Lucretius' time, a condition that was believed to be induced by a god through his power, capable of binding the lover to the beloved. Nussbaum, in book *Therapy of Desire* (1996), tells us that in our time, the erotic passion of the individual, since there is no longer any religiously based passion, must bear all the intensity of desire where, now, we only must reckon with fragile worldly projects that have to incorporate all life's hopes that were once directed towards the divine. Perhaps we need to wonder again what is the reason that throughout our history has led us towards a "disenchantment" with erotic–romantic love that was once experienced by men and women as the central goal, at least during a part of life? Is this not the cultural and social temperament within which the forms of human flourishing are inscribed, especially in relation to desire and affection in their very precarious declines? If the true and proper end of love, which is also expressed in sexuality, is to achieve a closeness that allows intimate co-responsibility with the other, it is nevertheless true that lovers who experience a profound need for the other as painful dependence, from which they feel a weakness originates, will seek to destroy the otherness of the beloved; there is too much suffering in being aware of one's own incompleteness! In *The Fragility of the Good*, Nussbaum (2001) suggests that the best human life is one that can take the risk of loss and suffering, that can encounter Eros as well as its dangers.

Stoller (1968) claimed that, with the same confidence as an art critic, he would reaffirm his conviction that the construction of erotic arousal was just as subtle, complex, inspired, profoundly moving, fascinatingly impressive, problematic, ingrained in the unconscious, and visited by the genius as the creation of a dream or a work of art. Clinical work, when we can listen to our patients without saturating the field with our pervasive beliefs, teaches us that such complex and sometimes inescapable erotic scenarios not only allow us to safeguard sexual pleasure, but sometimes present themselves as peculiar forms of psychic subjectivation, the only ones capable of safeguarding the feeling of self, of subjective identity. We do not yet have sufficient clinical experience, in this new scenario of the pluralisation of gender not necessarily consistent with sex, of the fate of the extended sexual in adolescence, for example, in those subjects who will produce what is currently diagnosed (with all the associated problematics) as gender incongruence. In adolescence, the need for subjective appropriation of gender identity and sexual dimension urges for a potential definition in which to be "really oneself", in some possible articulation, even plural and fluid.

I am thinking of the reflections of a mother of a young man who has decided to undertake a sexual transition towards femininity. She is aware of various traumatic impingements in his history, especially in the problematic relationships entertained with primary objects, in his relationships with his father and her. There is however a significant element, peculiar to this historical era: the young man feels the need to reject a devalued and feared masculine with which he cannot identify, which he cannot appropriate for numerous individual and social reasons. Can we assume that identification with the feminine is experienced as capable of repairing and temporarily allowing a disidentification from that masculine experienced as "not me", whose inscription is in the folds of a turbulent and poorly psychicised relational history? But we must still ask ourselves: to whom does this drive belong? To the young man and the extent of his singular traumatisms, or does it perhaps herald radical transformations around the articulation of the masculine and the feminine as they are taking shape in this beginning of the new millennium?

In other words, it is a sign that might herald an attempt that comes from afar and that in every historical period has tried to make its way into every new generation, to integrate those elements of human bisexuality, the voices of excluded bodies, too long expelled from the construction of the subject and treated as residues, unassimilable remains. I am reminded, in this regard, of Fachinelli's reflections and on an unarmed psychoanalysis in the face of the new unforeseen processes – young men and women – as well as all the essential human experiences that had remained outside the political dimension. Rethinking culture and politics starting from what were traditionally considered "waste", "residues", unpresentable experiences, meant in some way becoming "barbarians", distancing oneself from the continuity of the known, questioning the optimistic relationship that western civilisation had entertained with its techno-scientific goals. "Even the young people of 1968", wrote Fachinelli (2022), "had appeared 'unexpectedly', like 'barbarians' from outside an exhausted civilisation, as if by "a trick of Eros". Along with them, "unthought-of perspectives" emerged, proving the incompleteness of the alternatives granted to the human species. Who knows, if one of the perspectives to which young men and women fighting the rigidities of identity expressed in binary conceptions to affirm the fluidity of gender, with changing and contrasting gender identifications, might not also become unconscious interpreters of new needs that the human species is encountering in a new form of articulation of the human? In other words, bisexuality, the irruption of the feminine, expelled and non-integrated sexuality in search of a new place in the economy of the contemporary subject are attempting to make their way, to open up avenues.

Perhaps, there is an analogy with the unconscious psychic work that some individuals experience through their bodies as a kind of affective semiosis, a kind of emotional grammar entrusted to bodies – bodies that sometimes hate each other, with which one cannot live, and through which in any case one can carry out complex forms of unconscious communication, which stimulate the need for psychoanalysts to continue to search for links between the body, the individual and the social bond, links capable of grasping a broader spectrum of meanings. After all, Freud, in *Psychogenesis of a Case of Homosexuality in a Woman* (1920), already considered the heterosexual object choice to be just as enigmatic a phenomenon as the homosexual one, to the extent that, "in the sense of psychoanalysis, even the exclusive sexual interest of a man in a woman is a problem in need of clarification and by no means a matter of course". He continued to express himself as follows: "All human beings, as a consequence of their bisexual disposition, as well as of cross hereditary transmission, unite in themselves the masculine and feminine characters, so that pure virility and femininity remain theoretical constructions of indeterminate content" (Freud, 1925).

Furthermore, in a perspective of dialogue with the contributions coming from the neuroscientific field, through which we continue to question our assumptions, I would recall Ramachadran's studies (Ramachadran & McGeoch, 2008) about the phantom penis. These studies confirm that in transsexuals, the sensation of having a phantom penis, the acquisition of a neurally based representation of gender organs as their image in the brain, resists all kinds of visual feedback and cultural reference, e.g., being raised as a woman. The gender-specific body image is perceived from within because it is entirely wired into the brain. Researchers have traced areas of investigation into genetic and epigenetic factors from gender identity tendencies in twins.

As psychoanalysts, it feels essential to continue to question the pathways of subjectification and subjective appropriation necessary for the unfolding of psychic life. We continue to ask ourselves about which psychic forces and through which identificatory economies the contemporary psychic subject, taking shape in such transformed historical, social, and cultural contexts, will maintain its libidinal balance in preserving the sense of self and the investment of internal and external bonds. Let us bear in mind the forms of subjective appropriation resulting from traumatic experiences that profoundly alter the sense of self. We need to succeed in guaranteeing our patients a possibility of an authentically analytic encounter and listening that go beyond, as far as possible, certain stereotypes and the many ideologies and constraints that can harness a way of listening that must instead become able to create the conditions for a dialogue with those forms of "psychic plurality" of the other, recognised and understood through our "analytic function of the mind". This function allows us to enter a relationship with the other while being able to reflect and maintain a dialogue with ourselves. Perhaps, "to go beyond opposites, it is necessary to think of something more multiform and more decentred than a simple equality-difference axis, than the idea of a single difference" (Benjamin, 2006).

It should also be made clear that the questions and reflections inherent to the different forms of psychic life and the processes of becoming a subject ubiquitously run through every experience of psychic life, every functioning – hetero-, homo-, and trans-sexual – and for these reasons our task is to continue to research to understand the specificities of each singular expression of life and psychic bonding. Human feeling, Freud reminds us, is characterised by the sense of self. Recently, Malabou (2020) reminds us that freedom under certain conditions seems possible only beyond the body, in a disembodied subject, as a freedom detached from that existence determined by the constraints put by the body. If the subject is innervated by its own psychic plasticity – in the sense of its dual capacity to receive and to give itself a form, psychic movements in constant dialectic with each other – it is then that psychic plasticity involves forming and dissolving forms, but it also determines a condition: to be what one is on the condition of being formed by other forces. Subtle balance, subtle interchange,

Winnicott would say, which must never exceed the subject's possibility of receiving and digesting any form of nourishment. The excess, however, for that couple system (which always includes the potentiality of three) *will remain inscribed in the subject's psyche as a trace of invasive encroachment, a form of identification alienating the emerging self.* In this perspective, we refer to forces, psychic economies, capable of mirroring and negotiating the emerging subjective idiom (Butler & Malabou, 2010). In this perspective, how can we fail to bear in mind the theme of the identificatory project (Aulagnier, 1979), when the nascent ego begins to invest identificatory thoughts through which mother and father begin to offer their love?

We are born within psychic matrices in which "the identificatory desire" is formulated by the unconscious of those who generated us. I am thinking of the interweaving of stories that come from back in time, i.e., from previous generations. During her treatment, a mother reveals with a dawning emotional awareness that she was abused in adolescence and that her own mother also suffered the same fate in childhood. An abusive male as a traumatic trace in both women takes shape in the latest generation: a rejected male body and an initial wish to become a woman through gender transition. Later, in the young man, in a new attempt at subjective appropriation of his own unconscious history, the need to go beyond the binary dimension appears as a provisional possibility to open the possible alienating bonds that colonised the young man's psyche early on. What becomes of that psyche embodied in a body called upon to represent psychic pain, never named and thus never represented in previous generations? The ways through which love can be transformed from an indispensable factor in life to a form alienating the idiomatic core of the self are multiple. I believe that an analytical experience must first and foremost be a guarantor of listening not only to what has invaded and colonised the subject's psyche, the traumatic nuclei that we will invariably encounter, but it needs to listen to all as yet unborn future psychic potentials, without exerting any interpsychic pressure to prematurely give it a form: you are a man, you are a woman, you are trans, you are binary... Instead, it needs to listen to the profound dialogue of the different drives that can come to life and lean in various directions. It is in this delicate encounter/passage that the analyst's countertransference dimension is placed. The analyst, carrying out a constant self-analytic work, will encounter his/her own history inherent to the sedimentation of his/her own internal objects. I am thinking of Nietzsche's *Untimely Meditations* (1997) in which he defines the plastic force as that force to grow in one's own way from within oneself, to transform and incorporate past and extraneous things, to heal wounds, to replace lost parts, and to reshape broken forms in oneself, receiving and giving a form. Bearing in mind the horizon evoked by Nietzsche, we should refer to the plasticity of development as a perspective in which the subject's autopoietic potential constantly dialogues with the forms of lived experience in the singular contexts of growth.

In *Analysis Terminable and Interminable* (1920), Freud assumes that the severity of psychic suffering represents a "depletion of that plasticity, that is, the capacity to change and develop further that we normally expect". In that text, he reminds us that in addition to encountering an excessive rigidity, psychic stickiness, we sometimes also must deal with the opposite mode, a particular fluidity in affective investment that very quickly turns towards the potential new goals that analysis envisages, just as quickly abandoning previous investments. Such psychic plasticity changes shape too quickly, either in an excess of fixity or of fluidity. Once again, we are forced to rethink the development of every living thing in the *entre-deux* of biology and history. Today, we would say, an epigenetic history, in which biological, psychic, and cultural factors are condensed, a work of epigenetics, often described by scientists as "an improvisation, a practical or artistic elaboration, a creative spontaneity. As if it refers to the register of interpretive freedom" (Malabou, 2020).

To conclude, I would like to return to Freud's (1922) thought about the double inscription of the sexual. It is in his testamentary work, "*Some elementary lessons in Psychoanalysis*" that I collect the threads. He says that in all its mystery, the biological piece of data regarding the duplicity of the sexes stands before us, the ultimate element of our knowledge, stubbornly irreducible to anything else. Psychoanalysis has not contributed in any way to the clarification of this problem, which clearly belongs entirely to biology. Sometime earlier, he had stated that morphological difference cannot but be reflected in disparities in psychic development. Much theoretical–clinical progress has been made since then, especially by female psychoanalysts around the themes of female psychosexuality, especially Melanie Klein. Each generation has the task of passing on their knowledge inherited from previous generations into new avenues of exploration and acquisition, through the original contribution of their own thought to contemporaneity, in which we are immersed.

References

Aulagnier, P. (1979). *Les destins du plaisir. Aliénation, amour, passion*. Paris: Le fil rouge.

Bastianini, T. (2017). Processi di identificazione nelle famiglie omogenitoriali: uno sguardo psicoanalitico. In R. Baiocco, N. Carone, & V. Lingiardi (eds.), *La famiglia da concepire*. Roma: Sapienza Università Editrice.

Benjamin, J. (2006). *Shadow of the Other. Intersubjectivity and Gender in Psychoanalysis*. London: Routledge.

Butler, J. (2004). *Undoing Gender*. London: Routledge.

Butler, J., & Malabou, C. (2010). *Sois mon corps. Une lecture contemporaine de la domination et de la servitude chez Hegel*. Paris: Bayard.

Fachinelli, E. (2022). *On Freud*. USA: MIT Press.

Freud, S. (1914). On narcissism: An introduction. *S.E.*, 14, 67–102.

Freud, S. (1920). The psychogenesis of a case of homosexuality in a woman. *S.E.*, 18, 145–172.

Freud, S. (1922). Some elementary lessons in psychoanalysis. *S.E.*, *18*, 235–238.

Freud, S. (1925). Some psychical consequences of the anatomical distinction between the sexes. *S.E.*, 19, 243–258.

Kaës, R., Faimberg, H., Enriquez, M., & Baranes, J.J. (1993). *Transmission de le vie psychique entre générations.* Paris: Dunod.

Kaës, R. (2004). Elementi teorici generali per costruire il soggetto e il soggetto del legame. *Ricerca Psicoanalitica*, 12, 260–299.

Laplanche, J. (2019). *Sexuale. La sexualité élargie au sens freudien.* Paris: PUF.

Malabou, C. (2020). *Divenire Forma: Epigenesi e Razionalità.* Milano: Meltemi Editore.

Maturana, H.R., & Varela, F.J. (1985). *Autopoiesi e cognizione: La realiszazione del vivente.* Venice: Marsilio Editore.

Nietzsche, F. (1997). *Nietzsche: untimely meditations.* Cambridge, UK: Cambridge University Press.

Nussbaum, M.C. (1996). Compassion: The basic social emotion. *Social Philosophy and Policy*, 13, 27–58.

Nussbaum, M.C. (2001). *The fragility of goodness.* Cambridge, UK: Cambridge University Press.

Ramachadran, V.S., & McGeoch, P. (2008). Phantom penises in transexuals evidence of an innate gender-specific body image in the brain. *Journal of Consciousness Studies*, 15(1), 5–16.

Roussillon, R. (2014). L'oggetto coppia. *Psicoterapia e Scienze Umane*, 2, 289–300.

Stoller, R. (1968). *Sex and Gender: On the Development of Masculinity and Femininity.* London: Hogarth Press.

Winnicott, D.W. (1966). On split male and female elements. In *Explorations in Psychoanalysis*. Milan: Raffaello Cortina Editore, 1995.

Winnicott, D.W. (1945). Primitive emotional development. In *Through Paediatrics to Psycho-Analysis* 145–156. London: Tavistock Publications.

5 Trans-identifications

Luca Bruno

Introduction

By the term, "trans-identifications", I refer mainly to the identification processes of *transgender, gender fluid and queer* people, but also to the intersections and complex identificatory crossings of everyone. Trans-identifications, processes that cannot be completely homologated and assimilated, are more complex pathways than the already tortuous pathways through which identifications take place in cisgender people, who identify with the gender assigned at birth and corresponding to their biological sex.

Freud, throughout the development of his thought, from the 1895 *Project* to the 1938 *Some elementary lessons in Psychoanalysis*, developed the idea of a discontinuity between the somatic and the psychic. The work of establishing the psyche in the body and the body in the psyche is particularly bumpy and complex. The concept of trans-identifications refers to an area of interpenetration between two or more psyches or, more precisely, to the multiple areas of the unconscious exchange between the subject and his/her environment and objects, which will have important effects on identity developments. It is an intermediate space, lacking defined borders, between the me and the non-me, where identity oscillations and ambiguities are played out. De M'Uzan (1977, 2005) has called it the *"identity spectrum"*.

The prefix "trans" is to be understood precisely as "going through" but also "beyond". On the one hand, this going "beyond" of identifications implies a greater degree of blending of introjective movements, on the other hand to "go beyond" one can venture towards the assumption of hyper-feminine, hyper-masculine or hyper-ambiguous physical and psychic characteristics, getting to caricatured, showy, excessive expressions. In a study called "Was Snow White transsexual?", Michel and Mormont (2002), at the University of Liège, analysed the psychological functioning of candidates for gender reassignment, observing a set of recurring characteristics and desires, which lead to a stereotypical accentuation of the gender they identify with, according to socio-cultural models and representations. Lemma (2013) points out how this "excess" can problematically

DOI: 10.4324/9781003534440-9

draw attention to the incongruence between the gender assigned at birth and the gender they identify with, intensifying the state of suffering rather than alleviating it.

I will punctuate this text with some quotations from *An apartment on Uranus: Chronicles of the Crossing* by Paul Preciado (2019), a FtM transgender philosopher and writer, who has been lesbian, then gender fluid, transgender and transsexual. Preciado tells the story of their transition, or rather of their transitions, of a very complex identificatory wondering, which I believe will help us understand a little more about the complicated and painful journey of people with gender variance. "Trans" as transgender, therefore, but also as an indication of crossing borders, transits, which is common to all migration and which confronts us with non-evidence, with foreignness, with diversity.

Preciado (2019, 41) compares the status of the transgender person to that of the migrant:

> *sex change and migration are two practices that … place a living human body inside the limits of citizenship, even of what we understand by 'humanity'. Beyond the geographical, linguistic or corporeal movements which characterize both journeys, it is the radical transformation not just of the traveller, but also of the human community that welcomes or rejects the traveller.*

Gender transitioning is a journey marked by multiple frontiers, requiring multiple acquisitions and losses for both the traveller and for those who, like the analyst, are called upon to welcome those who address them.

There are numerous examples of trans-identifications also in the arts. Think for instance of Flaubert's famous statement *"Madame Bovary c'est moi"* "(Madame Bovary is me") or of the person and work of Louise Bourgeois, an artist who, putting herself at stake, worked to a considerable extent on the intersections between masculine and feminine, fluidity and transitions. Considering the fluidity of identification, it is evident that a patient's absolute certainty about his/her identification expresses a confusion of registers, causing him/her to consider as real something that belongs to the symbolic sphere (Perelberg, 2019).

Anatomy is not destiny

Can anatomy still be considered destiny? Preciado writes

> *It called binary epistemology and the naturalization of genders into question by asserting that there is an irreducible multiplicity of sexes, genders and sexualities. We understand today that libidinal transformation is an important as epistemological transformation: we must modify desire. We must learn to desire sexual freedom … sexuality is a political theatre in which desire, not anatomy, writes the script (274).*

One in every 2000 babies is born with genitals that can be considered neither male nor female; they are called intersexuals. Most of the times they undergo surgery to be assigned a specific sex, thus raising a very complex ethical question. Do these babies have the right to be neither male nor female? Can we think of allowing them an independent pathway to identity, without an artificial anatomical caesura "guiding" their sexual identity?

The body is the original constitutive place of identity, but also the place of maximum transformability and change. It is the object of many projections such as fears, desires, fantasies and expectations, in search for a physical and phenomenological identity that could coincide as much as possible with internal representations and deep perception of one's own gender. These desires, expectations and fantasies may have belonged to previous generations and may have conditioned the gender of the individuals, with conscious and unconscious relational ways that are not always respectful of the offspring's personal inclinations.

Sexuality involves both drive- and object-related (sometimes traumatic) issues. Bodies represent possible configurations of unconscious parental objects, as well as a meeting place for regressive conflictual drives (themselves linked to primary identifications), Oedipal phantasms (in the context of secondary identifications) and the revival of partial infantile drives. The body is one of the main representatives of object-related connection with parents as well as with the conflicts with them.

Bodies are also places where maximum transformability and change occur. Bodies are again the object(s) onto which fears, desires, fantasies and expectations are projected, while searching for a physical and phenomenal identity that can align as much as possible with the internal representations and the deepest perception of one's own gender. Affective positions, blocked aspirations, as well as the unresolved conflicts burdening both *caregivers* and previous generations, can unconsciously influence the construction and shaping of gender identity within subsequent generations.

The attacks and rejections aimed at the body or a part of it reveal the conflictual features of the investments in the body, as well as the masked conflict with parental objects and/or the identifications with them. Such dynamics may, at least in part, play a role within the suffering related to gender non-conformity: a re-actualisation of both pre-existing issues reflected in a poor subject/object differentiation (especially in the case of primary identifications) and a conflict related to secondary identifications may become evident, especially within the context of the Oedipal configuration, i.e., in regarding the representations of the parents as the bearers of the differences of the sexes.

Another core passage involves the changes of puberty. The more brutally such transformations take place resonating with previous conflicts linked to passivity and dependence, the more they risk taking on traumatic features, themselves likely to induce an actual dissociation between the psyche and the body of any given patient. Within such dissociation, the body may be unconsciously experienced as the place where childhood conflicts resurface, together with its connection with passivity and dependence on the primary object that has not been adequately processed or resolved. Faced with such a passivity, adolescents may look for an opportunity of control and power by distancing themselves from their biological body and from the ambivalence and conflicts linked to any given identification, while rejecting the biological sex experienced as alienation with respect to the objects of investment, therefore allowing for a sort of "negative identity", owing nothing to objects. Such a process of rejection and re-appropriation of the self under a "negative" lens can describe and explain, at least in part, the unconscious psychic phenomena connected to gender non-conformity. Such non-conformity denies a part of the body (namely sex) to respond to discomfort and identification-based suffering.

During adolescence, it is more complex to discriminate those psychic aspects which are already more defined and structured, compared with the others that are still within an area of extreme changeability. Sometimes, such changes are genuinely subjective, while other times they resonate with group and cultural influences. Mental functioning in adolescence evokes a mixture of liquids of different natures and densities, temporarily mixing, before each liquid takes its place once again (Green, 1986). Such are conditions where the impact of primeval processes on the psyche is very intense and can cause discontinuities – or sometimes disruptions – in the process of identity research and subjectivation. Adolescents are usually torn between the re-emergence of Oedipal issues and the rise of the new, as they are grappling with the mourning of childhood ties, while they need to govern brand-new forces and drives (Cahn, 1998). This is complex psychic work, involving the narcissistic and object axis, balancing between permanence and change, where identity undergoes important rehashes and transitions.

Patricia Gherovici (2018) states that patients with gender variance question and demonstrate that anatomy is not destiny. Sexual difference is neither sex nor gender, sex must be symbolised, and gender must be embodied. What matters is not to have a body or to be a body, but to become the body that will embody being.

In many conceptions of contemporary psychoanalysis, we are faced with a potential overcoming of considering anatomy as mere destiny, both in theory and clinical work, in favour of a concept of identity no longer imposed by biology, but affirmed by desire, a desire subjectively perceived, psychically validated and in search of psyche–body correspondences.

Identity through identifications: the multiple

The formation of gender identity refers to processes of fantasy construction, conditioned both by the unconscious and by linguistic and cultural factors, the original centrality of the sexed body and desire that is at the centre of psychological functioning (Aisenstein & Moss, 2015). Freud understood that the role played by identification in mental life was not only that of a defence mechanism, but of a process that structures the ego, the super-ego and the ego ideal. Identity can be seen as an unconscious attempt to organise conflicting identifications to achieve transient forms of cohesion, a feeling of internal coherence and an illusion of unity (Perelberg, 1999). Above all, relational psychoanalysis has explored the multiplicity of genders and sexuality, adopting a particular attentiveness to differences and with what Mitchell (1993) has called the "multifaceted self". The construction of identity, and thus also of gender identity, is based on difference and is affected by multiple and complex intertwined processes of identification (and de-identification). These processes are multiple and can make the gender experience fluid or non-conforming to the biological gender assigned at birth: such phenomena are manifestations of a painful "multiple" that shows the suffering while searching for temporary forms of the balance between psyche and soma. We already find this "multiple" in a passage of Freud's from 1908: in *General Observations on the Hysterical Attack*, he states that the coexistence of different fantasies, male and female, presupposes a *"Mehrfache Identifizierung"*, *multiple identification* and he does not write *"dual"*. This term will not be found in later writings on the subject.

Trans-identifications contemplate psychic pluralities in which subjectivation pathways seem to take shape that, in delineating complex identity forms, underline the interplay of multiple identifications (Bastianini, 2008). Trans-identifications are thus also manifestations of a painful "multiple" that show the suffering and pain in the search for transient forms of psyche–soma cohesion. In trans-identifications, the mechanism of the condensation of the multiple and of the irreducible to a masculine/feminine simplification is in the foreground, much more so than in cisgender identities. Also contributing to the complexity of the phenomenon of identifications is the question of the transmission of psychic life between generations (Kaës et al., 1993). Unconscious alliances, identifications and modes of identification are transmitted (Kaës, 2008).

An important role is played by the impact on the psyche of the *sexuale* of which Laplanche (2003) speaks, which is multiple and finds its foundation in the unconscious. It is the extended sexuality, essentially based on the infantile; it is the sexuality that goes beyond sex and reproduction, that transcends sexual differences, linked to the fantasy, extremely mobile with respect to the goal and the object. It possesses its own functioning regime, i.e., it does not aim at discharge, but seeks excitement, increased tension.

It is also true that identifications are inscribed in ambivalence, as the identification "drive" and the pressure towards identity autonomy come into conflict. The discontinuity that follows a condition of identification refusal of an assigned role handed down from previous generations can assume significant meaning and consequences for the subject and sometimes influence the same gender identity modes: the imposition of discordant names, the assignment of a previously decided role and problems related to hereditary issues represent the field in which identity difficulties declined as gender difficulties are most frequently constituted (Pozzi, 2008). The issues of gender identity formation remain rather open and uncertain to this day, and it does not seem sufficient to refer only to the theory of unconscious psychic bisexuality or its symmetrical/complementary which André Green (1983) defined as the "gender-neutral fantasy".

Maternal mirroring (Winnicott, 1971) has the function of allowing an initial integration of the drives by restoring to the infant a first sketch of the self, thus initiating the integration of the ego and the acquisition of gender identity. However, inevitably, mirroring cannot encompass being in its entirety and leaves a "remainder" that does not transform and instead remains in a state of non-integration which I believe plays an important role in trans-identifications.

Transformations of the body in dialogue with the psyche

This is how Preciado (2019, 139–144) describes the transformation of his voice and body following the hormone replacement therapy:

> *Testosterone has an impact on the vocal cords, and recently my voice has become husky. Since I haven't yet figured out how to manage it, I sound like a cigar-smoker with pneumonia … I'm getting used to my new voice. The testosterone I administer is making my vocal cords grow thicker, producing a lower timbre. This voice emerges like a mask of air coming from within … I do not recognise myself. But what does 'I' mean in this sentence? … Apparently other people don't recognise this voice shaped by testosterone either. The telephone has ceased being a faithful emissary; it has become a traitor. I call my mother and she answers, 'Who is this? Who is calling?' The rupture of recognition makes explicit a distance that has always existed. I would speak to them and they would not recognise me … A voice that up to now was not my own is seeking refuge in my body, and I am going to give it refuge … The body is not property, but relationship. Identity (sexual, gender, national or racial) is not essential, but relational … The changing face, too, cannot serve as a stable place for the voice to seek as a territory of identity. On the contrary, it declines its subjectivity in the plural: it does not say 'I', but 'we are the journey.*

Many patients, especially *gender fluid* and *queer* ones, show constant transformations of their identifying structures, which among other things allows them to think about the different, the elsewhere, those identity landscapes that are more difficult to reach with understanding and empathy. These trans-identifications are not comparable to the identity confusions in the case of psychosis or to the experiences of multiple personalities. In trans-identifications, the different identifications and their various components are informed by each other, are in contact with each other and live together, unlike other circumstances where denial, splitting or dissociation may prevail.

Morel (2000) and Lemma (2013) emphasise the importance of the visual aspect: hormonal or surgical procedures (vaginoplasty, phalloplasty, mastectomy or mammaplasty) are sought less for reasons related to sexual pleasure and more for reasons related to the perception of the body self and the pleasure and desire to be able to "see" oneself with a body corresponding to one's gender identity. Is this a new mirroring pathway?

Trans-identifications as a pathway that meets and works through psychic pain: towards a "new birth"

This passage from Preciado's (77–79) book succeeds in movingly describing the pain of those who need to make a long personal journey to work through trans-identifications:

> *Transsexuality is a silent sniper who plants a bullet in the chests of children … I was three years old when I felt the weight of the bullet for the first time. I knew I was carrying it when I heard my father call two foreign girls walking hand-in-hand in the street 'disgusting, dirty dykes'. My chest started to burn. That night, without knowing why, I fantasized for the first time that I was escaping my city and that I was leaving for another country. The days that followed were days of fear, and shame … At night [the children with a bullet in the chests] go to bed with the shame of being the only ones to know that they are a disappointment to their parents, they go to sleep with the fear that their parents will abandon them if they find out, or would prefer it if they died. And perhaps they dream, as I did before them, that they are running away to a strange land, in which children who bear the bullet are welcome.*

Courage and the psychic possibility of facing "the bullet" lead to an even greater awareness of disillusionment, acceptance of limits, working through loss.

Max, a FtM transgender teenager in analysis, tells me that he has felt a strange intense despair, like a helplessness that feels ancient. He sits in silence for the first five minutes of the session and then says in a low voice "I'm tired" and lets himself fall on the couch, staying on his side, motionless, in a hopelessness that makes me feel very close to his loneliness as a little man cub.

> *Max: While coming here today I got lost. I don't know how it happened.*
> *Analyst (thinking about transits, travelling identifications and loss): Did you get lost?*
> *Max: Yes. I didn't recognise the streets around your office, as I got off at a different underground stop … Last night with a friend we watched an old Bertolucci film, "Tea in the desert", and that ending really got me involved. The protagonist is lost when she enters the café… and the narrator associates this loss with the ultimate loss, that of death and the fact that we don't know when it will happen… sometimes we live as if we had no limits and instead, we have to carefully consider them.*

Analyst: How long will your analysis last? How long will we still see each other and be together?

It seems to me, in addition to the ability to contact, feel and work through grief, this is a testament to his ability to access the depressive position, to renounce those residues of childish omnipotence to be able to contact such loss and its drifts that take shape in the transference. Without finding refuge in mechanisms of denial of one's own history, of the suffering associated with gender dysphoria, without escape into mania and without avoiding a most needed mourning process. With the awareness of limits, punctuated by the castration that is the foundation of our very existence and allows us to process even the limit of death, of transience. Identity is revealed, experienced and defined in the subject's capacity to psychically bear loss, meaning both the original loss and the loss resulting from the narcissistic wound of our incompleteness and therefore of castration, of the death of the object, of our own death (Decourt, 1999). In many respects, trans-identifications are pathways of subjectivation in the sense of "re-birth". The transitional pathway is specifically characterised by the repetition of the caesura of birth, which occurs whenever there is a significant change of state, of self and of one's body, a process that is at least experienced as the birth of a new identity.

Tiny, 24 years old, identified herself first as MtF transgender, then gender fluid, now Queer. She has very evident male and female characteristics, sometimes caricatured, but she recognises herself with female pronouns, and in one session, she catches my partial disorientation which she immediately needs to dismiss. In fact, the next day, she arrives to the session dressed in a white perforated dress, wearing vertiginous heels and her eyes heavily highlighted by mascara: "*I was dressed like this last night at a party*", she gets up from the couch and makes a sort of catwalk in the room. "*Don't you think I looked very cool?!*"

Beyond the acting-in and the obvious motion of seduction, she moves me. She tells me that she has found the courage to be herself, even though she has suffered much violence, physical and psychological. In childhood and adolescence, she felt excluded, mocked and ashamed, but also guilty for feeling not as others would have wanted her to be. Then, she took on and started a process that she calls "deconstruction", a de-identification that she partly describes as a mourning process: "*I left behind what others wanted for me and started to feel free, becoming trans, which is not just the transition from one gender to another, it is not adopting a new conventional normative, it is transforming, being reborn, finally entering a shape in which I recognise myself and feel alive, since a part of me – that I was not – has died*".

Conclusions

Sex, gender and sexual orientation may not be aligned with sexual identity. For many individuals, it is a relatively stable part of their self, defined and consistent with biological sex and it may undergo partial fluctuations that are affected by the complex phenomena of identification, both with the feminine and the masculine in turn (Winnicott, 1966). Such identifications are stratified both in our mind and in our body. Moreover, they are partly linked to the fundamental psychic bisexuality, as well as to the psychic phenomena determined by the dynamics of the Oedipal complex, while being modulated by the original phantasms concerning passivity, primary scenes, seduction and castration. The buildup of the core sense of gender identity is also affected by the influence of the parental unconscious desires and fantasies, as well as by the transgenerational legacies and by any given cultural environment.

Gender identity (itself a part of the broader sphere of sexual identity) does not only intersect with the impact of social, environmental and cultural aspects but also deals with the unconscious representations of the self. Psychoanalysts need to pay particular attention to the junctions of the complex processes of identification, as they are entering particularly complex paths for *transgender, gender fluid and queer* people, or for those whose sexual identity distances itself from the logic of male/female binarism.

Current clinical work of transgenderism remains the primary source for theoretical exploration, in order not to risk abstract speculation or an easy ground for establishing ideologies and prejudices. It can, as in the area of trans-identifications, not only put our theories to the test, but become a stimulus and an element of friction with those and an occasion both for creative and cognitive advancement in our discipline and for the refinement of useful tools for psychoanalytic treatment.

The construction of identity relies on identifications, and it is particularly linked to sensations and representations of the body, but it takes place within a personal narrative, the creation of an inner narrative that deforms and transforms the self and objects. It is the work of the family novel, and a plot that is based on the fantasies of origins. Identity is a process that is never quite finished, never finished at all. A continuous work of construction, demolition and reconstruction that takes place through fruitful exchanges and cross-fertilisation between conscious and unconscious processes. Affective positions, blocked aspirations, unresolved conflicts of previous generations can unconsciously influence the formation of gender identity in generations to come.

Fluidity, which is at the heart of identification processes, contrasts with the individual's need to find a coherent identity, a sense of cohesion that is in fact denied by the very nature of the psychic apparatus. As Piera Aulagnier (1979) writes, everything proves to the ego *"that it can only persist by becoming other, by altering itself, by accepting to discover itself different from what it is in an actuality that is always ephemeral, always in a state of instability"*. Paul Denis (1999) distinguishes between "relative identity" and "absolute identity". Identity is a permanent construction site in which there is a certain degree of mobility, oscillation and fluctuation that the subject must tolerate and rework. Relative identity is symbolic and polyphonic and is characteristic of the neurotic personality. It is the identity that characterises many people with gender variance. The need to assert an absolute (non-symbolic and monolithic) identity is a sign of suffering or pathology, as in character or personality disorders, perversion and psychosis. Throughout our lives, with varying degrees of intensity, we experience a vacillation of identity, which is more tolerable the more we have assumed and learnt to manage fluidity. Not only is the psyche "extended" (Freud, 1938), but it is also fluid.

Psychoanalytic thought and practice undergo constant revision in the encounter with human-based group and cultural changes. It appears necessary to think about the different forms of sexuality and gender manifestations away from any narrow and dogmatic vision, since multiple identifications and their expressions in fantasies and on the corporeal, intra-psychic and relational planes exist within everyone.

The current health and clinical protocols of gender non-conformity should remain the primary source for theoretical exploration, in order not to risk abstract speculation, itself an easy ground for the establishment of ideologies and prejudices. Healing-related and clinical activities test theories, becoming both a spur and an element of friction with them, therefore also an opportunity for both creative and cognitive advancement, as well as for refining the tools more useful for psychoanalytic therapy. In trans-identifications, we observe this assumption and management of fluidity, and on the other hand, when the distancing from one's biological sex is more of a clear cut and absolute, the possibility of symbolically reintegrating elements of sexual identity related to sex and gender attributed in childhood can allow a broader and more integrated representation of the self, a self that is more in touch with the unconscious. In this case, patients can be helped to deal with conflicting parts of their sexuality, to reapproach psychic bisexuality, to represent and reintegrate gender dysphoric aspects of their corporeity into the self (Bruno, 2023; Saketopoulou, 2014, 2023).

The "flight from femininity" and the "flight from masculinity" contain a very important unconscious conflictual dimension to be analysed, although in the analyses of these patients, the unconscious rejection and horror of the penis or breasts, the horror of the masculine or feminine, as Colette Chiland (1999) argues, need not to be postponed or confused with castration anxiety or penis envy. In transgender people, the genitalised body is experienced as particularly disturbing and dangerous because it is foreign and incongruous to gender identity and can become the object of major attacks.

The aim of therapy remains to analyse and enable, by taking care of the fragility of the preconscious (Guignard, 1996), the acquisition of a real psychic work that is itself a process of transformation and re-organisational reappraisal of identification processes.

References

Aisenstein, M. & Moss D. (2015). Desire and its discontents. In: Lemma A., Lynch P. (eds.), *Sexualities*. London: Routledge.

Aulagnier, P. (1979). *Les destins du plaisir. Aliénation, amour, passion*. Paris: Le fil rouge.

Bastianini, T. (2008). *"Amor sui*: essere se stessi, essere gli stessi. Il faticoso travaglio dei percorsi di soggettivazione". In: *Generi e Generazioni. Ordine e disordine nelle identificazioni* (ed. Centro Psicoanalitico di Roma), Milano: Franco Angeli.

Bruno, L. (2023). Ricontattare la bisessualità inconscia nella psicoanalisi di pazienti transgender, Paper presented at *SPI Congress with Multiple Seminars*, Bologna.

Cahn, R. (1998). *L'adolescent dans la psychanalyse*. Paris: Presses Universitaires de France.

Chiland, C. (1999). L'identité sexuée. *Revue Française de Psychanalyse*, 4(LXIII): 1251–1263.

De M'Uzan, M. (1977). *De l'art à la mort*. Paris: Gallimard.

De M'Uzan, M. (2005). *Aux confins de l'identité*. Paris: Gallimard.

Decourt, P. (1999). L'identité et la perte. *Revue Française de Psychanalyse*, 4(LXIII): 1153–1164.

Denis, P. (1999). Soi-même pour un autre, identité relative et identité absolue. *Revue Française de Psychanalyse*, 4(LXIII): 1099–1108.

Freud, S. (1895). Project for a scientific psychology. *S.E.* 1, 281–291.

Freud, S. (1908), Some general remarks on hysterical attacks. *S.E.* 9, 227–234.

Freud, S. (1938). Some elementary lessons in psychoanalysis. *S.E.* 23, 279–286.

Gherovici, P. (2018). Botched bodies: inventing gender and construing sex. In: Tsolas V., Anzieu-Premmereur C. (eds.), *A Psychoanalytic Exploration of the Body in Today's World. On the Body*. New York: Routledge.

Green, A. (1983). *Life Narcissism, Death Narcissism*. New York: Free Association Books, 2001.

Green, A. (1986). Interview. In: Baranes J.J., Cahn R. et al., *Psychanalyse, adolescence et psychose*. Paris: Payot.

Guignard F. (1996). *Au vif de l'infantile*. Lausanne: Delachaux & Niestlé.

Kaës, R., Faimberg, H., Enriques, M. & Baranes, J.J. (1993) *Transmission de la vie psychique entre générations*, Paris: Dunod.

Kaës, R. (2008). La trasmissione delle alleanze inconsce, organizzatori metapsicologici e metasociali. In: Centro Psicoanalitico in Rome, *Generi e Generazioni. Ordine e disordine nelle identificazioni* . Milano: Franco Angeli.

Laplanche, J. (2003). Le genre, le sexe, le sexual. In: Laplanche, J., *Sexual. La sexualité élargie au sens freudien*. Paris: PUF.

Lemma, A. (2013). The body one has and the body one is: the transsexual's need to be seen. *International Journal of Psychoanalysis*, 94(2): 277–292.

Michel, A. & Mormont, C. (2002). Blanche-Neige était-elle transexuelle? *L'Encéphale*, 28(1): 59–64.

Mitchell, R.W. (1993). Mental models of mirror-self-recognition: Two theories. *New Ideas in Psychology*, 11(3): 295–325.

Morel, G. (2000). *Ambiguités sexuelles*. Paris: PUF.

Perelberg, R. (1999). L'interaction entre identifications et identité dans l'analyse d'un jeune homme violent: question de technique. *Revue Française de Psychanalyse*, 4(LXIII): 1175–1191.

Perelberg, R. (2019). *Sexuality, Excess and Representation*. Milton Park: Taylor & Francis.

Pozzi, O. (2008). Il doppio senso generazionale delle identificazioni nella formazione dell'identità di genere. In: Centro Psicoanalitico in Rome, *Generi e Generazioni. Ordine e disordine nelle identificazioni*. Milano: Franco Angeli.

Preciado, P.B. (2019). *An Apartment on Uranus: Chronicles of the Crossing*. MIT Press, Semiotext(e).

Saketopoulou, A. (2014). Mourning the body as bedrock: Developmental considerations in treating transsexual patients analytically. *Journal of the Psychoanalytic Association*, 62(5): 773–806.

Saketopoulou, A. (2023). *Sexuality Beyond Consent. Risk, Race, Traumatophilia*. New York: NYU Press.

Winnicott, D.W. (1966). The split-off male and female elements to be found in men and women. In: *Playing and Reality*. London: Routledge.

Winnicott, D.W. (1971). Mirror-role of mother and family in child development. In: *Playing and Reality*. London: Routledge.

6 Gender identities and identifications in a changing world*

Vittorio Lingiardi

As a crucial component in the process of identity construction, the notion of "identifications" is an inherently plural concept spanning various domains, ranging from developmental psychology to defence mechanisms. From the skein of assumptions woven by psychoanalysis around this concept, I will try to unravel a thread that leads us to a core question at the heart of our contemporary times: What role do gender identifications play in the construction and shaping of identity?

To approach possible, though hardly generalisable, answers, I will shed light on two critical lived experiences in our daily clinical, social, and even juridical spheres:

1 growing up with same-gender parents, and
2 being a non-binary teenager.

In the *first scenario*, by juxtaposing research data with theoretical reflection, I will explore the fate of gender identifications when the exercise of parenthood transcends the physical embodiments of the father and mother, as well as the symbolic figures of male and female.

In the *second scenario*, after presenting some data and reflections on the significant rise in the incidence of gender-variant experiences in adolescence, I will share some observations gleaned from interviews with adolescents whose identity construction is not inspired by gender binarism (i.e., cis or trans), but rather non-binary solutions that are more or less integrated.

First scenario: from the oedipal complex to oedipal complexity

As emphasised in previous published works with Nicola Carone (see, e.g., Lingiardi & Carone, 2019), socio-cultural changes and advancements in assisted reproduction over the past 40 years have led to a rise in new family

* Portions of this contribution are reworked from Lingiardi and Carone (2019) and Di Giannantonio et al. (2024). Thanks to Nicola Carone, Bianca Di Giannantonio, and Guido Giovanardi for their research work on the topics discussed here. Presented at the 37th EPF Conference: "Identifications," Florence, March 22–24, 2024. Adapted from a shorter version published in the Italian psychoanalytic journal "Psiche" (Lingiardi, 2024).

DOI: 10.4324/9781003534440-10

forms. Among these are same-sex parent families formed through donor insemination or surrogacy, wherein the loving couple does not coincide with the generative couple and the parents do not embody sexual difference. Under these circumstances, can we still understand gender identification processes and the path taken to access one's origins through the lens of the Oedipal complex? In continuity with some developments in psychoanalysis (see Loewald, 1979; Winnicott, 1989), attachment theory, and infant research, I will revisit the Oedipal "complex" as Oedipal "complexity," arguing that the latter may apply irrespective of parents' anatomical characteristics (Davies, 2015). This of course does not mean to remove the importance of parents' bodies and sexuality in the development of children. However, I would like to emphasise that the two elements that, in my opinion, constitute the most important legacy of the Oedipal psychoanalytic Freudian myth today are the concepts of: (1) "the third" within the parental couple and (2) "position within generations."

The aim of my chapter is to rethink the contemporary meanings of the Oedipus complex without robbing it of its function as an inescapable passage in psychic and sexual development. If indeed the myth of Oedipus is about knowledge of one's origins and sexuality, then it is precisely families headed by gay and lesbian parents – who have used assisted reproduction to conceive – who reveal the Oedipal complexity, rather than its complex. In these family forms, the need to work out one's origins by confronting the anonymity/knowability of the donors and the presence/absence of the birth mother (i.e., the surrogate), and likewise the structuring of the child's gender identity from the starting point of same-sex parents, inevitably invites psychoanalysis to think about new and unprecedented possibilities for psychic and affective life.

Allow me a quick digression. We all know that Oedipus is a story of abandonment and adoption. One aspect that we generally neglect, but on which the dramatic plot hinges, concerns the existence of two parental couples: Laius and Jocasta, a non-functioning biological couple who abandon Oedipus and are potentially murderous, and Polybus and Merope, an adoptive couple who care for Oedipus and love him tenderly, but do not know his origins. Thebes and Corinth are the two places of Oedipus's origin: the first is the place of his birth and his abandonment – of persecutory and incestuous fantasies that conceal a transgenerational secret (i.e., Laius's love for Chrysippus), while the second is the place of containment and growth, and of confrontation with the unknown (i.e., the Sphinx's riddle), which will begin the laborious process of subjectivation.

1 What is the fate of gender identifications when the exercise of parenthood is detached from the concrete figures of father/male and mother/female?

2 In what way will children born through donor insemination or surrogacy have access to knowledge of their origins when the man who

donated his sperm or the woman who donated her ova and carried the pregnancy are present at the scene of the conception but play no part in the family scene?

Long considered the core of psychoanalysis, the architrave of the unconscious on which our psychic development stands, the Oedipus complex risks becoming a stumbling block for psychoanalysis now that sexual difference does not take flesh in the bodies of the parents. Extending this to families with gay and lesbian parents therefore entails a double somersault: overcoming the controversial relationship between psychoanalysis and homosexuality and engaging in a paradoxical confrontation with what Freudian psychoanalysis did not foresee, despite assuming the Oedipus complex to be universal. And yet, in the at times contradictory complexity of his positions on the topic of psychosexuality, Freud himself provided the basis on which the Oedipus complex would survive the decline of the nineteenth-century "traditional" family on which it was modelled. In fact, recognising the polymorphism of infant sexuality and the extreme plasticity of the drive, Freud (1915) showed how object investments are subjected to continual re-elaboration and how complex and polyvalent the identificatory constellations of psychic life can be. In this vein, Freud proposed a "psychosexuality" and not a "biosexuality," and so we must acknowledge that the shaping of one's object relations depends on the way in which each individual addresses sexual difference and attributes meaning to it. From this perspective, alongside the Freudian affirmation of a reality principle, coinciding with the acknowledgement of laws about sexual and generational difference (Freud 1911), another claim is posited: that Oedipal resolution originates and evolves from different desires and Oedipal processes, which, in all of us, express the need for both a gender identity and a multiplicity of genders (Benjamin, 1995).

Leaving behind the metapsychological concepts of drive and goal, subsequent developments of psychoanalytic theory – attachment theory and infant research (see, e.g., Stern 1985; Winnicott 1989) – have focused on the role played by object relations and experiences with caregivers, not only as opportunities for discharge and the gratification of needs, but as constituent elements of the psychic structure. This has certainly – though it was not the authors' intention – permitted the "de-gendering" of the Oedipal scenario and its extension to include same-sex parent families. In particular, infant research reminds us that, from the first moments of life, the newborn does not confuse their parents but is able to classify the experiences they have with one or the other, grasping modes of affective regulation early on, including the quality of the parents' interaction as a couple. This leads to the construction of what Stern (1995, 2004) calls "schemes of being-with." This pattern has also be confirmed by neurobiological research indicating that infants' recognition of, and preference for, parent's faces is driven more by the caregiving activity (i.e., time spent together or a parent's regulatory modes) than parent gender.

There is a further vertex, besides parents' gender and sexual orientation, from which to think about the Oedipal configuration. Alongside the infant's innate capacity both to perceive the quality of responses to their emotional signals and to internalise, assimilate, and identify with the object, the transmission of psychic contents from parent to child and the path by which gender identifications are formed is by no means linear. The infant appropriates some of the other's qualities because they need recognition and a secure attachment, and they unconsciously organise their responses to correlate with certain aspects of the parents' psychic functioning. Adapting this modality to the identification of gender, little boys and girls try from the first moments of life to maintain an identification with both sexes in the need/desire to have both parents as objects of security and recognition. In harmonious situations, identification with the parents allows the child to assimilate the characteristics of both, so that the child's identification with their own sex coincides with their identification with the other. Similarly, we cannot dismiss the fact that, from the beginning of life, infants are also exposed to other significant adults who may interact with them on a regular basis (e.g., grandparents, aunts, uncles, and babysitters) and contribute to their gender identifications.

From birth onwards – Ogden's (1989, 152–153) observation that, in the transitional phase from the dyadic to the triadic relationship "the mother is simultaneously experienced as father-in-mother and mother-in-father" could also be discussed here – the infant is in relationship with otherness and develops an internal representation of these dynamically variable functions, which are no longer rigidly codified based on sex or generation, as was previously the case. In this respect, the objection "boys and girls need both figures," so common when same-sex parenthood is perceived as the prelude to undifferentiation, grasps a central feature: that the necessary figures are images in the mind – psychic functions that relate to "doing" and "being" (Winnicott, 1966). The fact that these maternal and paternal symbolic codes cohabit in every one of us may explain why children with gay and lesbian parents grow up satisfactorily, achieving a mature and not confused, but, if anything, more flexible sexual identity (Biblarz & Stacey, 2010). This idea is well supported by more than 40 years of research, including that which has been conducted by my own research group (e.g., Carone et al., 2018a, 2018b, 2020, 2023a, 2023b, 2025), showing that children of gay and lesbian parents do not significantly differ from children of heterosexual parents in terms of psychological adjustment, attachment security or gender development. In fact, where differences are detected based on parents' sexual orientation, they typically indicate better adjustment in children of gay and lesbian parents and higher gender flexibility in the activities and characteristics of especially children of lesbian mothers. So, we can say with some certainty, "the kids are all right."

Based on my previous observations, it follows that the subject is constituted not only through gender identifications, but also through developmental sequences. These developmental sequences are not always coherent and linear, but constructed intersubjectively with caregivers, giving rise to compromise formations between multiple affective states, the bodily self, and the styles of language and thought that our cultural, biographical, and familial transitions make available (Birksted-Breen, 1993; Lingiardi, 2015). The more or less favourable outcomes of this idiomatic construction depend not only on the interweaving of the child's Oedipal and pre-Oedipal levels, but also on how the parents have structured their own gender identities, how they have mutually agreed upon more containing or normative functions, the authenticity of their desire for a child, and their readiness to acknowledge the child's otherness.

In any family form, it is inevitable that children will, at a certain point, seek answers to questions about their origin, their identity, and the identities of those who conceived and bore them, and this is irrespective of the more or less harmonious complexity of their identificatory processes. In this respect, families headed by gay and lesbian parents are nothing new (Heineman, 2004), and the oedipal myth survives because, through triangulation (i.e., both "ovule–sperm–product of conception" and "parent 1–parent 2–child"), the child learns that ambivalence exists alongside pre-existing bonds from which they are excluded. Within the triadic relationship, the child must confront differences between generations, the intuition of adult sexuality, similarities and differences between the sexes, gratification linked to inclusion and belonging, and frustration linked to exclusion and lack. The difference between these families and those headed by heterosexual parents lies in the way in which the invariants of the Oedipus complex (i.e., the incest taboo and differences between the sexes and generations) are reread as acquisitions that children and parents gain by integrating mental functions prior to physical models, instead of through automatic associations between sex/gender and certain psychological functions.

The task of psychoanalysis is neither to justify conservatism nor to maintain an extravagant enthusiasm for every way of having children that raises the bar of what is possible. Once again, it is the way of observing, listening and understanding what parenting is, regardless of whether its prefix is homo- or hetero-. One of my favorite definitions, deeper than the American Psychological Association's delicate "Love makes a family," is written in a paper by Meltzer and Harris (1976): parenting is to generate love, to promote hope, to contain depressive pain, to teach independent thinking.

Second scenario: transgenderism and non-binarism

With my second scenario, I would like to investigate the topic of gender identifications from a different perspective, that of gender-variant experiences in adolescent and young adults. Every metamorphosis contains an aspiration and a pain. I never take a pathologising or sentimental or novelesque view of the infinite gender variances that life presents us with, and increasingly does. I do, however, regard as intellectualistic those theoretical narratives that downplay the components of grief and melancholy in the vicissitudes of gender, particularly when related to the so-called "dysphoric" forms. Among the gender variations and transformations that are increasingly experienced and/or narrated by adolescents, some bring freedom, others fright; some are imperceptible, others conspicuous; some live in expectation, others in nostalgia. Is there a metamorphosis without identification?

Always – from the ancient myths to the first clinical studies of Harry Benjamin and Robert Stoller – we have asked ourselves questions about the causes and effects of that non-coincidence between sex and gender that fuels the unpredictable dialogue between "anatomy and destiny." This essentialist phrase of Freud's, according to which we are (he was referring to women) the gender from which we come, is however reversible in a constructionist key, for which we are the gender to which we arrive. Things were once (apparently) simpler because they were in opposition: male versus female, man versus woman (and, in the case of sexual orientation, hetero versus homo). Today more than ever, the different components of identity (e.g., gender identity, gender role, sexual orientation, paths of identification, and landscapes of fantasy) confront us with an embodied complexity – *gender embodiment* – that continuously poses questions about the personal and collective meanings of words like "identity," "gender," and "body" (Glocer Fiorini, 2017; Lemma, 2023; Lingiardi, 2007). With Stoller (1968), we learned to conceive transgender identity as a "core gender identity" rooted in a central core. Today, more recent psychoanalytic developments, predominantly of a relational matrix increasingly classify gender using new metaphors, from "soft assembly" (Harris, 2004) to "self-theorisation" (Saketopoulou & Pellegrini, 2023).

I would like to compare two recent works, both released in 2022: the philosophical/historical/anthropological essay by Paul B. Preciado, *Dysphoria Mundi*, and the novel/memoir by Kim de l'Horizon, *Bloodbook* (2022). Preciado, harshly criticising psychoanalysis, rejects the medical–psychiatric artifact of gender dysphoria (considering it a deteriorated product of the hetero-patriarchy) and somehow makes it "explode" into an intersectional network of various contemporary dysphorias, intertwined with the conditions of migrants, women, and the sick bodies of pandemics. Kim de l'Horizon, on the other hand, tells us about the painful and in some ways impossible tension between the need for subjective identification and the possibility of being "a stream of water." If Preciado is radical in their political invective, to the point of neglecting every sign of renewal in progress (especially in contemporary psychoanalysis, which they directly attack), de L'Horizon lives in the uncertainty of the present psychological moment and poses questions that fail to impart new knowledge and visionary revelations. Preciado and de L'Horizon are diverse twins: their paths, as discordant as they may be, aspire to the same future. It is necessary to read both: the impetuosity that triggers change and the word that swims in the psyche. I have cited non-psychoanalytic works not by chance: photography, literature, and movies have been able to tell the stories of gender metamorphoses better than the traditional psychiatric and psychoanalytic literature in which my generation grew up.

In the clinical field, historical (I was about to write "traditional") cases of transition are those that foresee a starting station assigned at birth and an arrival station dreamt of for rebirth. Today, we listen more and more to stories characterised by new variants, not always in view of bodies to be transformed into stable dwellings, but often in search of intermediate possibilities, transitory transitions, pathways, and passages to make the gender experience more fluid and less binary. There is not just one trans identity: the lives that gather under this umbrella term are varied and articulated. There are people who identify with the sex opposite to that assigned at birth, others who do not recognise themselves in the male–female binarism, and still others who do not identify with any gender (agender). An assigned female at birth adolescent patient of mine calls himself trans, asks to be called by masculine pronouns, is interested in hormone therapy and not in surgery, and sometimes dresses non-binary while at other times more "traditionally" feminine. When asked how he holds feminine outfits and the masculine pronoun together, he says that he feels like a gay boy who likes to feel feminine with certain feminine outfits. For some, alignment between their gender identity and sex (with paths that include surgical interventions and/or hormonal treatments) is vital, while for others, it is not important. Trans identity, gender incongruence, gender fluidity, and gender queerness are themselves labels in transition.

Has anyone truly understood gender dysphoria? Over the decades, theoretical hypotheses have greatly evolved. While classic interpretations focused more on psychosocial than constitutional factors (e.g., traumatic experiences in caregiving relationships, enmeshed relationships with parental figures, secondary symptoms of more pervasive disorders, or extreme dissociative defences), today, gender variances are viewed as multifactorial conditions developed through numerous biological and, depending on the case, also psychosocial factors. Classical psychoanalytic theories, mostly formulated on the basis of individual cases, have never been substantiated by empirical data. Regarding biological–constitutional factors, research has focused on chromosomal anomalies or prenatal exposure to specific hormones. Some correlations deserve further investigation, but the data are ambiguous and still scarce. It is probable that gender dysphoria has a constitutional basis upon which environmental factors can intervene, such as interactions with parents and complex identifications with the gender roles typical of one's culture. In need of further investigation is ongoing research on the possible co-occurrence of "gender dysphoria" and "autism spectrum disorder" (Fortunato et al., 2022; Kallitsounaki & Williams, 2023; van der Miesen et al., 2018).

The gender fluidity of our adolescents – and for some of them a declared dysphoria – is a growing phenomenon: the prevalence of a generic gender non-conformity in adolescence is currently estimated at 0.5–2% of the general population, and the demand for intervention by centres specialised in gender dysphoria in childhood and adolescence has seen an increase of 1500% over the last 10 years (Claahsen-van der Grinten et al., 2021). Another peculiar piece of data from these centres is that, whereas previously most cases involved transition from male (at birth) to female, this trend has reversed in recent years, with requests for transition from female (at birth) to male or to other non-binary solutions becoming much more frequent. Puberty represents an age threshold beyond which only a minority (approximately 20%) of adolescents with gender incongruence maintain a non-conforming identity. Most (60%) become cisgender homosexual adults and a smaller proportion (20%) become cisgender heterosexual adults. These last two groups represent "desisters," a term used to describe individuals for whom gender dysphoria disappears or significantly decreases after puberty. Conversely, adults who experience continued gender incongruence after pubertal development are defined as "persisters." Moreover, in some individuals, gender dysphoria arises after puberty (i.e., late onset). For these individuals, it is rare for the incongruence to desist. It is not yet possible to reliably indicate which factors predict desistence or persistence (Drescher & Pula, 2014; Roberts, 2022).

All these clarifications serve to explain that, to different degrees and in varying modalities, gender identity, even before birth (can we deny the weight of parents' fantasies and expectations, or the role of maternal hormones during intrauterine life?), is constructed, "suspended" between biology, psychology, and culture, representing an artifact of the more or less conflictual coexistence of nature and nurture. At the crossroads of these sliding doors, today's adolescents can seize opportunities for listening and self-realisation, in harmony with Jessica Benjamin's (1998) idea that being pulled in more than one direction at once is central for our psychic life. In this moment of a collective rethinking of gender, amid true opportunities and false starts, adolescent disorientation can, on a case-by-case basis, creatively reflect the need to experiment, contradict oneself, and integrate unexplored parts of oneself. Yet, we often see disoriented adolescents: victims of lives falsely liberated to be trivialised on the web and lives truly devastated by sexist stereotypes of binary dominance that oppose a masculinity of domination and a femininity of dependency.

It appears compelling, at this juncture, to delve into the essence of nonbinary textuality by presenting excerpts from interviews from a research conducted by Bianca Di Giannantonio et al. (2024) titled "The Third Table Where I would Sit Comfortably: Narratives of Nonbinary Identity Routes." For this work, we interviewed 40 young adults aged 19–36 years ($M = 26.81$,

SD = 4.95) who identified as non-binary, inviting them to narrate the history of their identity development from childhood to the moment at which they became aware of their non-binary identity. Exploration, uncertainty, deconstruction, and mirroring emerged as key themes in their narratives. Their childhoods were often marked by gender-creative behaviours (i.e., those not typically associated with the gender assigned at birth) and by a genuine spontaneity in expressing their own authenticity. As they grew and entered the social world, this freedom was often replaced by the pressure to conform to gender roles, resulting in feelings of shame and discomfort in response to reactions from the external world.

The stories we listened to spoke of families with strongly polarised and traditional gender representations. Even in more equal and flexible contexts, a traditional and heteronormative view of gender and relationships could often be perceived. Our participants' developmental contexts, characterised by a predominance of binary gender roles and representations, provided few coordinates for their navigation and understanding of themselves and their discomfort outside masculine and feminine geographies. Let us consider two representative excerpts:

> *In my family, gender identity exists, but not identity itself. If you have a uterus, you must have children; if you have a penis, you must work. There's no other possible destiny.*
>
> (36 years old)

> *If I were to define how I feel my identity, it's a bit like there being a room that is masculine, for boys, and a room for girls, and maybe they even have a porthole, a window through which one can look into the other room, but they are like separated by a wall. To me, it has always seemed like living in the cracks, in the corridors between these two rooms. In an area all to be mapped out.*
>
> (19 years old)

However, the interpersonal context is not just a theatre of identity invalidation. For many of the interviewees, romantic and sexual relationships, friendships, access to queer spaces, social networks, and literature were essential sources of information and mirroring. Speaking of sexuality, for some, encounter with the body of another shed light on the complex interplay between attraction and identification:

> *There was a body that allowed me to realise that what I desired was that kind of body and that I identified with the bodies that, instead, I was trying to pick up.*
>
> (33 years old)

In the interviewees' identity journeys, encounters with trans and non-binary people played a crucial role. Reflecting on and coming into contact with the experiences of others led to a broadening of their conceptions of gender, accompanied by a deconstruction of previously internalised meanings around these constructions. Furthermore, their discovery and acknowledgment of the non-binary possibility constituted moments of harmonisation and a re-signification of past experiences of non-conformity and discomfort, whose causes were impossible to identify. For some, non-binarism represented a liberatory alternative to the rigid constraints of male and female – what Preciado, in "Can the Monster Speak?" (2020), describes as an "escape route" "from the circus of the binary heteropatriarchal regime."

> *When they mistook me for a man, I would go crazy, really crazy … consider that I am also a trans-feminist and intersectional feminist … so when they mistook me for a man it bothered me. When they mistook or mistake me for a woman, it's still something I don't feel as mine; it's not something I feel fits me. … Now I'm 26 years old and I identify as a non-binary person.*
>
> (26 years old)

For others, non-binary identification allowed for the integration of elements that, to that point, had been split and experienced with conflict, thereby opening the door to a more positive and conscious relationship with their body.

> *Determining myself as a non-binary person, paradoxically, or maybe not, has made me get closer again to the feminine. I can finally wear pink again, because I am not female.*
>
> (30 years old)

From the examination of these excerpts (I had to select only a few, for brevity, but the interviews were indeed full of deep and personal gender experiences), it seems that the journey towards non-binary identification often begins against a backdrop of highly polarised familial and social gender images, with well-known attributes: the dominant masculine, the passive feminine. These images clash with a natural and enigmatic childhood polymorphic drive of "queer" creativity. When, with pubertal development, the body becomes coloured with the dark tones of stereotypical oppositions, an internal plane of bodily dysphoria is created, due to the transformations of the body, as well as an external plane of social dysphoria, based on a perceived lack of recognition in the two socially segregated genders (in the family, at school, in friend groups, in sports activities, etc.). Thus, the individual feels disoriented and in search of new personal meanings. Unlike binary transgender identities, which are often based on beliefs and perceptions of belonging to the other gender (even at a very early age), in non-binary adolescents, the solution to these experiences of incongruence is not found in a complete transition, but in an understanding of oneself as a subjectivity "beyond the genders." As we have seen, this identity, whose construction is always dynamic and relational, can rigidly reject every gender attribute, or be a "soft assembly" in which different gender identifications coexist. The latter represents possibilities for new mindscapes that speak to us of critical (dis)identifications or creative personal syntheses.

The task of psychotherapy, as I move towards the conclusion, is then to safeguard the creative impulses on the path of identity formation, creating space for listening and meaning-making that gives depth and "conflict" to the horizontal plane of the multiplication of categories. Dialogue with the adolescent discovering a non-binary identity must be capable of integrating all elements of the internal experience, even the most sidelined. For example, the physical and symbolic emergence of a changing body, negative expectations towards puberty, and the impact of new social containers capable of offering a dwelling place at a time in life when there is an extreme need for belonging, affiliation, and identification. Therefore, in my work, I try to nourish the body of meanings that boys and girls attribute to binary differences, while also working with the melancholy of what is inevitably lost (Butler, 1995). Always questioning the crystals of the identity kaleidoscope, whether they are too solid or too fluid. In my experience as a therapist, I have met people intent on seeking an identity that made them feel comfortable with the idea they had of themselves and their gender, even beyond the male/female binarism. Others, starting from a sense of being lost (ranging from "simple" disorientation to full gender dysphoria), have asked me to help them reach positions of greater certainty, with literal, binary, and psychobiological anchors. It is not always possible to process, let alone tolerate, the melancholy that stems from what we do not have, from what we are not. Most of us have benefited from the interweaving of identifications and inventions capable of producing third solutions that dialectically overcome the binary constraint. My work aims at decentralising the notion of gender identification and referring to the plurality of developmental positions, rather than a nonlinearity of development, in order to help my patients assimilate difference without repudiating similarity. In so doing, they may create a space between opposites that can conceptualise a tension, rather than an opposition that overvalues one pole by devaluing the other (Giovanardi, Mundo, Lingiardi, 2021).

Words and relationships in a binary world, especially in the Italian language, are simpler. The work of listening inclusively, paying attention to pronouns, and questioning our countertransference is strenuous. But it is also instructive: we learn many things – for example, attention to others, respect, and complexity. As a psychoanalyst, I would like to add that the encounter with gender variant people (from nonbinary to transgender) represents not only an opportunity for new insights in the countertransference, but also a true epistemological "gift."

Awareness of complexity must not distract us from the importance of adequate ego functioning. Concepts such as "multiple identities," "fluid genders," and "discontinuous selves" can be fascinating theoretical options, but unless they are to remain merely academic, they must also deal with everyday life and an individual's available psychological resources. "Painful" is a term that too often has been missing in postmodern narratives about gender.

A line from Virginia Woolf's *The Waves* (1931) come to mind: "I am rooted but I flow." Our freedom of movement – our "gender gradient" – is proportional to our rhythmic, integrative, and relational capacities. It is these capacities that determine whether we are playing a creative game with our identity or staging the script of an exile that is both painful and full of hope. The phenomena I have tried to describe are so new and complex that it makes no sense to marry them to a single explanatory or therapeutic model, let alone one that is pathologising or corrective. We must learn to listen and consider, on a case-by-case basis, the most appropriate approach. But one thing we know precisely (and especially as psychoanalysts and people who dedicate our lives to the construction of a sufficiently good psychic functioning): gender incongruence calls us to the deepest respect for subjectivities, which in the current age are sometimes sacrificed in the name of identity politics, with easy media traction. We must be able to stay close to patients in their journeys towards something unknown or not yet known, tolerating the uncertainty of paths that may take one direction, then turn back, then forward again, in a new direction. We must remain attentive, observe, and participate with care, empathy and, when necessary, courage, in the future developments of metamorphoses that may take shape before our eyes.

References

Benjamin, J. (1995). Sameness and difference: Toward an 'overinclusive' model of gender development. *Psychoanalytic Inquiry*. 15, 125–142.

Benjamin, J. (1998). *Like Subjects, Love Objects: Essays on Recognition and Sexual Difference*. New Haven: Yale University Press.

Biblarz, T. J. & Stacey, J. (2010). How does the gender of parents matter? *Journal of Marriage and Family*. 72, 3–22.

Birksted-Breen, D. (1993). *The Gender Conundrum: Contemporary Psychoanalytic Perspectives on Femininity and Masculinity*. London: Routledge.

Butler, J. (1995). Melancholy gender-refused identification. *Psychoanalytic Dialogues*. 5, 165–180.

Carone, N., Baiocco, R., Manzi, D., Antonucci, C., Caricato, V., Pagliarulo, E. & Lingiardi, V. (2018a). Surrogacy families headed by gay men: Relationships with surrogates and egg donors, fathers' decisions over disclosure, and children's views on their surrogacy origins. *Human Reproduction*. 33, 248–257.

Carone, N., Lingiardi, V., Chirumbolo, A. & Baiocco, R. (2018b). Italian gay father families formed by surrogacy: Parenting, stigmatisation, and children's psychological adjustment. *Developmental Psychology*. 54, 1904–1916.

Carone, N., Baiocco, R., Lingiardi, V. & Barone, L. (2020). Gay and heterosexual single father families created by surrogacy: Father–child relationships, parenting quality, and children's psychological adjustment. *Sexuality Research and Social Policy*. 17, 711–728. https://doi.org/10.1007/s13178-019-00428-7

Carone, N., Manzi, D., Barone, L., et al. (2023a). Disclosure and child exploration of surrogacy origins in gay father families: Fathers' adult attachment interview coherence of mind matters. *Journal of Reproductive and Infant Psychology*. https://doi.org/10.1080/02646838.2023.2214583

Carone, N., Mirabella, M., Innocenzi, E., Quintigliano, M., Antoniucci, C., Manzi, D., Fortunato, A., Giovanardi, G., Speranza, A.M., & Lingiardi, V. (2023b). The intergenerational transmission of attachment during middle childhood in lesbian, gay, and heterosexual parent families through assisted reproduction: The mediating role of reflective functioning. *Attachment and Human Development*. https://doi.org/10.1080/14616734.2023.2292053

Carone, N., Quintigliano, M., Benzi, I. M.A., Brumariu, L., Speranza, A. M., & Lingiardi, V. (2025). Parental sensitivity and child-parent attachment security in lesbian and gay parent families through assisted reproduction. *Journal of Family Psychology*. https://doi.org/10.1037/fam0001324

Claahsen-van der Grinten, H., Verhaak, C., Steensma, T., Middelberg, T., Roeffen, J. & Klink, D. (2021). Gender incongruence and gender dysphoria in childhood and adolescence - Current insights in diagnostics, management, and follow-up. *European Journal of Pediatrics*. 180, 1349–1357.

Davies, J. M. (2015). From oedipus complex to oedipal complexity: Reconfiguring (pardon the expression) the negative oedipus complex and the disowned erotics of disowned sexualities. *Psychoanalytic Dialogues*. 25(3), 265–283.

De l'Horizon, K. (2022). *Blutbuch*. Köln: Dumont.

Di Giannantonio, B., Milanese, K., Mirabella, M., Rosati, F., Lorusso, M. M., Pistella, J., Baiocco, R., Lingiardi, V. & Giovanardi, G. (2024). 'The third table where I would sit comfortably': Narratives of nonbinary identity routes. *International Journal of Transgender Health*. 25(1), 1–19.

Drescher, J. & Pula, J. (2014). Ethical issues raised by the treatment of gender-variant prepubescent children. *The Hastings Center Report*. 44(4), 17–22.

Fortunato, A., Giovanardi, G., Innocenzi, E., Mirabella, M., Caviglia, G., Lingiardi, V. & Speranza, A. M. (2022). Is it autism? A critical commentary on the co-occurrence of gender dysphoria and autism spectrum disorder. *Journal of Homosexuality*. 69(7), 1204–1221.

Freud, S. (1911). Formulations on the two principles of mental functioning. *S.E.* 12, 213–226.

Freud, S. (1915). Instincts and their vicissitudes. *S.E.* 14, 109–140.

Giovanardi, G., Mundo & Lingiardi, V. (2021). Paola on the couch: The quest for feminine identity in an empirically supported psychoanalytic psychotherapy of a trans woman. *Psychoanalytic Psychology*. 38(4), 239–253.

Glocer Fiorini, L. (2017). *Sexual Difference in Debate: Bodies, Desires, and Fictions*. London: Karnac Books.

Harris, A. (2005). *Gender as Soft Assembly*. Hillsdale, NJ: The Analytic Press.

Heineman, T. (2004). A boy and two mothers: New variations on an old theme or a new story of triangulation? Beginning thoughts on psychosexual development of children in non-traditional families. *Psychoanalytic Psychology*. 21, 99–115.

Kallitsounaki, A. & Williams, D. M. (2023). Autism spectrum disorder and gender dysphoria/incongruence. A systematic literature review and meta-analysis. *Journal of Autism and Developmental Disorders*. 53(8), 3103–3117.

Lemma, A. (2023). The seductions of identity: Thinking about identity and transgender. *Psychoanalytic Quarterly*. 92(3), 407–434.

Lingiardi, V. (2007). Dreaming gender: Restoration and transformation. *Studies in Gender and Sexuality*. 8(4), 313–331.

Lingiardi, V. (2015). No Maps for Uncharted Lands: What does Gender Expression have to do with Sexual Orientation? In A. Lemma & P. E. Lynch, (eds.) *Sexualities: Contemporary Psychoanalytic Perspectives*. 101–121. London, New York: Routledge.

Lingiardi, V. (2024). Identità e identificazioni di genere in un mondo che cambia. *Psiche*. (1), 317–332.

Lingiardi, V. & Carone, N. (2019). Challenging Oedipus in changing families: Gender identifications and access to origins in same-sex parent families created through third-party reproduction. *International Journal of Psychoanalysis*. 100(2), 229–246.

Loewald, H. W. (1979). The waning of the oedipus complex. *Journal of the American Psychoanalytic Association*. 27, 751–775.

Meltzer, D. & Harris M. (1976). *The Educational Role of the Family: A Psychoanalytical Model*. London: Karnac Books, 2013.

Ogden, T. H. (1989). *The Primitive Edge of Experience*. Lanham, MD: Jason Aronson.

Preciado, P. B. (2020). *Je suis un monstre qui vous parle*. Grasset: Paris.

Preciado, P. B. (2022). *Dysphoria mundi*. Grasset: Paris.

Roberts, C. (2022). Persistence of transgender gender identity among children and adolescents. *Pediatrics*. 150(2), 1–3.

Saketopoulou, A. & Pellegrini, A. (2023). *Gender Without Identity*. New York: Uit Books.

Stern, D. N. (1985). *The Interpersonal World of the Infant. A View from Psychoanalysis and Developmental Psychology*. New York: Basic Books.

Stern, D. N. (1995). *The Motherhood Constellation: A Unified View of Parent-infant Psychotherapy*. New York: Basic Books.

Stern, D. N. (2004). *The Present Moment in Psychotherapy and Everyday Life*. New York: W. W. Norton & Company.

Stoller, R. J. (1968). *Sex and Gender: The Development of Masculinity and Femininity*. London: Karnac Books.

van der Miesen, A. I. R., de Vries, A. L. C., Steensma, T. D., Hartman, C. A. (2018). Autistic symptoms in children and adolescents with gender dysphoria. *Journal of Autism and Developmental Disorders*. 48(5), 1537–1548.

Winnicott, D. W. (1966). The Split-off Male and Female Elements to be Found in Men and Women (Published as a Section of Creativity and its Origins). In Winnicott, D.W., *Playing and Reality* (1971), 72–85. London: Tavistock.

Winnicott, D. W. (1989). *Human Nature*. New York, NY: Routledge.

Woolf, V. (1931). *The Waves*. Wordsworth Classics, New edition, 2000.

7 Reclaiming psychic bisexuality

Revisiting Winnicott's "The Split-off Male and Female Elements to be Found Clinically in Men and Women" (1966)

Anat Schumann

In this chapter, I'll explore the dialectic interplay between the "masculine" and the "feminine" as a creative psychic movement relating to the *bisexual subjectivity* in both men and women. Psychoanalytic inquiry into the concept of *psychic bisexuality* ranges between the archaic and the Oedipal, addressing various modes of internalisation at different levels of integration. Drawing on Freud's conceptualisation of primary and secondary identifications, a distinction is suggested between *primary bisexuality* that represents the rudimentary encounter with otherness, akin to the archaic bisexualities described by Winnicott and Tustin, and *secondary bisexuality* which is consolidated through later introjective processes, involving the m/other and father within the Oedipal scenes. In revisiting the concept of *psychic bisexuality*, sexual and gendered states of mind which may reflect a *dissociation* of psychic bisexuality are considered and clinical illustrations are presented, describing analytic processes that involve the *reclamation* of psychic bisexuality in its primary and secondary manifestations. Finally, this chapter discusses the challenging and infinite question of *transitionality* in the Winnicottian sense, aiming to distinguish creative and playful psychic movement between the "masculine" and "feminine" from an anxious and repetitive pseudo-movement, which may reflect an inability for thinking and dreaming in the spheres of sexual and gender-related states of mind.

David came to see me shortly before his wedding, in severe distress. He felt that he could not marry his girlfriend and wanted to end their relationship. He later told me about his masturbation habits, which involved the fantasy that he is a woman: "Do you realise what that means? I'm inside the woman there. I am her... When I was in kindergarten, I loved putting on princess dresses, the teacher freaked out and called my mother".

I said: "Maybe you are asking for a quiet listening here, not to be alarmed like the kindergarten teacher, not confusing like the voice inside". He was silent and then asked: "That woman inside me, is she me? I don't know. Sometimes I feel like she is, especially in sexual situations, but not only then...".

DOI: 10.4324/9781003534440-11

Daniel, a married man and father, came to therapy feeling depressed without knowing why. Over time he revealed his addiction to sexual encounters with random women. In his associations, he would bring these women to life by granting them the most powerful sexual experience. As analysis unfolded, it seemed that through these women he was facing inside him a helpless maternal introject which had to be continuously revived in a manner that left Daniel depleted of his physical and mental resources.

In terms suggested by Winnicott (1966), David and Daniel may be described as men in whom a *split-off "female" element* has indwelt, creating a state of *dissociated psychic bisexuality*. This split-off female element is contrasted with the so-called *pure female element*, originating in the early m/other-infant unity, which is internalised into the psyche, laying the foundation for *integrated* psychic bisexuality. Later, the so-called *"male element"* object-relating will arise, signifying the introduction of drive into the psychic realm and the movement towards separateness. I will return to David and Daniel later.

Freud (1905) claimed that "Without taking bisexuality into account ... it would scarcely be possible to arrive to an understanding of the sexual manifestations that are actually to be observed in men and women" (220). Drawing on Freud, Winnicott (1966) used the term "psychic bisexuality" to refer to the subjective sense of self in terms of "masculine" and "feminine". He perceived psychic bisexuality as a transitional phenomenon, a developmental achievement among other intermediate phenomena such as cultural experience, creative scientific work and art, all of which "belong to the realm of illusion ... made possible by the mother's special capacity for making adaptation to the needs of her infant" (1971, 17).

Winnicott (1966, 170) preferred not to associate psychic bisexuality with object-choice, as he stated in his discussion of the "non-masculine" element in his patient's psyche: "I wish to emphasise that this has nothing to do with homosexuality". Freud regularly relates to the concept of "psychic bisexuality" without making a distinction between gender-related states of mind and sexual object-choice. It is remarkable to note his following comment (1920, 170):

A man in whose character feminine attributes obviously predominate, who may, indeed, behave in love like a woman, might be expected, from this feminine attitude, to choose a man for his love-object; but he may nevertheless be heterosexual ... The same is true of women; here also mental sexual character and object-choice do not necessarily coincide ...

It is instead a question of three sets of characteristics, namely -

Physical sexual characters

(physical hermaphroditism)

Mental sexual characters

(masculine or feminine attitude)

Kind of object-choice

which, up to a certain point, *vary independently of one another, and are met with in different individuals in manifold permutations.*

(emphasis added)

Freud distinguishes here between biological sex, the feminine or masculine attitude (later termed gender identity) and object-choice, similar to the distinction proposed by Winnicott (1966/1989), introducing a preliminary conceptualisation of sexual and gender diversity. These claims were later discussed by many authors (such as Chiland, 2009; Perelberg, 2018) and Mitchell (2018, xviii) summarised as follows: "independently of any identifications or object choices, subjectively our sexuality is always bisexual".[1]

Psychic bisexuality between the Oedipal and the archaic

Psychoanalytic thinking on *psychic bisexuality* ranges between the primordial and the Oedipal, addressing various modes of internalisation at different levels of integration. The earliest introjective processes, which precede the "me/not-me" differentiation, were described by Winnicott (1966) as a "pure female" relatedness, defined as primary identification: "in the sense of the baby becoming the breast (or the mother), in the sense that the object is the subject" (177, no emphasis in the text). Tustin (1981) also related to these archaic identification processes, focusing on the "nipple-breast" as the *primary bisexual object*. Subsequent modes of internalisation emerge later, involving secondary identifications with whole objects being perceived as "others", the m/other and father within the Oedipal scenes (Freud, 1923), creating the internal parents through introjective identifications in both "masculine" and "feminine" roles, including the sexual relation between them (Meltzer, 1973).

The term "psychic aspect of bisexuality" appeared for the first time in a letter Freud sent to Fliess in 1901 (Masson, 1985), in which he sought to add his understanding of bisexuality as a subjective essence, to the anatomical–biological emphasis that Fliess attributed to it. Freud (1905) depicted an innate, universal psychic bisexuality that emerges through the child's identifications with his m/other and father in the dual, positive and negative, Oedipal situation. This identification process eventually culminates in the repression of one aspect, either the "feminine" or the "masculine", which thus becomes unconscious (1923). Freud found it difficult to define the factors that affect which parent the child ultimately identifies with, and resorted to the constitutional explanation, pointing to "the relative strength of the masculine and feminine sexual dispositions" (Freud, 1905, 33). Over the years, Freud vacillated in his understanding of human bisexuality, moving between body and mind, biology and object-related identifications, as part of his contradictory movement between instinct-centred and object-related views of sexuality (Birksted-Breen, 1993; Blass, 2016).

Theorising psychic bisexuality, Freud ponders how to define "masculine" versus "feminine" as distinct psychic entities, while trying to avoid the simplistic equation of masculinity with activity and femininity with passivity. He therefore proposes the *libido* as a "masculine" psychic element in both men and women (1915, a later addition to the "Three Essays"). Given that the universal psychic structure is bisexual, the question arises what could represent the "feminine" element within it? Following Freud, Winnicott (1966) suggested the *"pure female element"* object-relating, originates in the early m/other-infant unity, as the foundation for bisexual subjectivity in both men and women. This primordial "pure female" relatedness is described as *primary identification:*

> Two separate persons can feel at one, but here at the place that I am examining the baby and the object are one. The term 'primary identification' has perhaps been used for just this that I'm describing, and I am trying to show how vitally important this first experience is for the initiation of all subsequent experiences of identification.
>
> (Winnicott, 1966, 177)

Winnicott emphasised the significance of the good-enough primary object, whose ability to be attuned to the infant's needs may relieve the anxiety of otherness, enabling the internalisation of a *"pure female element"* relatedness, to create an integrated psychic bisexuality. However, when early environment is perceived as traumatic and the continuity of being is broken, the primordial object might be experienced as a persecutory otherness incorporated into the psyche. According to Winnicott, this infant, who couldn't internalise the environmental m/other as a "pure female" relatedness, incorporates a concrete split-off "female" element instead, resulting in a rigid and anxiety-ridden dissociated bisexuality. This incorporated "female" element is sometimes felt as a foreign body implanted inside the self. Thus, Winnicott described the process of bisexualisation as affected by genetics as well as by the early maternal environment and the quality of its "pure female" relatedness, ranging from the capacity to maintain the infant's going-on-being to an intrusive or overwhelming presence that unravels it:

> In health there is a variable amount of girl element in a girl, and in a boy. Also, hereditary factor elements enter in ... Add to this the variable capacity of mothers to hand on the desirability of the good breast ... and it can be seen that some boys and girls are doomed to grow up with a *lop-sided bisexuality*, loaded on the wrong side of their biological provision.
>
> (1966/1989, 83; emphasis added)

In recent decades, psychoanalytic discourse on the concept of *psychic bisexuality* has given rise to diverse thoughts and interpretations. While some authors, like Winnicott, see it as reflecting psychic movement between "masculine" and "feminine" elements, which fosters creative states of mind (Aisenstein & Rich, 2018; Eigen, 2004; McDougall, 1995; Perelberg, 2018; Quinodoz, 2002), others perceive it as a concept that may confine gendered subjectivity (Drescher, 2007; Gulati & Pauley, 2019) and perpetuate the feminine-masculine binary as a social construction which is alienated from the individual's unique sense of self (Butler, 1990; Corbett, Dimen, Goldner & Harris, 2014).

Given this controversy,[2] one may wonder what could define *"transitionality"*, in the Winnicottian sense, in the spheres of sexual and gender-related states of mind? When listening to the free associating analysand, what would enable us to distinguish creative and playful psychic movement between the "masculine" and "feminine" from a repetitive pseudo-movement, reflecting an inability for thinking and dreaming? Nowadays, these clinical concerns seem to arise around the psychoanalytic discourse regarding gender dysphoria and various wishes for gender transitioning, when a feminine psyche is experienced as imprisoned in a male body or vice versa. In terms suggested in this chapter, some of these gender-related states of mind may be perceived as reflecting a *dissociated psychic bisexuality*.

As I will show later, Winnicott (1966) portrayed different kinds of dissociations in the inner bisexual configuration. When the dissociation is deep and may involve early trauma, distress related to gender-related states of mind may reflect a condition in which psycho-somatic cohesion is lost as a defence against an underlying annihilating anxiety (Quinodoz, 2002; Stein, 1995; Winnicott, 1945). Such psychodynamics may be found in certain gender-related states of mind, much like the way primordial anxieties may underlie other mental conditions which "communicate" through archaic psychic languages, such as hypochondria, severe eating disorders and other psychosomatic conditions (Amir, 2014; Lemma, 2013; McDougall, 1995; Schellekes, 2017).

I shall now elaborate on some suggested clinical manifestations of a *dissociated bisexuality*, focusing on the archaic phenomena that involve the incorporation of a split-off "female" element, in relation to other primary identification processes such as *imitation* (Gaddini,1969) or *adhesive identification* (Bick, 1968; Meltzer, 1975), all of them related to the psychic necessity to hold together the infantile body-self in face of early traumatic vicissitudes.[3]

Archaic identifications and gender-related states of mind

Stoller (1968), who coined the term "core gender identity", was one of the first to distinguish between the biologically determined sex, and gender identity as a psychological construct. Many other authors referred to the emergence of gendered states of mind at the very beginning of psychic life, when the initial sensorial impressions, later associated with "masculine" or "feminine", begin to have psychic meaning through pre-verbal representations (Argentieri, 2009; McDougall, 1995). In this early developmental phase, sensorial data are not yet represented through linguistic signifiers or in terms of unconscious phantasy, but through primordial modes of representation, such as formal signifiers (Anzieu, 1990). These imprint the psyche with early forms of opposites, such as soft-hard, full-empty, sequence-interruption or passive–active, registered in the psyche as bodily sensory traces that may coalesce into archaic shapes of the "feminine" and the "masculine", internalised into the primeval bisexual self. Moreover, the masculine–feminine dichotomy is perceived as one of the first dichotomies internalised in human thinking, and therefore as a prototype for any binary represented in the psyche (Amir, 2018). Thus, psychic bisexuality, in its broadest sense, may become associated with the ability to contain diversity in the psyche: male and female, me and not-me, self and other. In that way, it reflects the essential capacity for encountering *otherness*.

Focusing on autism as the "pathology of otherness" (Houzel, 2021), Tustin (1981) described the primary "nipple-breast" bisexual object, which evokes the initial registration of bisexuality in the infantile psyche, with the soft element, the breast, which represents "me", turning into the "feminine", and the hard, thrusting element, which represents the "not me", turning into the "masculine". According to Tustin, when the early "flowing-over-at-oneness" is safe enough and the hard nipple is experienced as harmoniously related to the soft breast, this leads to the integration of the "feminine" and "masculine" elements in the psyche. Nevertheless, when the awareness of the "not-me" is premature and traumatic, the primary object is *split* into its "masculine" and "feminine" components as a defence against the catastrophic dread involved in encountering otherness. In such cases, the autistic defence involves a significant failure to integrate psychic bisexuality.

Back to Winnicottian terms, when the infant's continuity-of-being is engulfed by congenital excess and/or early environmental trauma, which Winnicott defined as the absence of "female element breast", a split-off concrete "female" element is introjected:

Clinically … the baby who has to make do with an identity with a breast that is active, which is a male-element breast, but which is not satisfactory for the initial identity which needs a breast that *is*, not a breast that *does*. Instead of *"being like"* this baby has to *"do like"*.

(179)

Following Freud (1921, 170) who depicted an introjective identification which "…in a regressive way (it) becomes a substitute for a libidinal object-tie, as it were by means of introjection of the object into the ego", Winnicott referred here to the introjection of a *dissociated "female" element*, similar to other archaic two-dimensional modes of identifications, such as imitation (Gaddini, 1969), adhesive identification (Meltzer, 1975) and other "second skin" formations (Bick, 1968), all of these reflecting the internalisation of concrete features associated with the m/other, functioning as a form of "self-holding" that illusorily *replaces* the lost object.

Gaddini (1969, 477) described the primordial imitation that emerges in early traumatic states:

> *'Imitating in order to be'* ... installs itself not in the presence of the object but in its *absence*, and that precisely because of this, its aim seems to be that of re-establishing in a magical and omnipotent way the fusion of the self with the object.
>
> (emphasis added)

Green (1986, 151) also defined an imitative identification, when relating to an early "dead mother":

> This reactive symmetry is the only means by which to establish a reunion with the mother ... There is no real reparation, but a *mimicry*, with the aim of continuing to possess the object (who one can no longer have) by becoming, not like it, but *the object itself.*
>
> (emphasis added)

All these introjective processes may reflect the splitting of the fundamental bisexual function due to early traumatic vicissitudes. Under such internal and/or external circumstances, mental functioning becomes devoid of transitional space, followed by a deep sense of emptiness.

I will turn now to clinical illustrations, describing analytic processes involving the *reclamation* of psychic bisexuality in male patients. It should be noted that there are various clinical phenomena that may reflect the internalisation of a split-off "female" element in girls and women, as may be manifest in Riviere's (1929) images of "Womanliness as a masquerade", related to the girl's early relations with the pre-oedipal maternal other (McDougall, 1995; Perelberg, 2018). Nevertheless, in many ways, the bisexual dynamic in girls and women seems to manifest differently than in men (Chiland, 2009) and merits its own discussion. Paraphrasing Freud's (1921) conceptualisation of primary and secondary identifications, I will refer to an early *primary bisexuality* which is akin to the archaic bisexualities described by Winnicott (1966), Tustin (1981) and Houzel (2021), in relation to *secondary bisexuality*, which relies on identifications involving differentiated others, based on "male element" object-relations within the Oedipal phase.

Between "dissociation of male and female elements" and psychic bisexuality

I will begin with Winnicott's (1966) well-known clinical case, which depicts the revival of *primary bisexuality* within the transference relations. During an analytic session with a middle-aged man, Winnicott noticed a new type of dissociation,[4] a split-off "female" element embedded in the self:

> I know perfectly well that you are a man but I'm listening to a girl, and I'm talking to a girl.
>
> (170)

After a pause, the patient replied: "If I were to tell someone about this girl, I would be called mad" (171).

When the patient returned sick the following Monday, Winnicott interpreted his illness as a psycho-somatic condition related to the protest of his "inner girl", struggling against "her" integration into his bisexual self:

> You feel as if you ought to be pleased that here was an interpretation of mine that had released masculine behaviour. *The girl that I was talking to, however, doesn't want the man released* ... What she wants is full acknowledgement of herself and of her own rights over your body
>
> (172, emphasis in original)

Winnicott viewed this introjected "girl" as an unconscious *dissociated* maternal aspect that had been internalised into the psyche, in an effort to hold onto an oblivious m/other who treats him as a girl. The infant thus introjects a pseudo *"female" element*, rather than a genuine *"pure female element"*. In another paper, Winnicott (1969/1989) described a similar dynamic in a six-year-old boy, who introjected his mother's madness as a "traumatic agent", a split-off "female" element. Abram (2013) suggested these kinds of psychic scenarios as clinical evidence for the non-survival of the original object, which remains implanted in the self as an alienated, concrete entity, unavailable for mental representation and symbolisation.

Returning to Winnicott's patient, one may wonder what became of his inner "girl"? Winnicott suggested that the dissociation of the female element was now healed and replaced by psychic bisexuality: *"The dissociation defence was giving way to an acceptance of bisexuality as a quality of the unit or total self"* (173, emphasis added). Elsewhere, Winnicott (1963a, 77) addressed the psychic change that occurred in this analysis:

> This in turn has to be freed from his far-reaching *delusion* which he has always had that *he is truly female*. The *playing* at being a woman of the *female identification* which is much more *flexible* had now come into the analysis.
>
> (emphasis added)

What was it that enabled transformation towards psychic bisexuality in this analysis? Winnicott emphasised the analyst's receptivity to an excessive sense of emptiness and nonexistence, "live an experience together" (1945) as "two in oneness" (Eshel, 2019), all of which reflect a deep analytic unity, the "pure female" relatedness:

> Now that the new position had been reached the patient felt a sense of relationship with me … It had to do with *identity*. The pure female split-off element found a *primary unity* with me as analyst, and this gave the man a feeling of having started to live.
> (Winnicott, 1966/1989, 174; emphasis added)

It seems that through an analytic "pure female" object-relating, this patient could internalise a genuine femininity, assimilated into an integrated bisexuality. Other authors have also addressed the importance of the analyst's surrender to deep interconnectedness in areas of sexual and gendered states of mind. For example, Quinodoz (2002) described the need to encounter her own intense confusion, to enable her analysand – who had already undergone MtF reassignment surgery – to liberate herself from a binding relation to some concrete split-off "female" elements, creating a genuine and lively sense of femininity within her own bisexual self.

I will continue with two clinical illustrations suggesting processes of psychic bisexuality reclamation, which involves internal movements between the "masculine" and the "feminine" as aspects of primary and secondary bisexualities. In David's analysis, changes towards psychic bisexuality seem to involve the shedding of pathological psychic envelopes (Anzieu, 1990), that rendered the patient's subjectivity impoverished and empty. In the case of Daniel, the inner split-off "female" element may be reminiscent of Green's (1986) "dead mother complex" as a clinical phenomenon which involves the internalisation of a "psychic hole", representing and thereby holding onto the absent m/other. I will suggest that the depth of *dissociation* in psychic bisexuality changes from person to person, as does the depth of regression in the transference, depending on the severity of the trauma and how early in life it had occurred.

David

David separated from his fiancée and began a four-times-a-week analysis; I will try to outline an eight-year-long analytic process through its reflections in dreams and in the unfolding transference relations.

In the realm of archaic anxiety

After ending his relationship, David was in crisis. She had made all the decisions, managed his schedule. He had no idea how to get by without her. He gradually began to share his overwhelming anxieties: *"I'm a big lump of*

anxiety… I'm mostly afraid of gaining weight, and my skin always feels dirty".
David looked underweight, adhered to a very limited diet and was preoccupied with aesthetic treatments and plastic procedures: *"If I don't watch
myself, I will look really horrible, it would be unbearable, I'd rather die".*

I contemplated the dismantled way in which David brought himself to
me, as a pile of organs, maybe as a corpse; there was no inside. David was
missing.

"You're deeply concerned about your body", I said.

*"I mostly wish there was less of it. I want to be as thin and invisible as rice
paper".* I wondered what made him want to get rid of his body. The woman
inside wasn't mentioned yet.

First dream in analysis: *I'm sick and I ask you to come to my place. We sit in the
bathroom, I'm on the toilet and you're next to me. Something up my nose is irritating
me – I find a dry leaf hanging from the end of a branch. I start pulling it out and there's
no end to it. I'm stunned, how is it possible that something like this is inside me?*

Listening to David's dream, I thought he may be telling me about an
"infantile seduction" scene repeated in the transference (Laplanche, 1989),
alongside his longing for an unobtrusive presence, accompanying him in a
process of dealing with a "foreign object" implanted inside him. I also noticed
some formal signifiers (inside–outside, passive–active, the movement of pulling out, of discharge) which may serve as rudimentary representations of primordial bisexuality, beginning to emerge through the transference relations.

In the first year of analysis, David sank into depression. He missed his
girlfriend and was also full of rage and hatred towards her, blaming her
for ruining his life. At the end of sessions, he found it difficult to leave: "I
want to stay here, to merge with that couch… The others can come and lie
on top of me, one after another, I promise not to remember anything they
say". He was expressing a deep sense of loneliness and an intense yearning
for a merged, soothing connection, like someone who had prematurely lost
the peace of infantile relatedness and was therefore unable to internalise it.

Another dream from the end of the first year:

> *Everything is happening here. Ruth, the woman who wanted to go out with
> me, is lying on the couch and you are sitting in front of me. You are trying
> to convince me to accept her advances, you keep insisting… I yell at you: "I
> don't want to, I won't, leave me alone".*

I said: "All these women… what do we want from you? Maybe you're
worried that I might force you into something here…"

David replied: *"I'm actually not that afraid of you. No offence, but you remind me
of Meryl Streep, who simply vanishes into her roles. Off-screen, she's completely grey,
she dresses like a nobody".* I heard him relating to an imposing introjected object,
alongside the emergence of an "environmental m/other" in the transference,
experienced as suspending herself and her colours. In Winnicott's terms, this
kind of analytic presence may reflect a *"pure female relatedness* which facilitates

the emergence of *primary psychic bisexuality.*" As he noted elsewhere: "only on the basis of monotony can a mother profitably add richness" (1945, 141).

Fear of breakdown

Two years into analysis, David met Jonathan, a married man and a father. This led to a relationship that unsettled David's psyche for years to come. After several weeks of elation and the thrill of discovery, David realised that Jonathan had no intention of pursuing a deeper relationship, saying that he does not want to hurt his family. David pleaded with Jonathan to see him at least once a week, once a month: *"I can't take it, something terrible has happened to me, I'm going to die".* He demands that I tell him when the pain will go away, that I promise him that it will not kill him. I realised that he is overwhelmed by an anxiety of unprecedented intensity. During this period, he shared archaic dreams:

> *I'm holding my nose in my hand; I need to put it back on my face.*
>
> *There's an ugly black stain on my skin. I tried to clean it, but nothing helps.*

These dreams seem to convey a terrifying sense of deformation, while various objects extrude from the body or invade it, both internal and alien. This anxiety seems to emerge around Jonathan, who stirs hope for an environment in which the self could be enlivened, simultaneously triggering David's fear of breakdown.

Jonathan's visits became rare. David fell into an abyss of despair and emptiness, overwhelmed by unremitting thoughts about Jonathan's wife, wishing violent and humiliating deaths for her. Facing this emotional turbulence, it seemed that David needs me as a safe environmental m\other, a silent "pure female" presence, offering psychic meaning to what was going on inside him.

Through persecutory anxieties to bisexual movement

Three years into analysis, David's anxiety increases, both within and outside the deepening transference relationship. He was preoccupied with men whose wives "speak out of their mouths", especially Jonathan, whose wife is an "aggressive throat cancer". He sometimes texts me to notify that he will not be coming that day: *"I need some time off, to make sure it's still me, that it's not your voice coming out of my throat".*

He shared a dream:

> *I walk into an apartment. The house is a mess. I'm very tired. I walk into the bedroom, mother's lying in bed, the sheets are soiled, leftover food, faeces and blood, it's terrible. I have to sleep. I ask mother to make room for me. I'm disgusted, she won't give me enough space.*

It seems that the associations of the "feminine" as an imposing entity inside the body, "throat cancer", together with the internal scene of filth and invasiveness arising in this dream, may reflect a "dissociated female element" object-relating, which has been soiled by a sick overload of sexualised messaging.

In those days, David seemed to live from one encounter with Jonathan to another: *"Jonathan is the only thing that's ever really happened to me, the only story I can tell, everything else is faded, meaningless, dead"*. He wondered why I wouldn't help him end this relationship with Jonathan – can't I see the amount of pain he is in? In one session, he said to me: *"You know, I think you're in love with Jonathan yourself. That's why you can't help me end this"*. I felt that he had a point. I could not find in myself any anger towards Jonathan. I thought that, despite his tantalising presence, he touched David's psyche in a genuine, meaningful and transformative way.

Another year goes by, Jonathan occasionally shows up at David's apartment. Their encounters are close and intimate. David is moved by new feelings: *"I don't feel as dirty when I'm with him, as if the garbage heap inside of me is cleaned up"*. He shared that, in his sexual fantasy, he no longer experienced himself exclusively as a woman: *"I think that's a gift Jonathan left me before he went away…"* In Winnicott's terms, one could say that the establishment of primary identification within the transference relations enabled the emergence of secondary identification processes, involving Jonathan as a third.

Four years into analysis, David feels an urge to strengthen his body. He starts eating. He enjoys feeling his body changing and growing stronger. Jonathan continues to play a meaningful role: *"with him, I feel like a human being, not an alien anymore…"* David shares more changes in his sexual fantasy: *"My yearnings have always been so passive, with Jonathan they're beginning to change"*.

Towards the transitional

Five years into analysis, he shared a dream:

> *I come here but your office is being renovated. I suggest that we go to another one. We walk down the street together and I point out my apartment. At first you don't spot it, so I lightly touch you, not in a sexual way, directing your gaze. The apartment is all lit up and the windows are open, which is strange because I never leave it that way. The apartment looks broken-into, something is wrong.*

I recalled the bathroom dream from the beginning of analysis, wondering whether David is inviting me on another analytic journey, signifying the emergence of "another office", a transitional one. His home is once again broken-into, like his body and mind, and the fear of intrusion is still present. Nevertheless, it seems that a different experience is emerging in the transference, one of walking together, gently touching ("not in a sexual way") within a growing ability for separateness and concern. During this time, David shared several dreams that took place in the stairway leading to my office:

> *At the end of the session, I wait for you outside. We go to a different apartment, one of us is leading and the other doesn't know the way, but I don't know which is which. It crosses my mind that I have never seen you standing upright. I'm surprised to discover that you're shorter than what I imagined…".* I replied, "Maybe it is safer for you here now. In a way, you really are noticing me for the first time, curious to find out who I am, which one of us is leading and where we go from here".

It seems that these "stairway dreams", taking place at the boundary between the psychoanalytic session and the world outside, represent a transitional Oedipal space emerging in the transference relation (Ogden, 1989). In the room, the movement between longing for intimacy and dread of its realisation continues. David is asking me to see him and love him in all his aspects, the so-called "feminine" and "masculine", to admire his changing body and acknowledge his love for me. He is keenly aware of any change in my facial expressions, conveying his fear that something has changed: "*I can feel you in the room now, you're not disappearing like before…*" It seems that the movement between environmental-m/other and object-m/other leads to increased intrusions of incestuous contents into the transference. I said: "Now, when you are using this space so intensely, you want to make sure that I am holding on, that I'm not losing my grip".

New beginning

Six years into analysis, David is trying to pursue other relationships, mostly with men, sharing further changes in his sexual fantasy. He misses Jonathan.

He shared a dream:

> *At the end of a session, you ask me if I am free to stay longer. I don't understand what you mean. You open a door in the wall that leads to your apartment. You change completely, you start talking incessantly…. I ask where your children are, and you say that they are at their father's. I'm surprised because I thought that you were married. From this point on, everything turns violent and goes downhill. A man walks in, he humiliates me. I feel that this is a catastrophe, that I'm losing my analysis, that it's irreversible.*

I think about his evolving ability to "dream" his traumatic narrative in the transference: destructive infantile seduction, a distorted Oedipal situation, collapsed boundaries and the fear of irreversible catastrophe. It seems that the transference relationship is safe enough now for the trauma to become psychic material that can be thought and dreamt. I say: "Maybe now you can have this dream, because you know that this is not going to happen here. I will never ask you if you are free to stay longer, even if I wanted to".

David arrived at our next session dejected, wanting to leave, to take a break from analysis: *"You and Jonathan... you both end up leaving me all alone... Now it's too late, so many years wasted on 'not-being-a-woman' and 'not-being-a-man,' years I didn't get to live. I can't remember anything about the person I used to be"*. It seems that David was now capable of representing in words a years-long experience of absence, of being empty of himself, which was also manifested in his gendered-related state of mind. Eight years into analysis, David applied for a senior position in an international company. He feels proud and excited as well as worried that he will not be able to achieve his goal. He shares another dream:

> *I'm preparing for my first day and notice a dead rat in my paper basket... It's huge. I'm disgusted by it and then I realise, to my horror, that it came out of my body, out of me.*

I think about his preoccupation with a foreign object that has taken up residence inside him. I say: "As you are preparing for a new beginning, you want to get rid of bad things that have penetrated you, to make room for the good that you're hoping to find in the world".

Discussion

In this clinical illustration, I have tried to portray the emergence of "gender space" (Amir, 2018), which entails psychic movement between "feminine" *and* "masculine" subjectivities, as aspects of *primary* and *secondary* bisexualities. These psychic transformations became possible within the analytic process, which initially involved a unified, "pure female" relatedness, allowing regression to dependence and thus a new opportunity for subjectivity to emerge.

David came to therapy before his wedding, in distress over his *gender identity*. In analysis, a deep sense of depletion and emptiness was unfolded, protected by concrete "second skin" manifestations, to preserve his continuity of being. In an earlier paper, "Nothing at the Centre", Winnicott (1959/1989) referred to the same patient who unconsciously carried a *dissociated* "female" element within him (1966), describing his search for a true sense of self. This patient is depicted as having a "false self" located in the area of his gender identity. David sadly acknowledged the years he had wasted on "not-being-a-woman" and "not-being-a-man", expressing his difficulty in internalising both genuine "masculine" *and* "feminine" elements as aspects of *primary bisexuality*. This resulted in an ambiguous, ambisexual state of mind (Meltzer, 1973), within a chaotic, alien-like identity suffused with early incestuous traumatisation.

Later in the analysis, the development of a transitional Oedipal situation and Jonathan's presence as a "third", experienced in David's phantasy as a love object that both of us shared, facilitated the emergence of *secondary identification* processes, based on *"male-element" object relations* which reflect the encountering of separated others. These enabled more elastic gender-related states of mind, sometimes experienced as "masculine with feminine elements" and sometimes as "feminine with masculine elements", both may be considered as manifestations of *secondary bisexuality*. Thus, psychic movement was generated within a *bisexual space*, movement towards *the feeling of being real and alive*.

Daniel

I shall now briefly present another analysis of a split-off "female" element, where the clinical manifestations and the level of integration differ from those depicted in David's case and may thus illustrate the variety of psychic derivatives of dissociated bisexuality, described by Winnicott (1966). Daniel is an esteemed academic in his late thirties, married and a father. He sought therapy because of vague feelings of depression and emptiness and began a three-times-a-week analysis. It turned out that he was addicted to sexual encounters, mostly one-time endeavours, with women he would find on dating apps. He described a compulsive need "to give my entire being to a woman, whatever her kind, age and size", focusing on her eyes, seeking the moment of her ultimate arousal. In his associations, he was awakening these women from a long slumber, providing them with the most powerful sexual experience. Once the sexual encounter was over, he would usually be plagued by a devastating feeling that they were using him, draining him of his internal resources. Therefore, he usually preferred never to see them again. It seemed that through these women, he was encountering a maternal introject inside him, which had to be repeatedly enlivened through endless enactments that left him emptied of himself.

In my attempt to "take in" and give meaning to Daniel's sexual state of mind, I found it resonating with Winnicott's (1966, 175) writing about a specific manifestation of the split-off "female" element:

> The man who initiates girls into sexual experience may well be one who is more identified with the girl than with himself. This gives him the capacity to go all out to wake up the girl's sex and to satisfy her. He pays for this by getting but little male satisfaction himself and also in terms of his need to seek always a new girl ... (a) man with a split-off female element who must satisfy many women is at a premium even if in doing so he annihilates himself.

Over the years, the transference relations seemed to oscillate between Daniel's wish for self-holding followed by efforts to keep the analyst alert, excited, fascinated and a yearning to surrender to the analytic holding, which gave rise to an intense anxiety of slipping through the arms of a loosely holding analyst-mother who might vanish, leaving him alone and helpless. These vicissitudes in the transference may suggest that this patient's split-off "female" element can be described in terms of Green's (1986) "dead mother complex", as a defensive manoeuvre which ends up internalised in the psyche as a presence of a "hole", an absence. When Daniel was a child, his mother became depressed following the adulterous behaviour of his father, who eventually left their home. Daniel recalled that, as a child, he would sneak behind his mother and scare her with a sudden "boo", trying to evoke her, to bring her back to him.

The psychoanalytic process apparently allowed him to gradually relinquish the compulsive need to use his sexuality to enliven his internal mother. Nevertheless, it seems that, akin to Winnicott's patient which I described before, he still lives in a constant internal struggle against a split-off "female" element internalised in his psyche. The following is part of a text of his, which I believe resonates his continues striving for the *reclamation* of psychic bisexuality:

> ...*Were we ever really connected or merely entwined. I, a nebulous seedling with roots and bark and branches... you, a sinuous, snaking vine, climbing and by your strangle, dictating and engaging my growth, depending on my vigil and patience and being.*
>
> *You know... A cock sees in everything a hole. In its eye, everything is the lack, and we all imagine presence...*
>
> ...*The lack, the hole, the cave, the abyss, the missing is the driving force of all – still you would gouge out all the eyes in all the sockets - and fill them only with your form.*
>
> *Enough! ... I'm the sweating exorcist, hand raised – "BEGONE" I say "Begone!"*
>
> *I banish you out of my spaces. Let me breathe the full spectrum of chaos, of emptiness, of a gap existing in its own right. Goodbye.*

Concluding thoughts

Winnicott (1960, 142) described the non-gendered quality of the primary object: "I am referring to early phenomena, those that concern the infant's relationship to the mother, or to the *father as another mother*. The father at this very early stage has not become significant as a male person" (emphasis added). Apparently, perhaps through his own experience as a male analyst who devoted himself to psychic areas that involve the primordial m/other, Winnicott is expressing his belief in the capacity of men *and* women, who internalise a "pure female" relatedness, to become a "good-enough m/other" as a manifestation of psychic bisexuality. Alongside these bisexual manifestations, I described excessive gender-related states of mind which may reflect a *dissociation* in the fundamental bisexual function, when gendered or sexual preoccupations become a "thing in itself" which cannot be played, dreamt or thought but only evacuated through repetitive actualisations. In this regard, early Winnicott (1936, 47) made a significant differentiation between transitional play, which enriches experience, and "play" which effaces psychic space:

> At the normal end of the scale there is play, which is a simple and enjoyable dramatisation of inner world life; at the abnormal end of the scale there is a play which contains a denial of the inner world, the play being in that case always compulsive, excited, anxiety driven and more sense-exploiting then happy.

The association between the dissociated bisexual function and gendered and sexual states of mind may be confusing, as the bisexual attitude is crucial for psychic movement in many other aspects of human subjectivity. Nevertheless, the distinction suggested here between *primary* and *secondary* bisexualities may fine-tune our listening and interpreting in areas of unrepresented mental states, embodied in the archaic sexual and gender-related states of mind. Clinically, it seems that profound distress at the "archaic edge" of gender-related states of mind requires a reliable and quiet analytic environment, willing to be receptive to excessive feelings of formlessness, emptiness and psychic deadness. This "purely female" parental or analytic presence is based on an internal *bisexual attitude*, which reflects the dialectic interplay between the "masculine" and the "feminine" in their broader sense, representing the endless challenge of encountering *otherness*, the unknown within the other and in ourselves. Nevertheless, when analytic listening is saturated with "memory and desire", searching for the familiar and known (Bion, 1970), clinging to ideals or social "isms", the analyst's bisexual position might be weakened, leading to the impoverishment of the creative analytic space that relies on it.

Brenman Pick (2018) referred to the bisexual analytic attitude as the capacity to do creative analytic work which is based in the bringing together of emotion and thought, mother and father, male and female, and good and bad parts of the self. When holding this bisexual analytic attitude, a binocular vision in Bion's terms, the analytic process may give rise to the emergence of a caesural, transitional space, through which patient and analyst can seek their own ability for thinking and dreaming, searching for ever-changing meanings in the realms of sexual and gender-related states of mind, feeling real and alive.

Acknowledgements

Special thanks to Amir Atsmon for editing and translating and to Zelda Padeh for her English language consultancy.

Notes

1 Furthermore, the conceptualisation of gender and sexual identities as distinct psychic constructs is consistently supported by current research studies (Jacobson & Joel, 2019), which indicate significant variance in object-choice patterns among groups defined by experienced gender identity, as well as low correlation between the kind of experienced gender identity (cisgender, transgender and gender-diverse) and sexual identity (i.e., object-choice pattern: heterosexual, homosexual or any intermediate variation).
2 Which touches upon the crucial and controversial issue of the differences between the sexes.
3 Winnicott (1966) focused on the female element, which he perceived as crucial to the early development of the self in men and women. He adds that he refrains from addressing those clinical manifestations in which women present with *split-off "male" elements*, because these are based on different, later developmental processes.
4 Winnicott (1966) stresses here the role of dissociation, rather than repression, when relating to the male and female elements within the bisexual self of men and women.

References

Abram, J. (1996). *The Language of Winnicott*. London: Karnac.
Abram, J. (2013). DWW's Notes for the Vienna Congress 1971. In J. Abram (ed.), *Donald Winnicott Today* (302–330). New York: Routledge.
Aisenstein, M. & Rich, H. (2018). On bisexuality: Being born with two eyes. In R. J. Perelberg (ed.), *Psychic Bisexuality: A British French Dialogue* (133–150). London: Routledge and The New Library of Psychoanalysis.
Amir, D. (2014). *Cleft Tongue: The Language of Psychic Structures*. London: Karnac.
Amir, D. (2018). The Two Sleeps of Orlando: Transsexuality as Caesura or Cut. In O. Gozlan (ed.), *Current Critical Debates in the Field of Transsexual Studies: In Transition* (36–47). London & New York: Routledge.
Anzieu, D. (1989) *The Skin Ego*. Tr. C. Turner. New Haven, CT: Yale University Press.
Anzieu, D. (1990). *Psychic Envelopes*. London: Karnac.
Argentieri, S. (2009). Transvestism, transsexualism, transgender: identification and imitation. In G. Ambrosio, (ed.), *Transvestism, Transsexualism in the Psychoanalytic Dimension* (1–40). London: Karnac.
Bick, E. (1968). The experience of the skin in early object relations. *International Journal of Psychoanalysis*, 49:484–486.
Bick, E. (1986). Further considerations on the function of the skin in early object relations: Findings from infant observation integrated into child and adult analysis. *British Journal of Psychotherapy*, 2(4):292–299.
Bion, W. (1970). *Attention and Interpretation*. New York: Jason Aronson.
Birksted-Breen, D. (1993). *The Gender Conundrum*. London: Routledge and The New Library of Psychoanalysis.
Blass, R. B. (2016). Understanding Freud's conflictual view of the object relatedness of sexuality and its implications for contemporary psychoanalysis: A re-examination of three essays on the theory of sexuality. *International Journal of Psychoanalysis*, 97(3):591–613.
Brenman Pick, I. (2018). *Authenticity in the Psychoanalytic Encounter*. New Library of Psychoanalysis. London: Routledge.
Butler, J. (1990). *Gender Trouble: Feminism and Subversion of Identity*. New York: Routledge.
Chiland, C. (2009). Some thoughts on transsexualism, transvestism, transgender and identification. In G. Ambrosio (ed.), *Transvestism, Transsexualism in the Psychoanalytic Dimension* (42–54). London: Karnac.

Corbett, K., Dimen, M., Goldner, V. & Harris, A. (2014). Talking sex, talking gender—A roundtable. *Studies in Gender and Sexuality*, 15(4):295–317. DOI: 10.1080/15240657.2014.970493

David, C. (2010). The Beautiful Difference. In D. Birksted-Breen, S. Flanders & A. Gibeault (eds.), *Reading French Psychoanalysis* (649–667). London: Routledge.

Drescher, J. (2007). From bisexuality to intersexuality. *Contemporary Psychoanalysis*, 43(2):204–228.

Eigen, M. (1996). *Psychic Deadness*. Northvale, NJ: Jason Aaronson.

Eigen, M. (2004). A Little Psyche-Music. *Psychoanalytic Dialogues*, 14:119–130.

Eshel, O. (2019). *The Emergence of Analytic Oneness: Into the Heart of Psychoanalysis*. London: Routledge.

Ferenczi, S. (1933). Confusion of tongues between adults and the child (the language of tenderness and passion). *International Journal of Psychoanalysis*, 30:225–230 (1949).

Freud, S. (1905). Three essays on the theory of sexuality. *S.E.*, VII:123–246.

Freud, S. (1908). Hysterical phantasies and their relation to bisexuality. *S.E.*, AIX:155–166.

Freud, S. (1920). The psychogenesis of a case of homosexuality in a woman. *S.E.*, XVIII:145–172.

Freud, S. (1921). Group psychology and the analysis of the ego. *S.E.*, XVIII:65–144.

Freud, S. (1923). The ego and the id. *S.E.*, XIX:1–66.

Gaddini, E. (1969). On imitation. *International Journal of Psychoanalysis*, 50:475–484.

Green, A. (1986). The Dead Mother. In Green, A. *On Private Madness* (142–159). London: Karnac.

Green, A. (2001). The Neuter Gender. In R. J. Perelberg (ed.), *Psychic Bisexuality: A British French Dialogue* (243-257). London: Routledge and The New Library of Psychoanalysis.

Green, A. (2010). Sources and vicissitudes of being in D. W. Winnicott's work. *Psychoanalytic Quarterly*, 79(1):11–35.

Gulati, R. & Pauley, D. (2019). The half embrace of psychic bisexuality. *Journal of the American Psychoanalytic Association*, 67(1):97–121.

Houzel, D. (2021). *Splitting of Psychic Bisexuality in Autistic Children*. Lecture given for the Frances Tustin Memorial trust series of Lectures.

Jacobson, R. & Joel, D. (2019). Self-reported gender identity and sexuality in an online sample of cisgender, transgender, and gender-diverse individuals: An exploratory study. *Journal of Sex Research*, 56(2):249–263. https://doi.org/10.1080/00224499.2018.1523998

Laplanche, J. (1989). *New Foundations for Psychoanalysis*. Tr. D. Macey. Oxford: Basil Blackwell.

Lemma, A. (2013). The body one has and the body one is: Understanding the transsexual's need to be seen. *International Journal of Psychoanalysis*, 94(2):277–292.

Masson, J. M. (ed.) (1985). *The Complete Letters of Sigmund Freud to Wilhelm Fliess, 1887-1904*. Cambridge, MA: Harvard University Press.

McDougall, J. (1995). *The Many Faces of Eros: A Psychoanalytic Exploration of Human Sexuality*. New York: Free Association Books.

Meltzer, D. (1973). *Sexual States of Mind*. Strath Tay, Perthshire: Clunie Press.

Meltzer, D. (1975). Adhesive identification. *Contemporary Psychoanalysis*, 11:289–310.

Mitchell, J. (2018). Forward. In R. J. Perelberg (ed.), *Psychic Bisexuality: A British French Dialogue* (xvi–xxv). London: Routledge and The New Library of Psychoanalysis.

Ogden, T. H. (1989). *The Primitive Edge of Experience*. New York: Jason Aaronson.

Ogden, T. H. (2016). *Reclaiming Unlived Life*. London: Routledge.

Perelberg, R. J. (ed.) (2018) *Psychic Bisexuality: A British French Dialogue*. London: Routledge and The New Library of Psychoanalysis.

Perelberg, R. J. (2019). *Sexuality, Excess and Representation: A Psychoanalytic Clinical and Theoretical Perspective*. London: Routledge.

Quinodoz, D. (2002). *Words that Touch: A Psychoanalyst Learns to Speak*. London: Karnac.

Riviere, J. (1929). Womanliness as a masquerade. *International Journal of Psychoanalysis, 17*:304–320.

Schellekes, A. (2017). Daydreaming and Hypochondria: when daydreaming goes wrong and hypochondria becomes an autistic retreat. In H. B. Levine & D. G. Power (eds.), *Engaging Primitive Anxieties of the Emerging Self* (21–41). London: Routledge.

Stein, R. (1995). Analysis of a case of transsexualism. *Psychoanalytic Dialogues, 5*(2):257–289.

Stoller, R. J. (1968). *Sex and Gender*. London: Karnac.

Tustin, F. (1981). Autistic States in Children. London: Routledge.

Williams, P. (2004). Incorporation of an invasive object. *International Journal of Psychoanalysis, 85*(6):1333–134.

Winnicott, D. W. (1936). Appetite and Emotional Disorder. In *Through Pediatrics to Psychoanalysis: collected Papers* (33–51). London: The Hogarth Press, 1975.

Winnicott, D. W. (1945). Primitive emotional development. *International Journal of Psychoanalysis, 26*:137–143.

Winnicott, D. W. (1954). Withdrawal and Regression. In *Through Pediatrics to Psychoanalysis: collected Papers* (255–261). London: The Hogarth Press, 1975.

Winnicott, D. W. (1959). Nothing at the Centre. In *Psychoanalytic Explorations* (49–52). London: Karnac, 1989.

Winnicott, D. W. (1960). The Theory of the Parent-Infant Relationship. *International Journal of Psychoanalysis, 41*:585–595.

Winnicott, D. W. (1962). Ego Integration in Child Development. In *The Maturational Processes and the Facilitating Environment* (56–63). London: The Hogarth Press and the Institute of Psycho-Analysis, 1965.

Winnicott, D. W. (1963a). A Note on a Case involving Envy. In *Psychoanalytic Explorations* (76–78). London: Karnac, 1989.

Winnicott, D. W. (1963b). Fear of Breakdown. In *Psychoanalytic Explorations* (87–95). London: Karnac, 1989.

Winnicott, D. W. (1966). On the Split Off Male and Female Elements. In *Psychoanalytic Explorations* (168–192). London: Karnac, 1989.

Winnicott, D. W. (1969). Mother's Madness Appearing in the Clinical Materiel as an Ego-alien Factor. In *Psychoanalytic Explorations* (375–382). London: Karnac, 1989.

Winnicott, D. W. (1971). *Playing and Reality*. London: Tavistock.

Winnicott, D. W. (1988). *Human Nature*. Philadelphia, PA: Brunner/Mazel.

Part III

Gender fluidity

A challenge for approaching the coexistence
of different states of the self

Introduction

Luisa Marino-Coe

In this part, the authors bring their reflections together with their own clinical experience when thinking about gender diversity, gender fluidity and working with non-binary people, considering at the same time the available theories and reformulating those with new angles, a permeable process that appear to be much needed when facing something we may be less accustomed to. Clearly a challenge, as much as that of theorising the self, a very complex concept within the psychoanalytic world (see IPA dictionary chapter on Self, 648). Reading this part, we may also be faced by inevitable difficulties, not only as our clinical and therapeutic work is delicate per se, and the fact that the "strange situation" of the person of the analyst immersed together in the same room with a patient is a very unique and unrepeatable matter, but also because all of the above carries a public impact that has to be taken into account. We will encounter a vast reviewing of old and newer literature; this will come together with a dive inside the authors' clinical work, providing a snapshot of their own inner worlds as well as their inner capacity as psychoanalysts, as human beings working and feeling with their patients, and in the last chapter we are introduced to group dynamics when clinical work with queer patients is presented in an intervision group of four psychoanalysts.

It is a challenge around the analytic listening from within, from within the self of the patient, that of the analyst, and the space in between them, and that of larger groups of belonging, whether it is our psychoanalytic society, the environment we live in, the country, and so on. We may discover how this requires a step further at listening to our own pre-conceptions, our conscious and pre-conscious theories, our implicit theories, our personal identifications, and so on. As for the title of this part, we will have to try to hold a variety of different theories within us and possibly at the same time, as well as different parts of ourselves that may appear in mutual opposition, and consider their impact on our work with patients who identify as non-binary/gender fluid.

We have learned elsewhere how pre-conceptions may slide easily into prejudice about gender, genders, dualities, pluralities, norms, and disruptions of the norms; this phenomenon is sometimes connected with our own

DOI: 10.4324/9781003534440-13

personal relation with gender, and a common confusion made by default by an unconscious that for instance may erroneously jump from those of gender to those of sexual choices, with an equation that is only valid for the specific non doubtful "logic" of the unconscious (see Matte Blanco, 1980). Again, the aim is inspiring our own journey as readers and clinicians that may orient our hopefully never-final considerations.

It may be relevant to inform the readers of some geographical references about the authors, as I consider this of some significance in how theories and clinical practices are expressed in our writings (Borgogno et al., 2016, 187).

Eva Reichelt is the first author in this part; she works in Berlin and is a member of the German Psychoanalytical Association. She takes us through her particular journey as psychoanalyst working with non-binary people. While entering less explored territories, not only we will be looking at finding appropriate words, also we will need to observe our listening capacity, a listening that occurs through our mind and body at once. The author may be gently warning us that we may need first to make a special space within ourselves and opening up to exploring new or less familiar universes and some different kinds of listening. To do so, the author encountered this book as her way to investigate new ways of writing, listening and understanding. As announced, art came to the rescue in the shape of Kim De l'Horizon's book, *Blutbuch*, a clever, poignant pseudonymous work of a young non-binary author who was awarded prestigious Swiss and German book prizes.[1]

Admittedly at times Reichelt says the book was a difficult and disturbing reading, and with her we found ourselves immersed in this journey (a writing that took ten years, a long auto-analysis?), where the protagonist engages into a deep understanding of their self, back and forward from past, present and ultimately hoping for a different future prospective and transformation. Together with Reichelt, we may keep an eye on our own bodily reactions that will emerge while reading.

De l'Horizon plays with words and sounds, rhymes, associations, and meanings, and Reichelt notices also how in this book "*form and content complement each other*". By association, in fact, we are reminded that in certain situations, the non-binary inner identity may reflect on the form, the external forms – the appearances conveyed by the body – and this is when identification with the larger queer community may come into place. Reichelt was at times surprised by the attention to this "form" of non-binary people – and understood how appearances may match or reciprocally influence the inner vicissitudes of the Self. In fact, reading parts of *Blutbuch* helped Reichelt to not get lost in her countertransference and deal better with the shrillness of some appearances. In this sense a specific way of intending the concept of "identification" is employed, for instance when Reichelt explains that:

> Now I understand better how important it is for trans people to orientate themselves on other trans people who bear witness on the worldwide web about how they have searched and found their way to their

own body and language. Nevertheless, in the consulting room it remains a challenge to find out what really belongs to each person and where someone tends only to imitate.

It was Gaddini (1969) in his paper on imitation that reflected on the central role of this mechanism in the early development of the baby and the ways their personality functions.

We are invited to take a further step with Reichelt's paper from confusion, rejection, an uncanny feeling of dissolving physically, of feeling blurred temporarily without contours. At last, through neologism unique perceptions and sensations are finally conveyed: "The words seem to creep under the skin and work from within. And this impression of permeability is what the protagonist experienced themselves". It seems that this process was necessary because,

> Several of my non-binary patients have been used in an extensive manner by one or more of their primary objects as a container for some of their split off feelings. It is sad for anyone to realise they have been subject of this kind of narcissistic abuse.

We could now say the same about the difficulties in reading the book, that its disruptiveness, a seduction to numbness, a variety of fluctuating bodily feelings, are not far from the pain that some people may endure:

> Some people don't have any feeling of their body and may feel only head and neck. Others may have a blurred perception of their whole physical existence, but since they are used to this kind of generally alienated body image, it takes time until this becomes clearer in the course of the treatment.

Nevertheless, "Transformation is possible", we learn from the intimate work of Zurich, the auto-fictional character of the book as well as that of an attentive analyst such as Reichelt.

Mauro Manica, a field psychoanalyst from the north of Italy and the Pavia Centre of Psychoanalysis, thought it was crucial to start from revisiting some of the literature on the Oedipal theories, to better understand certain risks of confusion between the origin of our identifications with that of our sexual orientation. We then scroll with a renovated interest through the main theories on Oedipus and that of the feminine and masculine. In fact, it is clear since the beginning that for Manica there is much more than the classical idea of Oedipal rivalry and murderousness to win the loved one; in a different prospective in fact, as hinted at in Bion, we should sort of "feel" for Oedipus himself as for all the protagonists in the myth as they may be lacking in their capacity of reverie (they are all blinded by the impossibility of looking and making sense of their emotions and experiences).

Manica explains that there are versions of the Oedipal experience and theory that are less violent, "a much quieter affair", that focus more on the slow relevance of the processes of developing love for family life warmth rather than a specific object; they have to do with themes of separation, differentiation, the limiting reality (Searles, [1959], the caesura in Bion words). Manica writes:

> I believe that the so-called Oedipus complex can currently be regarded as a fundamental organiser of psychic vitality, in which the child is called into life, even before sexual identification, by a loving and facilitating environment. In this perspective the Oedipus complex does not come to play a central role in the definition of a sexual or gender identity, especially in those conditions in which gender variances (transgender, gender fluid, agender) are realised beyond the limits set by a rigidly binary conception.

Manica ventures inside the Jungian broader vision on femininity and masculinity, and further shows how Bion used the two symbols of feminine for container and masculine for contained "imagining the mind as a *variegated (queer)* set of "container (♀)/contained (♂) relations"; we find here a hint on the use of the word "queer" that will be better explained later.

Not enough, we learn from the biologist, Anna Fausto-Sterling (1993) as a provocation too, that in some populations of the Melanesian archipelago, it appears there are at least five genders: men who love women, women who love men, men who love men, women who love women, and people who fit our definition of "Angel". I would like to think that Zurich, the protagonist of the Kim de L'Horizon book would be happy to be associated with the latter. In fact: *"With non-binary patients, we may need to make an epoche of the seemingly rigid dichotomies..."*, Manica continues. For him, Bion and Ogden are a compass around contemporary themes on gender as they suggest the relevance of an ontological psychoanalysis rather than epistemological. Manica associates the first to his own discourse around the idea of identity of the ego (a core self?), basically a way of "being", without the urgency of any other word, adjective nor verb to be attached to it. This could suggest that the contemporary social discourse on female and male binarism, the not being one or the other, rather than being about confusion, but belonging to the realm of "being" itself, and to authenticity. It is about the crucial question of "who am I", not who we may desire which is an ontological perspective, rather than the doing of understanding, the knowing epistemologically.

After this thoughtful theoretical introduction, we encounter two clinical cases, and it is here that we see those reflections in action. I would like to think that the initial rethink of the theories has informed the open and understudying approach to these cases that among many other difficulties, present gender-related themes. In a way it is also the other way around, we have the feeling that in a sentence like this:

> (...) only a psychoanalysis of "who I am" can look into this multidimensional space of being, without prejudices, not even diagnostic prejudices; without memory and without desire; aimed at a mathematics of being in unison (at-one-ment) and not centred on identification (...)

Manica is helping us shape more creative approaches to listening and "being", not only based on previous theoretical reflections and rushed psychopathologisations, but also on feelings and thoughts and words sourced from within his clinical experiences. Ontological questions appear in the first case and the white holes theory in the second one recalling Madama Butterfly's existential threats and sad destiny, but it is in Manica's words that we encounter this different listening:

> Perhaps this is what gender fluid patients require of us, to equip ourselves with a specific negative capacity that concerns the ability to tolerate the unknown: the unknown of being in an environment that has no call to a personal, authentic and original life.

Manica suggests that there is a need to develop a new variation of psychoanalysis, that we could call "queer psychoanalysis", but borrowing one of the original meanings of the term "queer": variegated "a psychoanalysis that should perhaps equip itself with new myths – that of Tiresias, for example – new theories as well as new technical tools". In fact, Manica concludes:

> (...) woman and man, female and male cannot be analysed as a kind of continuum. On the contrary, ssex and gender are best conceptualised as points in a multidimensional space, in which genetic, hormonal and anatomical levels interact, in a way not yet fully understood, with environment and experience.

Dana Amir is a psychoanalyst practicing in Haifa and a member of the Israel Psychoanalytic Society. In her rich and complex chapter, she deals with the question of gender binary versus gender multiplicity, while introducing us to new conceptualisations: an "emergent" component of gender that exists in parallel with a "continuous" component and entertains variable relations with it. She suggests that, alongside a continuous gender identity and gender identification, there exists a component characterised by its nonlinear, changing, varying gender experience, based on incessant movement between the gender poles, and on the subject's taking different positions in and between them. This experience does not come to take over or inherit the continuous component of gender identity but joins it by way of constituting an additional dimension, which exists in parallel to it throughout every subject's life. Some of these concepts are effectively employed by Amir from Bion's (1967) "catastrophic change", as for the two key principles of human psyche, the emergent and the continuous: the first perceives the world as undergoing a constant change, the second perceives the world as stable and fixed.

Not dissimilarly Amir challenges us when affirming that neither the canonical psychoanalytic binary model of gender nor the one derived from the second wave of contemporary gender theories, feminism, and postmodernism, that she calls the multiplicity model of gender, are sufficient to describe the complexity of these themes. In fact: "when used alone, both the binary and the multiplicity models are insufficient because they set up a false dichotomy: one either belongs to one of two genders or floats in between".

I will here paraphrase some of Amir's points: "*Gender, too, can be understood in terms of the relations between the continuous and the emergent. An excess of a continuous gender experience as opposed to an emergent gender experience can damage the possibility of establishing a gender subjective space that holds*", that contains both and at the same time "*the continuous and the emergent in a fertile dialectic relation*". Unfortunately, within certain developmental experiences, people encounter an excess of emergent gender experience, in which every shift, every movement/change, for lack of capacity to reverie (see Manica above) threatens a deep nucleus of the Self/"identity" and may undermine the possibility of a cooperative relationship between the two components described above. As I understand it, to create a sense of continuity, we need to consolidate the same stability of the experience and avoid and/or postpone change as much as possible, for this not to become an overwhelming disruptor of the continuity of the self. My paraphrase, I sense, is a simplification of Amir's theories and I am aware of its relativity, as I am reminded of the complexity of time and space and the easy confusion in relation to gender development as opposed to gender as soft assembly.

We may grasp the richness of Amir's theoretical approach better when in her clinical presentation we can dive into her analytic work with Raphael, a 30-year-old person, who appears to bring their difficulties in finding "their" own self. Years of school bullying, his parents preoccupied by their own difficulties, at times intrusive and abusive, may have an impact on how Rafael is troubled and in search of a more grounded sense of the Self. As an adolescent,

> In spite of his colourful, exhibitionistic looks, he did not feel sexual, couldn't tell whether he preferred boys or girls as partners, and didn't know whether his identity was male, female, both, or neither. Mostly, as said, he felt neither man nor woman.

Amir quotes here concepts such as Bick's second skin, or Meltzer's adhesive identification, but these may constitute, I would say, mainly sort of maps to orientate us and get closer to the inner life and difficulties of Raphael; these modalities, we believe, do not define for instance gender fluidity per se, these are specifically called into action to get us closer to Raphael's functioning, we are in the realm of a possible unique "how" for Raphael, not the "why". It is during the long and difficult work with Raphael that Amir explores also how a transference interpretation will open a new discourse and allow Raphael to name his pain. During a session, Raphael is explaining how, with a man who was ignoring him, he utilised some of Amir's words and felt sort of victorious and powerful on this man:

> When I (Amir) ask whether this also happens here, with me, in analysis, he replies: "That's it: Here it doesn't really work. I can't find the costume you prefer, at least not in my closet. I have no idea what you want. I don't know whether you want me passive or active, masculine or feminine. Each time I throw my ball at your wall it bounces back to me. And it doesn't simply bounce back: it turns on me, as though it were asking what it actually was that I wanted. Most of the time that's confusing and frightening, and most of the time it makes me hate you.

Amir is not taken aback too much by these sharp and provocative words and gently we imagine she continues: "And the rest of the time?", to which Raphael replies heartily: *"The rest of the time it feels like the closest thing I've ever had to what a true relationship is"*.

In her final remarks, Amir explains once again that Raphael's way of being and crossdressing is not in the realm of what we know is gender queer creativity expression via fluidity: "*[This is] not a creative, playful heterogeneous gender show (though it may be misleadingly seen as such) – but rather a hollow and mechanical negation of any gender subjectivity: a "story" that Raphael himself is enslaved to, but also repeatedly erased by"*. Amir concludes that "Analysis in this case can therefore be thought of as an attempt to reclaim the narrator: to allow Raphael to extract, out of the undifferentiated chameleon texture, his own voice, turning him into not just the owner, or the protagonist, of his story, but also its one and only narrator".

In the final contribution to this chapter, **Davide Bruno** and **Laura Balottin,** two psychoanalysts working in Milan, write from the core of their experience as clinicians – and show us what happens in the peer intervision group context reflecting and discussing together. We could say that is in the spirit of the fourth pillar concept by Bolognini (2022) that the authors show us the work of a group, considering the risk of such discussions derailing towards a stigmatised and violent road due to bias and a need for quick hyper-simplifications when approaching gender identity. Not by chance and with some effect on the content of their discussion, this working group was started during Covid times as a necessity to keep thinking together while apart, at least online. It is well known in literature how important working groups and intervision groups are when facing controversies and solving those with the constant reflection and crucial validation among its members, so important that it may have been considered part of the scientific core of the psychoanalytic work, if we consider for instance the scientific revolution theory (Kuhn, 1970).

Two very detailed cases are reported in this chapter, the first case is L., referred to the public service, a transexual (FtM) about 30 years old, who had already undergone gender assignment surgery. L. returned to the health service feeling generally better but lamenting about considerable states of anxiety for which previous psychotherapies proved, in L's words, ultimately ineffective. In a partial unconscious resonance with L. the therapist at first felt inadequate and perhaps unusually not up to the task of working with a patient with such issues, despite her long experience and having always perceived herself as open minded, an "ally", we could say.

The second is a young person in their teen years, A., a dancer, referred to the psychoanalyst by the parents after they lamented A.'s tendency to isolate, thinking that A. may be "Asperger": A. just hangs around with a "dead face", they would have lamented. The therapist in a similar way will have a first difficult contact with A. but once again art (a picture of the mysterious Gioconda) and a musical video called "*Fuga*" come to the rescue and help the pair establish a first contact and initiate a long and fruitful twice-a-week treatment.

As the reader dives into the deep understanding of these two patients via the work of the group and that of the clinicians, I'd like to focus here on the first bodily reactions experienced by both the therapists when encountering these patients, as it has been a *fils rouge*, among others throughout this chapter. In the first case, L., the therapist caught himself somehow accurately cleaning the chair in a robotic way before each session, in a default way that *was not* experienced before with other patients despite measures during the times of COVID. As for the second case, the therapist again recalls a first reaction of confusion, feeling uncomfortable in *his* own body while walking side by side into the room with the patient; then out of no conscious thinking, the therapist found herself saying: "I am aware you dance…", halfway between an acting out and a way to put into alphabetisation some beta uncomfortable feelings for both.

Once again, the body, its reaction within the therapeutic room when working with people expressing gender-related themes. Long subsequent work within themselves and in the inter-peer vision group will help them understand these feelings, in a constant reflection on how the transference/countertransference dynamics of the clinicians and of the group can either evolve and involve, at times regress to rigid positions, polarised views, and then with deeper exploration and discussion, can finally remerge into more dialogical positions and finally facilitate the work with patients and a fruitful theoretical discourse.

Stemming from Bionian and Winnicottian reflections within the group, the participants gradually witnessed for instance a slow transitioning (epistemologically very significant) from an inevitable heteronormative biased prospective, the logic of "why" (why this patient is ...) to that of the "how" (how is this person ...). We could now say that either perspective often allows us to avoid complexity and reduce theories to single easy and less controversial positions.

This comes with no surprise having read the previous chapters in this part. And it appears that the conclusion of this chapter once again points out the essential constant listening and review of the self-analysis of the therapist but also that of the dynamics within a functioning working intervision group, as the unique way to bring a sort of justice to our clinical work, helping our patients to find their own voice and self. We could say together with Bruno and Balottin that it is the work of psychoanalysts to accept that sometimes only in *après coup* will we be able to understand what multiple forces of our patients were combined and endured by them to conduct them to the authentic self (Saketopoulou, 2020). In fact, our more authentic attitude is to try and be good companions along the journey that brings each person to become themselves, as far as possible from elements of prejudice and censorship.

As for a conclusion we are also reminded of how all this work of reviewing together and in groups, theories, our clinical work, transference and countertransference, individual and group dynamics, the bodily embodiment, the listening within ourselves, within the patient's own bodily experience (see Lemma, 2018), all of this may bring us closer to an understanding of the specific pain of the patient who introduces, in our consulting room, gender-related themes for these to be better understood, reflected on and integrated within themselves.

> These processes led some psychoanalytic societies to issue public statements such as apology of the Finnish Society (29 June 2022), that expressed an apology "for all views expressed within its sphere of influence, which have contributed to individuals belonging to sexual and gender minorities being stigmatised as diseased, disturbed, developmentally challenged or in any other way abnormal, based on their sexual orientation or gender diversity".
>
> (Ballottin and Bruno in this book)

Note

1 Significantly, the song "Nightcall" was intoned by Kim de L'Orizon during the German Prize Award ceremony in 2022: "I am giving you a night call / to tell you how I feel / There is something inside you / It's hard to explain [...] They are talking about you, boy / But you are still the same" Nightcall, by Kavinsky.

References

Bion, W. R. (1967). *Catastrophic change*. Unpublished paper.

Blanco M. (1980). *The Unconscious as Infinite Sets: An Essay in Bi-logic*. Routledge: London.

Bolognini S. (2022). Reflections on the institutional family of the analyst and proposing a "Fourth Pillar" for education, in *Living and Containing Psychoanalysis in Institutions*, Ed. Junkers, G., London: Routledge.

Borgogno F., Luchetti A. & Marino-Coe L. (2016). *Reading Italian Psychoanalysis*. London: Routledge.

Fausto-Sterling, A. (1993). The five sexes: why male and female are not enough, *The Sciences*, 33(2): 20–24.

Lemma, A. (2018). Trans-itory identities: some psychoanalytic reflections on transgender identities. *International Journal of Psycho-analysis*, 99(5): 1089–1106. doi: 10.1080/00207578.2018.1489710

Gaddini E. (1969). On imitation, in Borgogno F., Luchetti A., Marino-Coe L. (eds.) (2016) *Reading Italian Psychoanalysis*. London: Routledge.

Kuhn, T. (1970). *The Structure of Scientific Revolutions*. Chicago, IL: University of Chicago Press.

Saketopoulou, A. (2020). Thinking psychoanalytically, thinking better: reflections on transgender. *International Journal of Psycho-analysis*, 101(5): 1019–1030. doi: 10.1080/00207578.2020.1810884

Searles, H. (1959). Oedipal love in the countertransference, in *Collected Papers on Schizophrenia and Related Subjects*. New York: International Universities Press.

8   Tolerating uncertainty. On reading *Blutbuch* by Kim de l'Horizon

Eva Reichelt

When psychoanalysts want to share some impressions, thoughts, and feelings that repeatedly occur during treatments with non-binary persons, it may be of some help to convey those by referring to a book of fiction or a memoir. Confidentiality is not an obstacle when referring to an auto fictional publication. Of course, there is a gap between fiction and an account of a psychoanalytic treatment. However, there are some books that can help to understand and communicate own treatment experiences in a different context.

Every year in October, Frankfurt hosts the International Book Fair. On this occasion, the German Book Prize is awarded annually to the best new novel of the year in German language. The jury consists of authors, journalists, literary academics, and booksellers. In autumn 2022, it was a real surprise that the jury voted for "Blutbuch", "Bloodbook", written by Swiss author Kim de l'Horizon. Why was this decision so exceptional? The public discourse about gender transitioning started only a few years ago in Germany. This book describes fluid gender boundaries on a scale never seen in the literature of German speaking countries before. A few weeks later, it was awarded the Swiss Book Prize, too.

The first-person narrator identifies neither as male nor as female. *"With an enormous creative energy"* according to the jury of the German Book Prize, the narrating figure is *"searching for a language of their own"*, called *"écriture fluide"*, "fluid writing" by the author. *"What narratives exist for a body that defies conventional notions of gender? (…) The novel form is in constant motion. Every attempt at language, from the vivid scene to the essay-like memoir, unfolds an urgency and literary innovation that provoked and inspired the jury"*. This was the jury's reasoning for awarding the prize.

At this point, it is necessary to reflect on the use of pronouns. In the USA, 'they' has become accepted as a gender-neutral singular pronoun. In German, the translation of the pronoun 'they' cannot be used since the pronoun for the third person plural (they) is 'sie': the same word as for the third person singular in the female form: 'sie' (she). In German-speaking countries, there is no universal pronoun for non-binary people. Probably, it is one of the tasks of a society to open up and keep developing inclusion in language use.

DOI: 10.4324/9781003534440-14

The reading of "Bloodbook" offers insights into the experiential world of a non-binary person. The narrator conveys in an overwhelming manner an existential unease in their way of perceiving external reality with the dominating binary dichotomy. The writing is marked by deep pain, and yet, the pain seems suspended or at least bearable through the writing. The auto fictional narrator has been able to find words and sometimes poetic images for their suffering and thus – as mentioned in the book – has been able to relieve themselves of it. We get to know that the process of writing this book has lasted more than ten years.

The reading is an adventure and at the same time a challenge, sometimes a provocation.

Often, I felt reminded of my experiences with non-binary persons during treatments when I met contradictions and many incongruences and reacted with incomprehension. The reading often is difficult, bulky. I had to interrupt many times. This novel is definitely "not a bedside reading", as a Swiss reviewer aptly put it, "because the danger is great that images accompany you into your dreams".

In this contribution, I would like to describe how form and content of "Blutbuch" complement each other and how this interlinking contributes to a particular reading experience. I hope to show how the reading helped me to find another approach to the worlds of my non-binary patients.

My reflections begin with the title. *"Blutbuch"*, "Bloodbook" refers to blood ties, that is, to family stories. Furthermore, it is a play on words: "Blutbuche" is copper beech in English. This tree took on an essential role in the protagonist's childhood and becomes a symbol of their own roots. The book alludes in its title a confrontation with the concept of and conflicts with home ("Heimat" in German).

The narrator sets off in search of clues by following a trail of non-linear memories of their childhood. After the grandfather died, they spent their time mainly with the grandmother, while their parents worked. In an immediate manner, we get invited in their life and their ambivalent thoughts and feelings towards their family members.

We learn that "mother" in the narrator's mother tongue is "die Meer", from the French "la mère", with a female article. At the same time, this word links with "das Meer", neuter in German, "the sea" in English, in French: "la mer". Accordingly, "der Peer" is the expression for the father ("le père" in French) and "Grossmeer", "Grandmeer", for grandmother.

The women of my childhood are an element, an ocean. I remember my mother's legs, I remember wrapping my arms around them, gazing up at her and saying: YOU ARE MY MEER. I remember a feeling of being home and of beingcompletelyenclosed. The Meer's love was so big we couldn't escape it, can't escape it, we swim for a lifetime to emerge from its depths.

(p. 16)

"Meer" is an example for the author's onomatopoetic play with words and sounds, with rhymes, associations, and meanings. The repeated use of capital letters stands for a special intensity with which the protagonist obviously experiences their own life. *"Beingcompletelyenclosed"* is paradigmatic for Kim's creative approach to language. Three words are glued together without any gaps. This neologism illustrates the claustral narrowness of being enclosed by the "Meere", Meer and Grossmeer. Throughout the text, neologisms convey perceptions and sensations. Past, present, and future become blurred. The language gives an oneiric impression, a primary-process-like pull.

With love for the smallest detail, the narrator describes observations and experiences with their Grossmeer that testify to affection and despair at the same time. The grandmother develops a dementia, and the narrator expresses their wish to talk meaningfully with her, to ask how she experienced her life, how she evaluates events in retrospect. Simultaneously, the longing for exchange is affected by the fear of being disappointed, the fear of hoping for more than the grandmother is able and has ever been able to reveal about herself and the family history. In childhood days, fear shaped the relationship with her, too.

> *I can feel you slowly disappearing. Dear Grandmother, I'd like to write to you before you completely disappear from your body or can no longer reach your memories. (...) I'd like to understand what it was like to be you: a normal, lower-middle-class woman in 20th century Switzerland. I'd like to understand why I have barely any memories of my childhood, and why the only ones I have are of you. I'd like to find a language in which I can ask you: 'Where are my people?' I'd like to know how this shit gets into our veins.*
>
> (pp. 13–14)

The first-person narrator grapples with feelings of pain and guilt of having a mother and grandmother who each had to *"give up their lives"* (p. 18) because they had a child. The idea that a woman has to give up so much when she becomes a mother reveals a lot about the family atmosphere: that mothers invest allegedly more than they ever can get back from their children. The guilt feels even greater because the protagonist's family stems from a less educated background, whereas the narrator today has the opportunity to study and change social class. The confrontation with oneself and one's own family history is broken up by breathless sentences without a full stop. When the search, respectively, the writing process, becomes too painful or is blocked, quick anonymous sex with men seems to serve as a compensation.

> *I try to write, and when I can't write, when I sink into the mudflats of the past, I shave, shower and ride my bike to the outer areas of the city, the 'outskirts' ('Aussenröcke'), as the English say, scour the petrol stations and football pitches, prowl back and forth outside the gyms, the Grindr app my dim torch in the night of agglomeration, guiding me to the men I'm searching for, the*

men I need and let myself be needed by, the men behind the bike shed whom I let push up my skirt and whom I let push into me, quick and emotionless, I have enough feelings and don't need any more, all I need from them is a hard cut.

(p. 12)

All these impressions can already be found in the ten-page prologue. Condensed or detailed descriptions of anal sex, of the pleasure both to penetrate and being penetrated, are interspersed throughout the book. Like a patchwork, the novel is made up of various shorter or longer episodes. The first chapters of this book have an effect as if they make the reader permeable. The words seem to creep under the skin and work from within. And this impression of permeability is what the protagonist experienced themselves.

In my memory, Grossmeer's hands are so alone with themselves; one hand keeps reaching for the other, and then the other clutches the one, they search incessantly, looking for something to hold, grabbing my child's legs and child's arms and stroking them relentlessly. I don't remember my child's legs and child's arms; I only remember the feeling of great roughness and the knowledge that I have to hold out, that Grossmeer needs this.

(pp. 20–21)

In retrospect, the grandchild realises painfully they have been used as a self-object. Between the lines, it becomes clear how bitter this realisation is. At the same time, these memories also seem full of affection and warmth. Several of my non-binary patients have been used in an extensive manner by one or more of their primary objects as a container for some of their split off feelings. It is sad for anyone to realise they have been subject of this kind of narcissistic abuse.

Interspersed in the text are repeated expressions in Swiss German. In one episode, we learn that the Grossmeer collected little boxes – made of a wide variety of materials – that she brought back from her travels to different places. Their name is TRUCKLI.

The boxes (…) were all empty and closed. Their emptiness worried me. (…) The Truckli looked back. (…) I felt things without understanding them. I felt that the Truckli were inner spaces of Grossmeer she had outsourced. The Truckli were Grossmeer's accomplices; I knew that she had cut off little chunks of her emptiness and stored them inside.

(pp. 22–23)

This passage shows in a literary way an intuitive understanding of projective identification. It seems as if Grossmeer's emptiness affected the grandchild who could not develop a suitable perception of their own body.

What surrounded the child was never outside of it, it had no skin; the world went out of the child and came into it. (…) I don't know where I begin and where I end. (...) I only feel my body when I give it away, when I offer it to others. (...) I don't primarily have the need to feel cocks inside me, I have the need to feel myself, that pulsating coat around the cocks. (...) I never resisted when other bodies forced themselves into me.

(pp. 28, 30)

Reading the protagonist's reflection on their own body helps me – retrospectively or currently – to better understand some of my non-binary patients. It is painful to understand how contradictory these feelings are.

I am writing this to you, Grossmeer, because for a long time I have been trying to dispose of my body as I wish: to speak about it as I wish, to move it as I wish, and to enjoy it as I wish. (...) How incredibly soft and alive a penetrated ass feels. As if we were carpentered entirely of silk. (...) I am writing to you to write against the contempt, which I feel for this body for as long as I can remember, and which is perhaps partly responsible for the fact that I have so few memories of it. How is it possible to hold on to something that always gives way, blurs, dissolves? I am writing this to you to write against the body negativity that I have inherited (...). I write this to you (...) because I felt that you never had a body, because I am still angry that you needed me, my body; angry that you tended me, held me, caressed me, to dump your unprocessed history into me (...). I write to you because I exist only through your body, because I am your continuation and because I don't want to continue certain things. I write to you because - like Meer and you - I cannot talk about the things that really occupy me, I write to you because: As long as I write, I do not speak, but I am not silent, either.

(pp. 31–32)

It seems to me that this difficulty in feeling secure about one's body and continuously libidinously cathecting it may account for why some queer people put so much effort into standing out through clothing, through hairstyle, or through fashion accessories. As if they lived by the motto: I am noticed, therefore I am. If I don't stand out to others, I risk being lost. Having experienced this anxiety of getting lost in my countertransference, I can deal better with the shrillness of some appearances.

I think that the child (...) perceived the things that the adults did not talk about. It had a sense, a tuning fork that resonated with the things it did not see. The past things, the feelings that were all the more present because they were not spoken of.

Childhood feels like a dead rabbit on the side of a field path, slowly being decomposed by ants, flies, bacteria, and fungi. This feeling of things disappearing, although it is not a disappearance but a transformation, a translation

from body to another body, from rabbit to worm, to flies, to world, from present to always-being-there past, from stories to silence, from Grossmeer to me.
(p. 44)

The metaphor of the tuning fork vibrating through invisible things helps me deal with the sensitivity of some persons – and not just the non-binary ones. The comparison of childhood with a decomposing rabbit seems disturbing and paradoxically also encouraging: transformation is possible.

In my opinion, the narrator manages in a remarkable way to develop words for their experience of alienation from their own body and shares a convincing hypothesis of aetiology:

If there's one feeling from my childhood that I remember clearly, it's the feeling that my body doesn't belong to me. That it is there for other people, for other things, and not for me to be in. I was always such a furniture, 'ein Kommödli' (a chest of drawers in Swiss German) for discarded items. I don't know how, but the adults deposited their things, themes, problems in me: the feelings that were unwanted, the fears, being a man, being a woman, the wounds.
(p. 49)

In manifold variations, the narrator expresses their own experienced powerlessness towards their Meer and Grossmeer. Some passages later, we get to know that Grossmeer had a garden with several trees, among them a copper beech, "Blutbuche" in German. As said before, this is another play with words: "Blutbuch" is Bloodbook; "Blutbuche" is blood beech.

In our garden were many trees. The trees are which I remember best, and the tree I remember best of all is the blood beech. (...) The child spoke to the blood beech. It sat under its red foliage as if under a second, real skin. (...) The child asked for lessons. The blood beech knew so clearly how to exist, how to find its own shape, how to fill a body. How not to let oneself be driven out of one's skin. (...) Dear blood beech, how to become a blood beech? How does one become as big and strong as you? (...) The lessons of the blood beech were: Stand. Shed the foliage. Hold out. Work on new foliage. Bud out. Transform. People were much more threatening than the monsters under the bed and in the closet. They always had this body, and the monstrous thing about that body was that it was never simply a form to be in the world, but that it always had a gender, no, was a gender – a man OR a woman.
(p. 57)

The lessons of the blood beech appear truly wise, as if gained during a long analytic treatment. You cannot change much; you can only accept the way things are going. *"Stand. Shed the foliage. Hold out. Work on new foliage. Bud out. Transform"*. For the protagonist, the blood beech is the symbol of a simple form of being in the world, beyond a gendered (binary) identification. In view of this juxtaposition of the blood beech body and the human body, one can guess how disturbing the perception of this uncanny difference must be for some people to realise that something unknown to them is however familiar for the majority: That human beings have bodies which represent gender. And consequently, there is no language for the unknown. The protagonist describes this non-existence of a language for one's own body and the search for it within the limits of the given.

> *I don't know any language for my body. I can move neither in the mother tongue nor in the father tongue. I stand in a foreign language. Perhaps this is one of the reasons for writing, for this fragmented, crumbling writing. (…) Perhaps this writing is the search for a foreign language in the words that are available to one. (…) I will sit down now and open the writing, this skylight in the fog of things, and see what comes. Because what I do not tell eats me.*
>
> (pp. 58, 63)

The difficulties to find words for the confusing perception of oneself are a feature, which I have repeatedly encountered in my work with Trans persons. It may take some time until this becomes tangible at all in the dynamics of transference and countertransference. Some people don't have any feeling of their body and may feel only head and neck. Others may have a blurred perception of their whole physical existence, but since they are used to this kind of generally alienated body image, it takes time until this becomes clearer in the course of the treatment. I remember some uncanny countertransference feelings of dissolving physically, of feeling blurred, temporarily without contours. This profoundly disturbing experience was difficult to grasp and describe.

The difficulty to find an appropriate language for the perception of the own body might also be read in the numerous quotations that precede each chapter; quotations by philosophers like Gilles Deleuze and Félix Guattari, writers like Virginia Woolf, non-binary thought leaders like Paul Preciado or Alok Said-Menon, or actors and singer–songwriters like RuPaul. They seem like a recourse to navigational aids in a world that is potentially dismissive and hostile when someone does not adhere to the gender assigned at birth. In the beginning of my work with transgender people, I repeatedly wondered how often many of them referred to such Trans 'celebrities'. I had the impression that it is difficult to distinguish what is truly an idea or a feeling of one's own and what is seemingly just taken over from someone else. If adopted, it often looked like a false self in my view. In the meantime, I better understand how important it is for trans people to orientate themselves on other trans people who bear witness on the worldwide web about how they have searched and found their way to their own body and language. Nevertheless, in the consulting room it remains a challenge to find out what really belongs to each person's own and where someone tends only to imitate.

The prologue and the first chapter of "Bloodbook" to me provided the most intense reading experiences. The second chapter is called *"Search for Childhood"*. Like in a dysphoric fairy tale, we get acquainted with more details of the protagonist's past. Magic thinking had to help against feelings of overwhelming guilt.

The title of the third chapter is *"Search for the Mother Blood Beech"*. The form resembles a scientific essay on the history of the blood beech in Europe, indeed interesting. Snarky comments about the efforts of scientific research, about several scientists and their past and about the storyteller are mixed with stories about gay sex adventures, again with long breathless passages without any full stop. In between, the protagonist knits a pullover for their Grossmeer. They seem torn between affection and anger at having been exploited as a child for the needs of their Meer and Grossmeer. The third chapter also deals with nationalism, racism and colonialism. It becomes clear that the search for the "mother blood beech" represents the preparation for a search for a family tree, too.

The language sometimes appears flippant. It is about a radical confrontation between language, form and content. *"Language can inflict wounds; language can heal wounds"*. Some sentences are condensed with neologisms and puns, truly challenging to translate. One example: *"What do texts look like when there is not a human master subject at the center, giftedly goetheing the world into the mould?"* (pp. 154–155).

The many Anglicisms in the book are striking. This also fits in with my treatment experiences with transgender persons. Books, films, podcasts, and blogs on transgender topics are used in the English original and are gradually manifesting themselves in everyday language use in German.

The fourth chapter is titled *"Search for Rosmarie"*. Meer gives the protagonist a typewritten manuscript with her research about a female genealogy back to the 14th century, with countless stories of witches and their persecution experiences. The narrator continues their confrontation with the past and with the present. In dealing with the history of the witch-hunt, one of the issues seems to be the identification with an unrecognised minority. Meanwhile, Grossmeer is losing more of her memory. Pain and affection become overwhelming. Sex adventures help. Writing helps.

Perhaps the last chapter, *"Coming full spiral"*, written completely in English, can also be understood in this context of the problematic finding of an appropriate language. It is a collection of eleven letters to *"dear Grandma"* and one letter to *"dear Mum"*.

English, (…) the language that has other eyes than my mother tongue, the language in which I did not inherit your eyes and your mother's and your mother's mother's eyes, the language I don't feel watched, the language that feels like a space of my own, no matter how incorrect, the language that you (grandma) don't really understand.

(p. 267, English and in italics in the original)

Appropriating and writing in another language functions as a demarcation from the maternally and grandmotherly occupied language and allows for a free and at the same time a protective space in which writing becomes a process of becoming, including becoming a body:

> *Maybe this is what is inherent about auto fiction: to start writing from a reality that repeats the fiction that we don't exist. To start writing from a reality that isn't real to us, that puts us in the realm of fiction. To produce ourselves through writing, to invent literary spaces that are other, hyperreal, utterly needed realities. Maybe this is why so many of us write 'auto fiction': because we are still stories, because we aren't real bodies yet.*
>
> (p. 270)

Over long passages of the book, one can get the impression that the author describes a course of analytical psychotherapy. Meanwhile, the writing seems more congruent. At one point, the narrator even speaks about their *"psychoanalyzed ego"* (p. 146). Nevertheless, it seems as if writing is the main therapeutic agent, whereby the reference to other literary protagonists function as a self-reassurance, like the many already mentioned quotations in the beginning of the chapters do.

> *I am a fluidity, my body resonates, I am in constant, deep resonation with you, with the past, with the ghosts you didn't bury, with the feelings you didn't live. (...) Writing this, I have come into resonation with my languages, our bodies, and all the ancestors that made both bodies and languages. And of course, I don't mean 'ancestors' in a biological way. Virginia Woolf is as much my mother as you are (...).*
>
> (pp. 287–288)

Reading "Bloodbook" might offer a possibility to open our eyes, our senses, and our minds. This book, of course, is not a manual or a guide; it is fiction, literature, a piece of art. Nevertheless, a genuine characteristic of art is that it can contribute to understanding the world, a world full of facets. Thus, reading "Bloodbook", the search of a non-binary person for their body and self, condensed into a literary art form, can help to accept, and endure the uncertainty facing the often-disturbing perceptions of my non-binary patients.

It seems meaningful that this book has been translated into 17 languages (Bulgarian, Catalan, Croatian, Czech, Danish, Dutch, English, French, Greek, Hebrew, Hungarian, Italian, Norwegian, Polish, Slovak, Spanish, and Swedish). Obviously, there is a broad interest and need to get acquainted with perspectives of non-binary persons. Kim de l'Horizon explains in an interview:

My pseudonym stands for the vastness of the horizon. I come from the horizon, from where you never get to, what is away from your own view. Many people who are from the edge of society know this. I feel the book prize in such a way that I am welcomed by broader parts of society. I am incredibly grateful for that. I may not be from here, but I'm here now and I want to fight for this here and now.

(NDR, North German Radio, 18.10.2022)

We understand that what may happen – both in the consulting room and outside of it – when you dare to get involved in a meaningful encounter with a non-binary person is a matter of perceiving and enduring existential uncertainty.

Material from *Blutbuch* by Kim de l'Horizon is included here by kind permission of DuMont Buchverlag. Kim de l'Horizon, "Blutbuch" © DuMont Buchverlag, Cologne. Translation by Eva Reichelt.

9 Gender fluidity

White holes in psychoanalytic theory?

Mauro Manica

I will start with a detailed literature search about psychoanalytic revisions of the Oedipus complex (Klein, Meltzer, Loewald, Searles, and Bion) and offer the following hypothesis: In this perspective, the Oedipus complex does not come to play a central role in the definition of a sexual or gender identity, especially in those conditions in which gender variances (transgender, gender fluid, agender) are realised beyond the limits set by a rigidly binary conception. I continue with a clinical vignette and end with some thoughts provoked by the physicist Carlo Rovelli: Paraphrasing the words of this quasi-poetic physics, we might perhaps ask whether gender variants might not constitute equivalents of "white holes" for that part of psychoanalytic research that studies the stars that make up the universe of personality. Gender fluidities might then be the elusive younger sisters of the galaxy that makes up an identity.

Re-visions of the Oedipus complex

Starting with the conception of an original psychic bisexuality, Freud's psychoanalysis generated a theory of sexual and gender identity that was fundamentally binary and informed by the vicissitudes of the Oedipus complex. While for Freud (1924) the Oedipus complex was to be brought to an end, not to be removed but rather "eliminated" and "destroyed" (under the aegis of the threat of castration) to neutralise its pathogenic effects, subsequent psychoanalytic developments have instead attributed to the Oedipal experience an increasingly evolutionary and vital function.

Already Melanie Klein (1926, 1932, 1933), in contrast to her master, had deepened the function of the Oedipus complex, considering it as an unconscious fantasy with a backbone of a mythical nature, present at the dawn of psychic life. In her view, it is almost as if life begins with Oedipus, in a kind of Dante's hell circle. The child's original fantasies about the parental pair have a particularly sadistic character, which then give rise to intense paranoid anxieties; most of the fantasies are conceived in terms of partial objects – the penis in the vagina, the nipple in the breast – continually sexually coupled, creating the terrifying fantasy of a combined parental figure,

DOI: 10.4324/9781003534440-15

and finally, the ambiguity of the positive and inverted Oedipus complexes, which by the fact of co-existing generate ambivalent tormenting feelings towards each parent. Be that as it may, the Kleinian Oedipus complex dramatises the primary relationships and increasingly orientates the individuation and subjectivation processes in a relational sense, as an outcome of the interactions between the self and internal and external, partial, and total objects.

Following Klein's revision of the Oedipus complex, further conceptions of the Oedipus complex came into being, aimed at emphasising its positive and evolutionary values, in fact, aimed at enabling us to understand the Oedipus complex as a true organiser of psychic vitality (Manica & Oldoini, 2023). Meltzer (1992), for example, goes so far as to develop the idea of a "geographical" composition of the mind that also includes claustrum spaces corresponding to different areas of the inner mother (head-breast, rectal space, and genital space). Meltzer attributes considerable importance to these areas in relation to the development of the child's future personality. Constructing an inner, integrated representation of this mother figure is a difficult task, because of the ambivalence aroused by the inevitable frustrations that the child will receive from this primary object and because of the intrapsychic projective identifications that drive him to segregate his parts inhabited by intolerable abandonment anxieties in the claustra of the inner mother. But it is at this point that Meltzer's (1992) most original insight comes in, for he writes: "It is precisely this inner mother in danger that drives the child not so much towards eliminating the father as a rival, but rather towards seeking an alliance with him in order to preserve this valuable and indispensable object". Meltzer's reversal of the Oedipus complex is revolutionary: the father is not only not a rival to be killed to possess the mother but becomes an ally. And this ally helps the child both to repair the damage he might have done to the object in fantasy and to enable him to keep it and nurture his love for it.

Albeit within a different horizon of discourse, Loewald (1979) also reconceives the Oedipus complex by disengaging it from the priority of guilt and destructiveness. In fact, he seems to reformulate it in a way that sees it as one of the fundamental human tasks necessary to evolve, to grow and to try to make of oneself an individual that can be used by subsequent generations to create, in turn, something unique. For Loewald, patricide becomes a dramatic, but necessary, indeed loving act that the child must perform to assert his/her own autonomy and sense of responsibility towards and for himself or herself and towards the ability to become a person who is, in many ways, more than his or her parents were able to be or become. Loewald's patricide is an act that takes place psychically, but it is an extremely raw and determined act, in which the son's breaking of a sacred bond, such as the one that unites him to his parents, does not represent a frightened response to a threat of bodily mutilation (castration), but manifests itself as the passionate affirmation of an "active drive for emancipation" (Loewald, 1979).

In an inimitable theoretical and clinical discourse, Searles (1959) is perhaps the author who has provided one of the most vital versions of the Oedipus complex, developing it from his extreme sensitivity and receptivity to the patient's unconscious communications, as well as his courageous capacity for self-disclosure and laying bare his own unconscious experience. Searles' version of the Oedipus complex is the story of the child's experience of a shared romantic and sexual love for the parent (a desire to "marry" and make a family and home with this parent). Rivalry with and jealousy towards the other parent are felt, but it is a much quieter affair than Freud's, Klein's, Meltzer's and Loewald's conception of the child's murderous desire regarding his or her parents. In this interpretation of the Oedipus complex, the child emerges with the feeling that his or her romantic and sexual love is accepted, valued and changed, together with the firm recognition of "a greater limiting reality" (Searles, 1959) within which he must live. Both elements – love and loss – strengthen the child psychologically. The first element – reciprocated Oedipal love – increases the child's feeling of his or her own worth. The second element – the loss implicit in the end of the Oedipal romance – contributes to the child's sense of "a greater recognised limiting reality". In fact, for Searles, the renunciation of Oedipal love is something new, it is a reciprocal experience for child and parent that is fulfilled by taking into consideration a greater recognised limiting reality, one not only substantiated by the presence of the rival parent, but also encompassing the Oedipally desired parent's love for their spouse. That love predates the birth of the boy or the girl, and is a love to which, in a sense, they, as children, owe their very existence. It is undoubtedly a love that must recognise and set a limit, as much as it must not be frightening in its fulfilment in a deeply intimate and inner dimension.

Bion's revision leads the Oedipus complex to carry out the most surprising and somewhat unpredictable functions in relation to the incorporation of this myth in psychoanalytic theory and clinical work. In Bion's view, it is not the incestuous fantasy that is central to Oedipus' tragedy, but rather a sin of *hubris*: it is the exposure of a child, deprived of the protections offered by the availability of an α-function, to a blinding emotional truth, to a terrifying and impersonal O. The consequence of this shift from the emphasis on sexuality to the centrality of arrogance is that other characters are brought to the centre stage of the myth: no longer Laius, Jocasta and Oedipus, the new king of Thebes, but the *sphinx* who terrorised the city by posing two riddles and who is destroyed (or destroys herself) when Oedipus solves them, winning the kingdom and marrying Jocasta; the blind soothsayer *Tiresias*, who has the knowledge of the truth and deplores the king's decision to go in search of it, and is nevertheless forced to reveal it to him; the *oracle of Delphi*, which provokes the seer's quest, which he deplores; and again the king, Oedipus, who, having completed his quest, discovers that he is responsible for the plague afflicting Thebes, and condemns himself to blindness and exile. According to Bion (1958), it is through the history of these characters that it is possible to grasp, "in the ruins of the psyche", the destiny towards which the scattered elements of curiosity, arrogance, and stupidity lead.

And Bion delivers a further revolution that overturns the most taken for granted paradigms of a psychoanalysis too convinced that it can know the absolute truth about ultimate reality. Oedipus' *hubris* concerns the patient as much as it concerns the analyst and as much as it concerns the analytic procedure itself, which is "precisely a manifestation of that curiosity which is felt as an intrinsic component of disaster. Consequently, the very act of analysing the patient renders the analyst an instrument of regression and transforms analysis into an acting-out". By placing the Oedipal vicissitudes in a relational and intersubjective field, Bion also transforms its developmental significance. Although he does not state it explicitly, we cannot help but think that the Oedipus of arrogance, curiosity, and stupidity also speaks of a failure of the primary relationship in which an object endowed with reverie and α-function capable of containing the primitive agonies and projective identifications of one's own child is lacking.

If the capacity for reverie fails, and if the α-function of the maternal mind (as well as that of the analyst) fails, the child (like the patient) is forced into envy. And the envious attack can result in the destruction of the α-element or the Oedipal pre-conception, and a parental (or analyst's) "conception" is prevented, so that the child (or the patient) cannot experience the Oedipus complex, precisely because he has never been able to constitute it. Curiosity, as a source of development, turns into the Sphinx's riddle (Bion, 1992), and Oedipus' need for knowledge becomes an insistent determination to know the truth at any cost[1] that overflows into *hubris*, an exaggerated pride.

Following the development of these Oedipal theories, I believe that the so-called Oedipus complex can currently be regarded as a fundamental organiser of psychic vitality, in which the child is called into life, even before sexual identification, by a loving and facilitating environment. In this perspective the Oedipus complex does not come to play a central role in the definition of a sexual or gender identity, especially in those conditions in which gender variances (transgender, gender fluid, agender) are realised beyond the limits set by a rigidly binary conception. On the contrary, the Oedipus complex as an organiser of psychic vitality maintains an entirely relevant function in a direction of a therapy that foresees an increase in the patient's vitality (and creativity) as an indicator of its effectiveness.

The feminine and the masculine

Within a different horizon of discourse, Jung (1913, 2009), placing the Electra complex alongside the Oedipus complex, had restored to the feminine in general, but above all to the feminine aspects in the personality of each human being, an essential function on the individuation path: it was the conjunction, the sacred marriage (*hieros gamos*) between the "anima" (feminine) and the "animus" (masculine) that performed the miracle of the definition of an identity.

Jung thus anticipated Winnicott's ontological turn (Winnicott, 1966), where the pure feminine elements of the personality and the pure masculine elements were brought back to the categories of being (feminine) and doing (masculine), respectively, where a lack of being leads to a disorganised and disoriented doing, and a lack of doing results in a rarefied and disembodied being, detached from a grounding in the body dimension.

And again, it is Bion (1962) who frees psychoanalytic theory from oversaturated concepts, imagining the mind as a variegated (*queer*) set of container (♀)/contained (♂) relations, where the α-function allows for the transformation of unthinkable proto-sensory and proto-emotional experiences (β-elements) into the building blocks that make up the visual images (α-elements) of dream and thinking.

The priest and theologian Pablo d'Ors wrote (2012, 60):

I came to these conclusions by asking the only necessary question: who am I? Attempting to answer, I realised that any attribute I added to this "I am" was, on closer inspection, outrageously false. For I could say, for example, "I am Pablo d'Ors": but the truth is that I would be who I am even if I replaced my name with another. Similarly, I could say "I am a writer"; but would that then mean that I would not be who I am if I did not write? Or "I am a Christian", in which case: would I stop being myself if I denied my faith? Whatever attribute one attaches to the "I", even the most sublime, is radically inadequate. The best definition of me that I have arrived at so far is "I am". Simply that.

Is this the reflection to which the issue of gender fluidity introduces us? Is it the *who I am* as an attribute that should be affixed to the I? Something that comes even before name, gender, feminine, masculine or any sexual identity.

The biologist Fausto-Sterling, in a now seminal 1993 paper called *The five sexes*, almost provocatively argued that there are at least five sexes in human nature (Balocchi, 2019; Fausto-Sterling, 1993). Thus, referring only to the genital organs and reproductive apparatus, it is possible to speak of: *males* with penis and testicles; *females* with vulva and ovaries; *herms* that have both testicles and ovaries at the same time; *merms* with testicles and some features of female genitalia; and *ferms* with ovaries combined with some features of male genitalia. The effects of Fausto-Sterling's work were disruptive because, while it made it clear that our society's binary sexual system was inadequate to encompass the entire spectrum of human sexuality, it also intensified sociological discussions on the social determination of sex and the identity of each human being. Fausto-Sterling showed the existence of intersex people, who do not fit into the female/male binarism, before the eyes of the scientific community and society. In the past, the existence of intersex people was known. They were defined as "hermaphrodites", a term that carries a stigma and for this reason is no longer accepted by the scientific community and those involved in intersex activism. The effects of this realisation have increasingly involved the legal and political worlds as well, giving rise to the need to legislate to protect the rights of non-binary people.

Anne Fausto-Sterling (2019, 35–36) writes:

> The concept of intersexuality is embedded in the very ideas of male and female. In the idealized, Platonic world, human beings are divided into two types: a perfectly dimorphic species ... This idealized representation conceals many obvious objections: some women have facial hair, some men have none; some women have deep voices, some men literally squeak. Less well known is the fact that, on closer inspection, absolute dimorphism also collapses to the level of biological foundations. Chromosomes, hormones, internal sexual structure, gonads, and internal genitalia all vary far more than most people recognise. Those who are born outside the Platonic dimorphic mould are called intersex.[2]

It is therefore biology itself that questions a rigid sexual binarism. And anthropological research has confirmed how sexual and gender identities are not simply dimorphic. In some populations of the Melanesian archipelago, it appears that there are again at least five sexual orientations: men who love women, women who love men, men who love men, women who love women, and people, who fit our definition of "Angel", who can love people of all other genders. And in these populations, for parents giving birth to an Angel is a celebration: giving birth to an Angel is a gift from the gods.

From a psychological (and psychoanalytic) point of view, where the sexuality of bodies, again, cannot be equated with the sexuality of minds, the polysemous figure of the *Angel* refers us to the ontological question of "who I am" (d'Ors, 2012). Perhaps we must begin to ask ourselves the problem of also writing a psychoanalysis of "who I am". We must begin to think that being is more important than knowing (Manica, 2023), rather an ontological psychoanalysis (Eshel, 2017; Manica, 2021; Ogden, 2022) than an epistemological psychoanalysis. And in an ontological psychoanalysis, it is not what the analyst knows, and the patient comes to know about himself or herself that is important, but rather the presence of the analyst – all that the analyst *is* and succeeds in "becoming" (Bion, 1970) the patient's emotional experience – becomes essential.

With non-binary patients, we may need to make an *epoch* of the seemingly rigid dichotomies of Freudian thought: the dichotomies between primary and secondary processes, between pleasure principle and reality principle, between thing presentation and word presentation, between conscious and unconscious, between external and internal, and between subject and object and in the very modulations of temporality. We must break the censorship, the overly rigid slashes of theory, in the same way that Freud, after all, had invented the limiting concept of "drive" to reduce the distance between mind and body, between soul (*Seele*[3]) and matter.

Perhaps, it was the Bionian turn that broke the caesura/censorship paradigm, revealing the intersubjective soul of psychoanalysis, the bipersonal psychological dimension that, already present in Freud's thought, had been unconsciously induced by the radioactivity of the material being treated to wear a one-personal suit. Bion (1966, 99) wrote: "Investigate the caesura, not the analyst, not the analysand; not the unconscious, not the conscious; not sanity, not insanity. But the caesura, the link, the synapse, the (counter-trans)-ference, the transitive-intransitive mood". Then, we can think that the "object" par excellence of psychoanalysis is the *in-between*: not the axon, not the dendrite, but the synapse that connects them; not the analyst, not the patient, but the *field* (Ferro, 2002, 2007, 2010) created by their intersubjective relationship.

She's Tittì (Tweety) like a sparrow

Francesca is a person who begins her analysis at the age of sixteen, with a sensitive and attentive colleague, because she feels lost in her own life, disoriented with respect to the future, and immersed in a present to which she cannot attribute any reality or meaning. Her main interest is following the events of an *anime*, based on a Japanese manga comic, which tells the story of Dazai (brunette, vaguely more masculine) and Chuuya (coppery blond, vaguely more feminine), a couple of guys bound by a homosexual, romantic, provocative, and passionate love. Francesca mostly identifies with Dazai. In fact, she would really like to be like Dazai: she combs her hair like him, dresses the same way, wears a bandage that compresses her breasts until they disappear. From the very first encounters she wants to be recognised as a man, she asks to be called Sergio, or preferably *Tweety*, the nickname she was given in early childhood. "For me, Tweety was a boy's name, I have always felt like a boy".

Tweety has a relationship with a fluid gender girl, but it is a romantic love that excludes all physical intercourse. And as the three times a week analysis continues, Tweety comes to feel more and more like Dazai and to desire, like him, a homosexual relationship with a man. Her/his parents, who seem very open-minded and tolerant of Tweety's non-binarism, have procured several articles for her/him about hormone treatments and sexual transition surgery, but for the time being she/he feels no desire to transform her/his body. In the course of a second opinion with a colleague, the cartoon character of Tweety, the canary constantly and clumsily chased by Sylvester Cat, initially appears. Which parts of Francesca/Sergio's self can the cartoon characters talk about? Must the sexually undifferentiated, identity-seeking canary ("I seemed to see a cat" is Tweety's childish interlude) still fight with a clumsy male/Sylvester cat, who, however, presses and hounds her too eagerly? Maybe the protection of a grandmother/analyst is still needed, so that Tweety's self can find the truth of its own spontaneous act.

Later, in the course of the supervision, verses from the poem, *In front of San Guido,* by Giosuè Carducci pop up:

> *She is Tittì (Tweety) like a little sparrow.*
>
> *But she has no feathers for her dress.*

Whether Tittì/Tweety is a she sparrow or a he sparrow, the question of female or male identifications does not seem to be at the forefront, but the identity and ontological question of "not having feathers for one's dress". It is as if Tittì/Tweety communicates a sense of lack of being, an inability to dream her/himself into existence (Ogden, 2022), which holds a definition of gender in abeyance.

She tries to erase her breasts but does not want to start a hormonal transition (because, she says, "it makes her fat"). She wants to be a man, like Dazai, she wants a homosexual love relationship with a male, but for now she does not want to have a penis. Is Tweety a transgender, with schizoid traits that are still poorly integrated?

Anne Fausto-Sterling (2019, 40) writes:

> Transgender people, individuals who have an emotional gender at odds with their physical sex, once described themselves in terms of dimorphic absolutism - males trapped in a female body or vice versa, and, as such, sought psychological relief through surgery. Although many still do, some so-called transgender people today are happy to inhabit a more ambiguous zone. A trans-sexual man-to-woman (person), for example, can turn out to be a lesbian. Jane, born a man physiologically, is now in her early forties and lives with her wife, whom she married when her name was still John. Jane takes hormones to feminize herself, but these have not yet interfered with her ability to have sex like a man. In her mind, Jane has a lesbian relationship with her wife, although she sees their intimate moments as a crossing between lesbian and heterosexual sex.

We can be tempted to consider gender fluidity simply as psychopathological manifestations and to prematurely assign intersex, transsexual, or fluid persons to a particular gender, or to regard them as existing somewhere between the poles of male and female. But woman and man, female and male cannot be analysed as a kind of continuum. On the contrary, sex and gender are best conceptualised as points in a multidimensional space, in which genetic, hormonal, and anatomical levels interact, in a way not yet fully understood, with environment and experience. And only a psycho-analysis of "who I am" can look into this multidimensional space of being, without prejudices, not even diagnostic prejudices; without memory and without desire; aimed at a mathematics of being in unison (at-one-ment) and not centred on identification; aimed at the search for the emotional truth of the patient, however ambiguous, variegated and composed of different shades of plumage, from Dazai's black to Chuuya's coppery blond.

White holes

The physicist Carlo Rovelli writes (2023):

> I don't know if the idea that black holes end their long life by turning into white holes is right. It is the phenomenon I have been studying in recent years. It involves the quantum nature of time and space, the coexistence of different perspectives, and the reason for the difference between past and future. Exploring this idea is still an ongoing adventure … What exactly are black holes, teeming in the universe. What are the white holes, their elusive little brothers. And the questions that have always chased me: how do we see what we have never seen? Why do we always want to go and see a little further…?

Paraphrasing the words of this quasi-poetic physics, we might perhaps ask whether gender variants might not constitute equivalents of "white holes" for that part of psychoanalytic research that studies the stars that make up the universe of personality. Gender fluidities might then be the elusive younger sisters of the galaxy that makes up an identity.

Psychoanalytic research has gathered a wealth of data on the "black holes" of the mind. We know all about the "black mother" (Green, 1973) corresponding to a fantasy who governs the world of perversions and who, at the oral level, suffocates, sucks, and devours while, at the anal level, crushes and controls. Similarly, we are familiar with the "dead mother" (Green, 1980), as an archaic and deadly mother that determines the proliferation of a malignant narcissism. And we also know the "black-hole depression" (Tustin, 1972), a primitive depression generated by a "black-hole mother" and constituting the nuclear traumatic dimension of some autistic spectrum disorders. After all, it was Freud (1920) who had taught us that there is a drive *Beyond the pleasure principle* that draws us inexorably, like a veritable black hole, towards the negative, towards destruction and towards death. If this is the case, however, these black holes do not tell us anything significant about the definition of identity, the processes of subjectivation and those anxieties – perhaps "white holes" – that are experienced on this side of the pleasure principle: life anxieties (Manica,

2010) and anxieties that accompany the process of becoming oneself. Rovelli (2023, 130) adds:

> Some of the dark matter could perhaps be made up of billions and billions of these tiny, delicate white holes, which turn the time of black holes upside down, but not too much, and float lightly in the universe, like dragonflies.

In his ever-poetic language, "white holes" are "dragonflies", but we cannot forget that they are also part of a mysterious "dark matter", that they are nonetheless the effect of a star's death and that they disrupt the articulations of known time. But what interests me most is the fact that the "white hole" represents a real reversal of perspective of the "black hole": if the black hole sinks, the white hole emerges; if the black hole attracts, the white hole repels, and so on.

We have explored the different dimensions of the negative and should continue to explore them. But is there something disturbing on this side of the pleasure principle, in the folds of the life instinct? Do life anxieties exist? Is it the fear of living that sometimes overpowers the fear of dying? If a child has not been sufficiently called to life, called to Oedipus, can they fear life more than they fear death. As Rovelli tells us, the white hole is the reverse of the black hole. We have learnt to defuse death anxieties, but we have perhaps not got used to dealing fully with life anxieties. What do we know about white holes, and what happens on this side of the pleasure principle? Perhaps fluid gender patients ask us about the issue of the fright that life can generate. Perhaps they tell us that the fundamental ontological problem does not concern the modulations of sexuality or gender but involves the dimensions of being and not being: the tragedy of not being called to exist and of an environment in which it is not possible to exist as one is. Perhaps after overcoming this dramatic caesura, every form of existence can find its own meaning.

Meltzer (1973) suggested that the question of sexuality implies a very sophisticated experience, which to be fulfilled requires overcoming the primary confusions between external and internal (external reality and psychic reality), between self and object, and between good and bad. After overcoming these confusions, a distinction can be made between a good and a perverse sexuality and between the sexuality of being and the sexuality of doing. I find myself thinking, however, that underlying these confusions is that between being and not being. And this primitive confusion leads us to reflect on the foundations of our theories about Oedipus, the pleasure principle and the reality principle. Are we willing to broaden and transform our theoretical, clinical, and technical perspectives? And to what extent?

What does Freud, at the time of the second topographical model, realise when he replaces the sexual and self-preservation drives with life and death drives? Perhaps he senses, preconsciously, that under certain conditions it is more difficult to live than to die. Because somehow, we know phylogenetically that we must die, but we do not know what risks, and what unknown, living implies. Perhaps, and somehow, in the face of the anxiety of not being, we are reassured by the certainty of death. Perhaps this is what gender fluid patients require of us, to equip ourselves with a specific negative capacity that concerns the ability to tolerate the unknown: the unknown of being in an environment that has no call to a personal, authentic, and original life.

The boy who played with dolls

Alex returns, at the age of nineteen, to seek treatment from the therapist who had known him when he was an eight-year-old boy. He now has an ethereal appearance, platinum blond hair, an ensemble that hints at something angelic. He says he is shy, kind, and welcoming, but has great difficulty in social relationships because the other people frighten him. Because of this fear, he says that he cannot stand people, that he hates everyone and that he would like to kill anyone who frightens him. He was a child who played with dolls, loved Barbie dolls, was fascinated by their clothes, but especially by the fact that he could put make-up on them. For this reason, his parents had requested a consultation partly because they were concerned that Alex preferred girls' toys. He also manifested excessive fears and alternating moods. During his teenage years, he compensated for a growth retardation with growth hormone treatment. He has often changed the colour of his hair, but for the past few months, he has chosen platinum blond, reminiscent of the hair on the Barbie dolls he played with as a child. He finished a vocational school for hairdressers and currently works as an apprentice in the shop of a hair salon, a family friend. He enjoys styling hair, washing it, cutting it, but most of all he prefers to do the customers' make-up. His deepest wish would be to be a theatre make-up artist. His favourite opera character is *Madama Butterfly*, and his dream would be to make up the singer who could play her in Puccini's opera. He also loves to sing and is attracted to Japanese culture. But what else does the child who seemed to become a frightened, delicate and angry Angel have in common with Cio Cio-san, the protagonist of *Madama Butterfly*.

As we know, Puccini's opera stages a love tragedy: the young geisha marries Pinkerton, a US naval officer stationed in Japan. She is soon abandoned by Pinkerton who returns home, aware that according to local custom, he has the right to abandon his wife after only one month. However, she has a child by him, whose birth she keeps hidden from everyone, including her husband. She lives expecting his return. Pinkerton will indeed return, but not to be reunited with her: he has married young Kate legally in the United States and wants to take the child back with him to educate him according to Western customs. Faced with the facts, Butterfly understands:

her great illusion, the happiness she dreamt of next to the man she loved, has vanished completely. So, she quietly decides to take her own life by stabbing herself in the neck with the same dagger with which her father had committed suicide, according to the Japanese custom known as *jigai*. In the dramatic final scene, Pinkerton goes to Cio Cio-san's room to apologise to her, but it is too late, and he finds her already dead, while the child, blindfolded and protected by a screen, plays with a doll and an American flag, unaware of everything.

Also in the story of Alex, as in that of *Madama Butterfly*, the tragedy is represented by an irreconcilability of worlds: if for Cio Cio-san it was the irreconcilability between western and eastern culture, between the superficiality of Pinkerton's feelings and the almost religious depth of her love; for Alex, it was perhaps the irreconcilability of a child playing with dolls on the one hand and the culture of the world of his parents who considered him inadmissible on the other. It was always as if his parents' world had been the opposite of his. They had faced poverty and deprivation and had been forced to grow up fast, regardless of frills; he had been a child who had needed growth hormone to grow up and had preferred female peers to his peers because he resented the competitiveness and aggressiveness of the male world. As a child, Alex seemed to play what he felt to be without being accepted and understood. Now he does what he feels he is, but only in the cramped space of the hair salon where he works. Perhaps one of the reasons he has returned to analysis is to nurture the hope that it is possible to find an environment that accepts him as he is. Even if he were an Angel.

Queer psychoanalysis

In the light of the possible re-visions of Oedipus, the study of the anxieties that might arise on this side of the pleasure principle, and post-Bionian field theory, it is perhaps possible to consider supplementing the more traditional psychoanalytic corpus with a chapter devoted to a different psychoanalysis.

Patients like Tweety and Alex might need Queer Psychoanalysis, to use the beautiful definition that Pietrantonio (2023) recently took up from Bourlez (2018). And in her perspective, "queer" (variegated) psychoanalysis becomes a psychoanalysis that should perhaps equip itself with new myths – that of Tiresias, for example – new theories as well as new technical tools. But let us turn to Pietrantonio: Tiresias' transgender experience seems first and foremost to be an ontological experience, in which by *becoming* the other's feeling, we can become able to *intuit* what we cannot know and understand through thinking and reasoning alone. Tiresias's capacity for clairvoyance seems to be born as the result of being exposed to experiencing and suffering what Bion would call continuous transformations in O: transformations that imply the terrifying but also extraordinarily generative disruption of catastrophic telluric changes. A gift of clairvoyance that in Tiresias is sharpened when he becomes totally blind. Tiresias was born a man, became a woman and then became a man again, due to the capriciousness of the gods: Zeus and Hera who, like a pair of traumatic and incestual parents (Racamier, 1995), invaded the "son" with their needs and narcissistic demands, rather than supplying him with that particular and indispensable form of love that is reverie (Bion, 1962).

Are these potential white holes traceable in the childhood universe of trans-fluid-gender patients? And are these the unsettling transitions of Tiresias that can tell us about the drama of coming into being, after having gone through the catastrophe of *not* being? I believe that these are the unsettling transitions that the analyst must be willing to become in his or her own emotional experience by abandoning the safe harbour of any known identity theory. And faced with the patient-Tiresias, or Tweety, or Alex, the analyst-Tiresias must also be willing to go beyond all the dichotomies and binarism, not only of his or her own theory but also of his or her own technique; for example, beyond the binarism of free associations of the patient and interpretations of the analyst, and, beyond the binarisms of transference and countertransference. Because in a psychoanalysis of "who I am" there is not a couple in the room, but a group of two people, whose boundaries must temporarily thin out and overlap, sometimes even dissolve, to recompose themselves after each analytical segment, to develop ever greater coefficients of *meità/me-ness* (Manica, 2010, 2014), of the possibility of being what one really is in one's own existence. Which implies on the part of the analyst the ability to intuit and become what the patient feels; that is, the ability to have a mathematics of being in unison that funds the possibility of dreaming with another mind the unknown by which we are inexorably inhabited.

Perhaps Tiresias is a hologrammatic character, the soothsayer to whom Zeus gave seven existences and bestowed prescience. He is the mythical figure who, over the centuries, has been moulded and re-moulded into infinite identity versions by the greatest poets of the West: Homer, Sophocles, Ovid, Horace, Juvenal, Statius, Seneca, Lucian of Samostata, Clement of Alexandria, Dante, Poliziano, Pietro Aretino, Ugo Foscolo, Milton, Borges, Hugo von Hofmannsthal, Stravinsky, Apollinaire, Jean Cocteau, Virginia Woolf, Cesare Pavese, Primo Levi, Pier Paolo Pasolini, Ezra Pound, culminating in a ponderous eight-hundred-page volume entitled *Tiresian Poetics* (Camilleri, 2018).

Or perhaps Tiresias is simply the protagonist of a manga, or an *anime* of western mythology, ready to come alive in any analytic cabinet where the questions of not being and who I am become essential and the analyst must be willing to let any hologram enter the field and pass through: be it Tweety canary, Tweety sparrow, the clumsy Sylvester, the copper-haired Chuuya or the dark-haired Dazai, a Barbie, perhaps Ken or, finally, the cynical officer Pinkerton and the unhappy Cio Cio-san, a butterfly with broken wings.

Notes

1 In this regard, the words Sophocles has the soothsayer Tiresias utter in *Oedipus Rex* are emblematic, "*How frightening it is to know when knowledge/provides no benefit to those who know*".
2 Fausto-Sterling (1993) reported an estimate made by a psychologist experienced in the treatment of intersex persons, who suggested that about 4% of all live births are intersex. In fact, in later research done by the same author with a group of Brown University students (Fausto-Sterling, [2000] 2019), the estimate suggested that the intersex rate should be reduced to 1.7% and that in any case the intersex rate is not uniform worldwide.
3 The term *Seele*/soul is the one most frequently used by Freud, in his entire work, to refer to the mind or psyche.

References

Balocchi, M. (a cura di), (2019). *Intersex. Antologia Multidisciplinare*, Pisa: Edizioni ETS.
Bion, W. R. (1958). On Arrogance. *International Journal of Psychoanalysis* 39:144–146
Bion, W. R. (1962). *Learning from Experience*. London: Routledge.
Bion, W. R. (1966). Catastrophic change. In: *The Complete Works of W. R. Bion*, Vol. VI.
Bion, W. R. (1970). *Attention and Interpretation*. London: Routledge.
Bion, W. R. (1992). *Cogitations*. London: Routledge.
Bourlez, F. (2018). *Queer Psychanalyse. Clinique mineure et déconstruction du genre*, Paris: Hermann.
Camilleri, A. (2018). *Conversazione su Tiresia*. Palermo: Sellerio Editore.
D'Ors, P. (2012). *Biografia del silenzio,* Italian translation. Milano: Vita e Pensiero, 2014.
Eshel, O. (2017). From Extension to Revolutionary Change in Clinical Psychoanalysis: The Radical Influence of Bion and Winnicott, *The Psychoanalytic Quarterly*, 86(4): 753–794.
Fausto-Sterling, A. (1993). The Five Sexes: Why Male and Female are Not Enough, *The Sciences*, 33(2), 20–24.
Fausto-Sterling, A. ([2000] 2019). Per una rivisitazione de *I Cinque Sessi*. In M. Balocchi a cura di *Intersex. Antologia Multidisciplinare*, Pisa: Edizioni ETS.
Ferro, A. (2002). *Fattori di malattia, fattori di guarigione*, Milano: Raffaello Cortina.
Ferro, A. (2007). *Evitare le emozioni, vivere le emozioni*, Milano: Raffaello Cortina.
Ferro, A. (2010). *Tormenti di anime*, Milano: Raffaello Cortina.
Freud, S. (1920). Beyond the Pleasure Principle. S. E.. 18:1–64.
Freud, S. (1924). The Dissolution of the Oedipus Complex. S. E. 19:171–180
Green, A. (1973). *Il discorso vivente*, Italian translation, Roma: Astrolabio, 1974.
Green, A. (1980). La madre morta, Italian translation. In *Narcisismo di vita. Narcisimo di morte*, Roma: Borla, 1985.
Jung, C. G. (1913). The theory of Psychoanalysis. *Psychoanalytic Review*, 1: 1–40.
Jung, C. G. (2009). *The Red Book. Liber novus*. New York: W. W. Norton & Company.
Klein, M. (1926). The psychological principles of early analysis. *International Journal of Psychoanalysis* 8:25–37.
Klein, M. (1932). *The Psychoanalysis of Children*. London: Hogarth Press.
Klein, M. (1933). Il primo sviluppo della coscienza morale nel bambino, Italian translation. In *Scritti 1921–1958*, Torino: Boringhieri, 1978.
Loewald, H. (1979). The waning of the Oedipus complex, In *Papers on Psychoanalysis*, New Haven, CT: Yale University Press, 1980.
Manica, M. (2010). *Fare Psicoanalisi, vivere la clinica, sognare la Teoria*, Borla: Roma.
Manica, M. (2014). *Intercettare il sogno. Sviluppi traumatici e progressione onirica nel discorso psicoanalitico*, Borla: Roma.

Manica, M. (2021). *"E quindi uscimmo a riveder le stelle". Il dialogo di Bion con la psico-analisi*. Roma: Armando.

Manica, M. (2023). L'arte di guarire: dal *conoscere* all'*essere*, *Psiche*, 1: 105–116.

Manica, M. & Oldoini, M. G. (2023). *Leggere la psicoanalisi. Il presente del passato, il presente del futuro*. Milano: IBS Feltrinelli.

Meltzer, D. (1973). *Sexual States of Mind*. London: Karnac.

Meltzer, D. (1992). *The Claustrum. An Investigation of Claustrophobic Phenomena*. Glenlyon: Clunie Press

Ogden, T. H. (2022). *Coming to Life in the Consulting Room*. London: Routledge.

Pietrantonio, V. (2023). *Ipotesi Tiresia: un mito per una Queer Psychoanalysis*, a proposito di L. Bruno, *Riflettere psicoanaliticamente sulle varianze di genere*, presentata al Centro Psicoanalitico di Pavia, 14 febbraio 2023

Racamier, P.-C. (1995). *L'incest et l'incestuel*. Malakoff: Dunod

Rovelli, C. (2023). *Buchi bianchi. Dentro l'orizzonte*. Milano: Adelphi.

Searles, H. (1959). Oedipal love in the countertransference. In Searles, H., *Collected Papers on Schizophrenia and Related Subjects*. New York: International Universities Press.

Tustin, F. (1972). *Autism and Childhood Psychosis*. London: Routledge.

Winnicott, D. W. (1966). On the Split Off Male and Female Elements in Men and Women. In *Psychoanalytic Explorations* (168–192). London: Karnac, 1989.

10   Gender in movement*

The emergent versus the continuous

Dana Amir

Muriel Dimen (2014, 807) opens one of her papers with the following words:

> Once upon a time, sex and gender were a team. Gender aligned with
> natal sex, and both aligned with desire (heterosexual, to be sure): male
> genitalia rendered you masculine and desirous of women; female
> genitalia made you feminine and inclined you toward men. Nowa-
> days everything is up for grabs. No longer do genitals and gender
> predict desire: same-sex and same-gender love, like changes in desire
> across lifetimes, are deemed normal. Our grasp of the shifting rela-
> tions among the categories once grouped under the rubric of "psycho-
> sexuality" is much more nuanced.

In recent years, indeed, the complex relations between biological sex
(genital morphology) and gender identification have been variously rede-
fined (Benjamin, 1998; Butler, 1993, 1995; Corbett, 1993, 2009a, 2009b; Dimen, 2014; Dimen and Goldner, 2011; Goldner, 1991, 2011; Gozlan, 2015;
Hansbury, 2017; Harris, 1991, 2011a, 2011b; Lemma, 2012, 2013; Quinodoz,
1998, 2002; Saketopoulou, 2011, 2014).

Hansbury (2017, 1015) writes in this context:

> Historically, canonical psychoanalysis has treated the sexed body as
> delivering a clear pronouncement on gender. From that perspective,
> there are only two genders, and attempts to occupy more than either
> position amounts to a kind of gender grandiosity where nothing can
> be mourned or given up. This is what I refer to as the binary model

* Permission to reprint kindly granted by Routledge 15.11.23 to reprint Dana Amir, (2021)
Gender in Movement: The Emergent Versus the Continuous. *Studies in Gender and Sexuality*, 22 (3). DOI: 10.1080/15240657.2021.1961476. The chapter was originally given as
"Gender in movement: The rhizomatic versus the oedipal" at the Contemporary Psychoanalytic Perspectives on Gender and Sexualities Study Day, Brussels 2019, and at
the Cannes EPF panel presentation 2023 as 'Gender in movement: Emergent versus
continuous'.

DOI: 10.4324/9781003534440-16

of gender. Contemporary psychoanalytic gender theory, building on second-wave feminism and postmodernism, dismantled this binary and offered an alternative concept of gender as existing on a continuum of masculinity-femininity that may or may not map onto the natal body in material ways. This is what I refer to as the multiplicity model of gender. What I am proposing is that, when used alone, both the binary and the multiplicity models are insufficient because they set up a false dichotomy: one either belongs to one of two genders or floats in between.

Here, I deal with the question of gender binary versus gender multiplicity, introducing an "emergent" component of gender that exists in parallel with a "continuous" gender component and entertains variable relations with it. What I would like to suggest here is that alongside a continuous gender development (relating to a cumulative gender identity and gender identification, no matter the degree of compatibility to natal gender) there exists an emergent component characterised by its nonlinear, changing, varying gender experience, based on incessant movement between the two gender poles, and on the subject's taking different positions in and between them. This experience does not come to take over or inherit the continuous component of gender identity but joins it by way of constituting an additional dimension, which exists in parallel to it throughout every subject's life.

In an unpublished paper entitled *Catastrophic Change* (1967) – later reprinted as *Container and Contained Transformed* (1970) – Bion touched on two key principles at work in the human psyche. The first of these two, the emergent principle, perceives the world as undergoing a constant change. The second, the continuous principle, perceives the world as stable and fixed. In this paper, which describes the interaction between what Bion (1970, 121) defines as "the Establishment" (representing the stable, sometimes rigid force that resists change) and "the messianic idea" (which represents the force of innovation and change), he argues that the aspect of the personality that always stays stable and fixed is the only force that can contain new perceptions of the self and of the world:

> The individual always displays some aspect of his personality that is stable and constant even though it may sometimes be very difficult to detect in the welter of evidence for instability; it may appear only in the regularity with which the patient attends his sessions. In this stability will be found the counterpart of what ... I have called the Establishment. It will be maintained with great tenacity as the only force likely to contain the counterpart of the messianic idea. Reciprocally, the messianic idea is the only force likely to withstand the pressures of the counterpart of the Establishment in the individual.

Britton (1992, 110–111), in his paper *Keeping Things in Mind*, also refers to these two elements:

> Bion, in a description of the 'container' in an unpublished paper entitled 'Catastrophic change' (1967), says that 'some aspect of the personality is stable and constant, and that this is maintained as the only force likely to contain emergent ideas which express new awareness of reality of the self or the world.' If the relationship between this continuous self and the recurrently changing emergent self is mutually enhancing, development takes place. This relationship he describes as 'symbiotic.' If, however, that continuous identity which he called 'the container' is disrupted by new self-development or new self-discoveries, then psychic change is experienced as catastrophic, since the changes disintegrate the sense of self-continuity. When this happens, the subjective experience is one of fragmentation. In these circumstances, in order to preserve a sense of continuity of existence, all change must be resisted, and no new experience allowed to emerge. This mutually destructive relationship of container and contained Bion called 'parasitic.' I prefer to call it 'malignant containment'.

Thus, if the interaction between the emergent principle and the continuous principle of the self is mutually reinforcing, development will occur, and change will be possible. If, by contrast, every change is experienced as a threat to the continuous identity – namely to the "continuous self" – any psychological change will be felt as catastrophic since it will be associated with the destruction of one's sense of continuity. When the continuous container cannot hold the emergent contained, the subjective experience is one of breakdown. In such circumstances, in order to maintain a sense of existential continuity, the psyche must resist all change and avoid the emergence of any new experience.

Bion never expanded on the unique significance of each of these elements of the self, and actually never dealt with them separately, but rather encompassed them in his general argument concerning the interaction between container and contained. But one can think of the continuous principle as the one which perceives the world as predictable, explainable and logical – and of the emergent principle as the one that perceives the world as unpredictable, unexplainable, and constantly changing (Amir, 2016a). The integration of these two modes of experience yields the capacity to presuppose constancy and continuity on the one hand, and to tolerate severe deviations from that constancy and continuity without losing one's sense of identity and biography, on the other hand.

Formulating his notion of the container/contained interaction, Bion (1970, 78) pointed, as referred to by Britton (1992), at three possible types of this interaction, of which the one with the most powerful capacity for change is the symbiotic interaction, while the one with the most destructive power is the parasitic (in between, Bion posited a somehow neutral interaction he entitled "commensal"). If we formulate the interaction between the emergent and the continuous principles of the self in these terms, we may suppose that wherever the interaction between the emergent and the continuous is parasitic in nature or takes the form of a "malignant containment" (Britton, 1992, 111), one of two things might happen: the continuous self may smother the emergent self, leaving the latter no space for movement or development, or, alternatively, the emergent self might stretch the continuous self beyond its breaking point, crashing through its boundaries. When the continuous principle prevails, the psychic space becomes lacking in depth and resonance, while when the emergent principle takes over, the psychic space turns into a terrifying nightmare. The more fertile the interaction between the two, the more likely one is to experience oneself as owning a historical and biographical continuum on the one hand, and as being a singular individual, whose creativity and vitality are allowed to interrupt this continuum, on the other hand.

Gender, too, can be understood in terms of the relations between the continuous and the emergent. An excess of a continuous gender experience as opposed to an emergent gender experience can damage the possibility of establishing a gender subjective space that holds the continuous and the emergent in a fertile dialectic relation. On the other hand, an excess of emergent gender experience, in which every shift threatens to change the deep nucleus of identity, may also undermine the possibility of a cooperative relationship between the two components. Gender is constantly in the process of emerging. Yet, every emergence needs a continuous container for its forcefulness and volatility. When there is a "continuous" gender that can contain the various gender emergences in a way that doesn't force the self to undergo a catastrophic identity change, a gender space is created (Amir, 2016a, 2018a).

We may say that the difference between the continuous and the emergent gender components is the difference between the saturated and the unsaturated states of being (Bion, 1962, 1970). Every unsaturated component, for Bion, becomes saturated when encountering a proper actualisation. Then, from an open condition, like that of a variable without a value, it evolves a value, becomes saturated and thence permanent. What I am proposing here is that alongside the continuous gender component that seeks saturation, directionality, and stability, there is a component that always stays open, unsaturated, and in a state of becoming. This latter component doesn't stand in contradiction with the former, but rather exists in parallel, forming with it relationships of constant challenge.

Hansbury (2017, 195) writes in a somewhat similar context:

The queered transmodern body, put through a process of inquiry that dislocates it from orthodoxy, does not split binary and multiplicity models, but holds them both in dialectical tension. As Aron (1995) has written, "we need both a notion of gender identity and a notion of gender multiplicity; more broadly, we need an emphasis on people both as unified, stable, cohesive subjects and as multiple, fragmented, and different from moment to moment."

The emergent gender component tends to expansion and multiplicity rather than to refinement and reduction. It is "a moving, limitlessly changing ensemble, a cosmos tirelessly traversed by Eros, an immense astral space not organised around any one sun that's any more of a star than the others," in the words of Hélène Cixous (1976, 889). It makes itself known in phantasies, in dreams, in the way one positions oneself in actual or imagined relationships, and in the subject's attitude toward him- or herself. It exists in varying degrees of awareness. Its expressions may be obvious for all to see, but may equally exist solely in the intimate inner space.[1] The interaction between the continuous and the emergent gender components is responsible for the infinite variants of gender identity, and is what determines, to an important extent, the subjects' ability to constitute themselves as subjects of gender rather than objects of gender, and thus to create their singular gender identity beyond the inevitable correspondence with social and cultural norms as well as with their natal gender.

The more fertile and productive this interaction between the emergent and the continuous, the richer is the subjective gender experience. When the interaction is a malignant one, on the other hand, the subject may collapse into a rigid reduction of gender experience or, alternatively, into the usurpation of gender continuity by gender emergence, leading to the absence of any cumulative gender experience and identity. These components interrelate differently within each subject, depending on external and internal circumstances.[2] Where the continuous gender principle grants freedom of movement to the emergent gender principle, there is fertile interaction and integration between them. Where, however, the continuous gender principle ties up the emergent gender principle in a rigid brace or, the opposite, collapses under the gender emergent principle in a way that allows no cumulative, continuous gender experience, then rather than a subject of gender, an object of gender comes into being. This object of gender may take one of two forms: It may either cling reductively to gender characteristics (in the case where the continuous component prevails), or alternatively take a pseudo-emergent form (in case where the emergent component has the upper hand): an alleged emergent spectacle that, rather than consisting of a living movement between gender polarities, creates a malignant negation of any movement.

Clinical illustration

On my first meeting with 30-year-old Raphael, I'm facing a handsome young man. His hair is long and fair, he wears long earrings and high-heeled shoes, his nails are varnished colourfully, and his eyes are heavily made up. He wears tight trousers, and his shirt has a feminine décolleté. In subsequent meetings, he appears alternatingly as a boy with macho features (wearing a cap, tall working boots, unshaven), and a provocatively and brashly groomed woman. These transitions between stereotypical feminine and masculine presentations are conscious and intentional, and he employs them not only in the encounter with me but in his general encounters with the world.

Raphael is the only child of two older parents, with whom he lives. His mother was diagnosed as suffering from bipolar disorder a few months after his birth and has since been treated with high doses of medication. She rarely leaves home in the last five years. Inside the home she does not function either, and often Raphael has to get her to leave her bed and force her to wash and eat. His father is immersed in his work as a senior civil servant and has almost no presence in Raphael's life. He is a good-looking, charming man who, according to Raphael, has always had extramarital relationships, which the mother knows about. He has always approached Raphael as a "gadget," another "necessary item" in the picture of the functional family, nothing beyond that. In Raphael's experience his father never took an interest in him – neither in his inner nor in his outer world. His mother, on the contrary, is deeply attached to Raphael, but he describes her as a dependent child rather than as the mother who raised him. She is a compulsive hoarder of unnecessary objects that have come to obstruct the whole interior: cardboard packaging of pharmaceuticals, sanitary pads, half-empty tubes of toothpaste that "one day she may need." As a child, he remembers, he avoided inviting friends because he was ashamed of the physical state of the house, which looked like a storehouse. The one place in which it was possible to stay was Raphael's room, which he defended with all his might from her hoarding. But it often happened that she took over there, too, for lack of another free space. At rare moments of grace, his mother would invite Raphael to take a look inside her secret boxes. Together, awestruck, they would rummage among the objects she had collected, like children who had laid their hands on a forbidden treasure. Touching these objects would, at such moments, create a peculiar sense of illicit sweet intimacy.

His parents slept in separate bedrooms for as long as he remembers. Officially, this was because they functioned at different hours of the day: while the father was an early riser, the mother was awake in the nights and slept during the days. Raphael remembers repeated incidents when he "caught" his father masturbating in front of pornographic films in his room. His father treated this simply as acts of mischief and refused to acknowledge the way it confused his son. Raphael remembers how he was haunted by recurrent dreams in which he would find himself facing his father's erect penis, unable to hide himself from it.

He began adolescence, he says, at an "inferior starting point" in relation to the other boys. He was shorter than them and had hardly any body hair.

He found it difficult to think of himself or experience himself as a boy – but nor did he experience himself as a girl. He was very lonely, and he remembers feeling that he was somehow hiding a secret which he himself didn't know – always anxiously awaiting the moment it would be revealed. One day, just before the Jewish festival of Purim where children wear costumes, his classmates proposed they should dress him like a girl. When he entered the classroom after the break, all eyes were on him. He remembers it as a formative moment: "Never, until then, had I felt I was someone or anything in particular. But when all the children, and even the teacher, set their eyes on me, I felt I had a special power, all my own."

From then on, he began to cross-dress, initially at home only, in the afternoons, and later throughout the day. One moment he dressed like a woman, and in the other he put on men's clothes and baseball caps that created a boyish look. His father, he remembers, despised his looks (both feminine and masculine) and reacted with rejection and disgust, while his mother was attracted by his feminine side, using it to share her own "feminine" secrets (teaching him how to close and open a bra with one hand, how to put on nylon stockings without tearing them, etc.). He experienced both male and female dress as disguise. He felt that the power he was gaining was because the surrounding world was at a loss in front of him, unable to associate him with one gender or the other. As he walked down the street, often discussions would start up whether he was a girl or a boy, and when people asked, he would sometimes present himself as a boy dressed up like a girl, sometimes as a girl pretending that she was a boy. He often had to swallow humiliations or endure physical violence due to his cross-dressing, because it "turned everyone on." Inside, however, rather than a "girly-boy," he felt neither a girl nor a boy. In the shower, naked and without his costumes, he felt transparent. That was the most difficult to bear.

Apropos of transparency, he recounts how one evening he passed by his father, who was waiting on a bus stop. Raphael was wearing women's clothes, and his father looked at him with curiosity, maybe even aroused. It was a shocking experience, says Raphael, but not only because of the fact that his father was attracted to him, taking him for a woman, but also because he understood at that moment that his father simply failed to recognise him. He never confronted his father with that encounter. But he remembers that a few nights later, his father tried to persuade him to join him watching heterosexual porn. "These are real men and real women," his father said, "they're not putting it on like you." He remembers the event, which seemed a conscious or unconscious response to what happened that evening in the street and was left unmentioned, as harassment. He felt his father was raping him by exposing him to his sexuality, forcing him to be what he, Raphael, wasn't: a "natural woman" or a "natural man."

Towards the end of adolescence, he joined a group of boys and girls who were coping with sexual and gender variation. Here, too, he felt a stranger. In answer to my question, he responds that they were different from him because they "had a direction": Some of them were thinking of sex reassignment surgery, some were in the process of figuring out that they were attracted to partners of their own sex, but all, without exception, could point out "where they wanted to go". Raphael was the only one among them who did not. In spite of his colourful, exhibitionistic looks, he did not feel sexual, couldn't tell whether he preferred boys or girls as partners, and didn't know whether his identity was male, female, both, or neither. Mostly, as said, he felt neither man nor woman.

In his recurring dreams, throughout the years, he has sex with both his parents: one moment as a female partner with his father, and in another moment as a male partner with his mother. He awakes from these dreams bathed in cold sweat. Raphael's vague gender identity serves as a way of regulating traumatic violence, a kind of second skin (Bick, 1968) that covers up for a natural skin that is experienced as perforated and breached. The explicit, excessive disguises constitute a barrier between him and his gender subjectivity, situating him in a lifeless gender zone for which the indeterminacy offers the one way out of the perversion that distinct gender is bound to create. In fact, Raphael's multiple gender can be understood as an act of resistance to the parental perversion and its modes of use and abuse of his bodily experience – which erased him both as a subject of gender and as a subject in general, causing him to treat his gendered body as always belonging to, or complying with, the desire of the other.

Bollas (1987) introduced the term "trisexual" for a person whose body image is genderless. The trisexual's body is desexualised, a body whose gender has been removed from the categories of sexual differences. The trisexual seeks to invert the Oedipal situation so that the two parents will compete over the sexual love of the child, rather than the child competing with one of them for the sexual love of the other. Trisexuality can be considered, in terms of this chapter, as a negation of the gender emergent component. While the gender emergent component is rich and stratified, trisexuality constitutes a barren reduction. While the gender emergent component fills out and enriches the continuous gender experience, trisexuality undermines it. Raphael's trisexuality is a result of a distorted gender experience, with the emergent component taking parasitic possession of the continuous component and eventually supplanting it. The early perversion of the relations with both his parents caused him to revert to a pregendered condition in which the two gender poles appeared in a blend.

The main analytical challenge here was to steer clear of a possible pervertisation of the analytic space as well, a pervertisation Raphael time and again tried tempting me into by infiltrating my private life, finding ways to pull me into his world or to become part of mine, changing shapes in every possible way to adjust himself to what he believed might be interesting and attractive to my eyes. Each time he felt I rejected him he fell into a suicidal depression. Each time he felt I was unresponsive, he was filled with hatred and anxiety. During one session, he told me he had used one of my earlier interpretations to draw the attention of a man who had been ignoring him so far.

When I ask him about it, he says he quoted something I said about him, but as though it had been his own idea. "It worked!" he laughed. "I managed to nail him thanks to that sentence of yours."

When I ask how that felt, he says: "Well, that's all I am able to do anyway. I dress up. So yesterday I masqueraded as if I were you, to see how you think and feel. I liked it. When I was you facing that man, I had your power of words."

When I ask whether this also happens here, with me, in analysis, he replies: "That's it: Here it doesn't really work. I can't find the costume you prefer, at least not in my closet. I have no idea what you want. I don't know whether you want me passive or active, masculine or feminine. Each time I throw my ball at your wall it bounces back to me. And it doesn't simply bounce back: it turns on me, as though it were asking what it actually was that I wanted. Most of the time that's confusing and frightening, and most of the time it makes me hate you."

"And the rest of the time?" I asked.

"In the rest of the time it feels like the closest thing I've ever had to what a true relationship is," he answered.

Donald Meltzer's (1975) notion of "adhesive identification" throws a certain light on this vignette. His concept refers to a kind of defensive adhesion of one person to another, an adhesion that involves neither love nor curiosity for that other, but rather an attempt to alleviate through the contact with that other person the anxiety of disintegration. This is a condition when one individual adopts facial expressions, body movements, or vocal inflections of another to use the latter's outer surface – and the visual, tonal, and tactile features of this surface – as if they were his or her own. Imitation of this type is rather an adhesion of bits of the other's surface onto the fragile, perforated surface of the self. This is not the same as an internalisation of the other, for there is no experience of any kind of internal space into which the other can be taken. Since the experience is of one's psychic envelope being full of holes, the individual creates permanent friction with the other, both to keep the other present and to keep their own self present, with the other functioning by way of delimitation. Raphael does not only stick bits of the other to himself, but also generates a kind of sticky identification with the other's desires and wishes, by adopting a "chameleon language" (Amir, 2013, 2014) which sneaks into the language of the other – seemingly in order to win them over, but in fact using them as a psychic shelter, away from the possibility of a distinct, separate existence that might be invaded and exploited.

In my book entitled "Bearing Witness to the Witness" (Amir, 2018b), I dealt with four modes of traumatic testimony, which were distinguished from one another in the degree of the psychic motility they succeed to form in relation to traumatic excess:

The *"metaphoric"* testimonial mode refers to those areas in the testimonial narrative where there is a constant movement between the "first person" and the "third person" of experience, or between the experiencing I and the reflective I, further enabling the shift between the "position of the victim" and the "position of the witness."

As against the metaphoric testimonial mode, the *"metonymic"* testimonial mode remains a "first person" mode of report that does not stray to the third person. It enacts the traumatic experience without being able to turn it into an integrated narrative, incorporating it without being capable of transcending it.

The *"Muselman"* mode of testimony destroys both the first and the third person, and thereby the very possibility of an experiencing subject. It joins the traumatic Real without being able to distance itself from it on the one hand, or to create a vital link with it on the other. It appears in the form of a semipsychotic type of discourse, both intrapsychic and interpsychic, a discourse that annihilates any contact with the psychic reality and the pain it involves.

The *excessive psychotic* mode is a much more illusory one. In this testimonial mode, traumatic excessiveness is available to consciousness neither by way of an elaborated link (as in the metaphoric mode) nor by way of repetition (as in the metonymic mode). Testimony in this case involves the traumatic memory becoming a saturated object (Bion, 1970): an object that refuses transformation. Underneath the rhetorical cover, this is a pseudo-language that attacks rather than produces linking, one that under the guise of "full testimony" presents what Cathy Caruth (1996) calls "empty grammar," a grammar that empties the event (Amir, 2016b, 2018b). These testimonial modes embody different levels of transformation of traumatic excess versus acting out of traumatic excess, or otherwise formulated – different levels of constitution of language versus the collapse of language.

Raphael can be thought of as embodying, through his gender manifestation, the excessive testimonial mode, which is characterised by a tendency towards acting out of excess rather than transformation of excess. The traumatic excess associated with the ways his primary environment used and abused him – is now embodied in what appears to be a form of self-exploitation and self-erasure. This is not a creative, playful heterogeneous gender show (though it may be misleadingly seen as such) – but rather a hollow and mechanical negation of any gender subjectivity: a "story" that Raphael himself is enslaved to, but also repeatedly erased by. Analysis in this case can therefore be thought of as an attempt to reclaim the narrator: to allow Rafael to extract, out of the undifferentiated chameleon texture, his own gendered voice, turning him into not just the owner, or the protagonist, of his story, but also its one and only narrator.

Notes

1 "Gender is. . . a matter of fantasy, internal imago, and symbolization, not con-creteness," writes Harris (2011b, 9).
2 Adrienne Harris (2000, 232), in *Gender as a Soft Assembly: Tomboys' Stories*, writes: "The assemblage of gendered experience in sexual life is contingent and emer-gent, not pre-programmed."

References

Amir, D. (2013). The chameleon language of perversion. *Psychoanalytic Dialogues*, 23:393–407.

Amir, D. (2014). *Cleft Tongue: The Language of Psychic Structures*. New York, NY, and London, UK: Karnac.

Amir, D. (2016a). *On the Lyricism of the Mind: Psychoanalysis and Literature*. New York, NY: Routledge (Translated from Hebrew).

Amir, D. (2016b). When language meets the traumatic lacuna: The metaphoric, the met-onymic and the psychotic modes of testimony. *Psychoanalytic Inquiry*, 36(8):620–632.

Amir, D. (2018a). The two sleeps of Orlando: Transsexuality as caesura or cut. In: O. Gozlan. (ed.). *Current Critical Debates in the Field of Transsexual Studies: In Transi-tion*. New York, NY: Routledge, 36–47.

Amir, D. (2018b). *Bearing Witness to the Witness: A Psychoanalytic Perspective on Four Modes of Traumatic Testimony*. New York, NY: Routledge.

Aron, L. (1995). The internalised primal scene. *Psychoanalytic Dialogues*, 5:195–237.

Benjamin, J. (1998). *Shadow of the Other: Intersubjectivity and Gender in Psychoanalysis*. New York, NY: Routledge.

Bick, E. (1968). The experience of the skin in early object relations. *International Jour-nal of Psychoanalysis*, 49:484–486.

Bion, W. R. (1962). *Learning from Experience*. London, UK: Heinemann. Reprinted by Karnac Books, 1984.

Bion, W. R. (1967). *Catastrophic change*. Unpublished paper.

Bion, W. R. (1970). Container and contained transformed. In: *Attention and Interpre-tation*. London, UK: Tavistock. Reprinted by Karnac Books, 1984.

Bollas, C. (1987). "The trisexual." In: *The Shadow of the Object*. London, UK: Free As-sociations Books, 82–98

Britton, R. (1992). Keeping things in mind. In: R. *Anderson* (ed.). *Clinical Lectures on Klein and Bion*, New York, NY: Routledge, 102–113.

Butler, J. (1993). *Bodies That Matter*. New York, NY: Routledge.

Butler, J. (1995). Melancholy—Gender-refused identification. *Psychoanalytic Dia-logues*, 5:165–180.

Caruth, C. (1996). *Unclaimed Experience: Trauma Narrative and History*. Baltimore, MD: Johns Hopkins University Press.

Cixous, H. (1976). *The laugh of the Medusa*, trans. K. Cohen & P. Cohen. *Signs*, 1(4):875–893.

Corbett, K. (1993). The mystery of homosexuality. *Psychoanalytic Psychology*, 10:345–357.

Corbett, K. (2009a). *Boyhoods*. New Haven, CT: Yale University Press.

Corbett, K. (2009b). Boyhood femininity, gender identity disorder, masculine presup-positions, and the anxiety of regulation. *Psychoanalytic Dialogues*, 19(4):353–370.

Dimen, M., & Goldner, V. (2011). Gender and sexuality. In: G. O. Gabbard, B. E. Litowitz, & P. Williams. (eds.). *The American Psychiatric Publishing Textbook of Psychoanalysis*, 2nd edition. Washington, DC: American Psychiatric Publishing, 133–152.

Dimen, M. (2014). Both given and made: Commentary on Saketopoulou. *Journal of the American Psychoanalytic Association*, 62(5):807–813.

Goldner, V. (1991). Towards a critical relational theory of gender. *Psychoanalytic Dialogues*, 1:249–272.

Goldner, V. (2011). Trans: Gender in free fall. *Psychoanalytic Dialogues* 21:159–171.

Gozlan, O. (2015). *Transsexuality and the Art of Transitioning: A Lacanian Approach.* New York, NY: Routledge.

Hansbury, G. (2017). The masculine vaginal: Working with queer men's embodiment at the transgender edge. *Journal of the American Psychoanalytic Association*, 65(6):1009–1031.

Harris, A. (1991). Gender as contradiction. *Psychoanalytic Dialogues*, 1:197–224.

Harris, A. (2000). Gender as a soft assembly: Tomboys' stories. *Studies in Gender and Sexuality*, 1(3):223–250.

Harris, A. (2011a). Gender as a strange attractor: Discussion of the transgender symposium. *Psychoanalytic Dialogues*, 21:230–238.

Harris, A. (2011b). "My gender is tender." *DIVISION/Review*, 3:38–40.

Lemma, A. (2012). Research off the couch: Re-visiting the transsexual conundrum. *Psychoanalytic Psychotherapy*, 26(4):263–281.

Lemma, A. (2013). The body one has and the body one is: Understanding the transsexual's need to be seen. *International Journal of Psychoanalysis*, 94(2):277–292.

Meltzer, D. (1975). Adhesive identification. *Contemporary Psycho-Analysis*, 11:289–310.

Quinodoz, D. (1998). A fe/male transsexual patient in psychoanalysis. *International Journal of Psychoanalysis*, 79:95–111.

Quinodoz, D. (2002). Termination of a fe/Male transsexual patient's analysis: An example of general validity. *International Journal of Psychoanalysis*, 83:783–798.

Saketopoulou, A. (2011). Queer children, new objects; The place of futurity in Loewald's thinking. *DIVISION/Review*, 1:38–39.

Saketopoulou, A. (2014). Mourning the body as bedrock: Developmental considerations in treating transsexual patients analytically. *Journal of the American Psychoanalytic Association*, 62:773–806.

11 Rethinking sexual and gender diversity

Some psychoanalytic reflections

Laura Balottin and Davide Bruno

We will explore the theme of gender diversity and sexual orientation starting from group thinking. How to build a new space open to dialogue and the experience of multiplicity and inclusivity? Transgender and non-binary patients consult therapists more frequently than in the past and raise important questions to which all human beings – psychoanalysts included – are confronted, concerning identity, including professional identities, social belonging and stigma. A psychoanalyst explores her countertransference reactions during the treatment of an adolescent with gender issues in the discussion in a working group of colleagues. A deep understanding of the countertransference issues implied in those treatments may help avoid reproducing stigmatising dynamics conveyed by psychoanalytical theories which risk equating transness to psychotic structure. Patients' fear of being stigmatised by society might occur alongside analysts' fear of not being considered sufficiently "orthodox" towards reference theories by psychoanalytic societies. However, an open dialogue amongst colleagues, as experienced in our working group, may help to access a third – a "trans" space, a liminal, transitional space in which gender become playable and new creative thoughts may arise.

Our reflections arise from an intervision group on gender. As a group of IPA candidates, we made a submission for the 2021 First Tiresias Award of the IPA Committee on Sexual and Gender Diversity Studies. At that time, the COVID-19 pandemic had led to government decisions that imposed isolation, so that usual social exchanges amongst individuals were precluded, and training necessarily took place remotely. Our question as candidates and individuals was: How to get out of this condition of isolation and helplessness? Reflecting together, albeit remotely, on a challenging study theme seemed a good opportunity to reactivate connections and thought. Our group spontaneously formed around this project. The participants were all candidates, but differed in multiple aspects including gender, geographical origin, preferences related to theoretical orientation, and profession (medical doctors versus psychologist), just to name a few.

The starting point of our work was linked to two different considerations. First, there was the institutional mandate to rethink issues related

DOI: 10.4324/9781003534440-17

to gender and sexual orientation from a perspective free from biases associated with stigmatising and violent positions. Moreover, our reflections emerged along the way, while "classic" readings of the clinical material we had begun to share seemed reductive as they appeared not to capture the complexity of the experiences lived by the patient–therapist couple. If, on the one hand, it seemed vital to "come out" of the isolation linked to COVID, on the other hand, and in parallel, it seemed increasingly essential to find paths that expanded our vision.

Adopting a constructivist perspective, we tried to deconstruct some equivalences that transcendentally linked sexual orientation and gender identity to given psychological categories and mechanisms. For example, is homosexuality *a priori* linked to a deficit in psychosexual development (Bergler, 1959) or to a personality disorder (Bergler, 1944)? Some aspects related to gender incongruence, as currently defined in the ICD 11, can always be convincingly explained by psychotic defence mechanisms (Greenson, 1966). Can sexual reassignment, made possible by current bio-medical technologies, be conceived otherwise than as an expression of infantile omnipotence that refers to undifferentiated aspects (Stoller, 1968). Unfortunately, some of these positions were at times widely spread in our Italian Psychoanalytic Societies. However, we became deeply aware that these positions not only risk stigmatising patients but also analysts who belong to gender or sexual minorities (Saketopoulou, 2020). As Bruce Levin (2018) reminded us, analysts belong to different social and cultural groups, different sexes, and genders, they are heterosexual and gay, liberal, conservative, and everything in between these polarities, just like their patients. This certainly represents one of the resources of psychoanalytic societies that engage with our plural contemporary societies. Stigma concerns not only the field of human rights but also fundamental epistemological assumptions. Regarding certain phenomena, what is my position as an observer? The perspective from which things are viewed inevitably influences our judgement of them. Thus, as Fausto Petrella (1993) would repeat during his lectures, recalling Heisenberg's uncertainty principle in physics, it is necessary to constantly question our position as therapists, because this can only enrich the search for the meaning we give to things as psychoanalysts. This issue also opens up ethical and scientific reflections concerning the responsibility inherent to the representation that care disciplines give to sexual and gender variations.

Some cultures recognise supernumerary genders, such as *winkte* amongst the Sioux. Some societies in fact seem to show a flexible approach to gender identity, which is conceived as multiple, differently from the fixity observed instead in Western societies, rooted in the Judeo-Christian heritage (Davis, 1998). Identity issues are therefore conceived differently by human beings, depending on the context in which they live, so much so that in some cases culture allows for the social expression of multiple identifications that vary over time. It can therefore be hypothesised that identification processes are not only multiple but also follow different destinies and vary in time and expressiveness. In this sense, the male/female dichotomy, normal/pathological would appear inadequate in accounting for such aspects, which have to do with the complexity of the human being in relation to oneself and the world.

In rethinking clinical material as a group, we often found ourselves questioning, disoriented, not only about the identifications of the patients but also about our own as therapists. This continuous questioning driven by transference and countertransference movements, in a broad sense, not only represents the gold of our discipline and the foundation of learning from experience but also the antidote to the temptation to solve gender issues in a dogmatic and judgemental way. Many possible biases may interfere in the analytic relationship when gender-related issues are at play since they are a potential source of deep anxiety not only for the patient but for the therapist as well. However, the analyst's anxiety should be illuminated by a beam of more intense darkness, to quote Grotstein (2007). There are things we still do not know, such as why many adolescents today are non-defining, fluid or non-binary in relation to gender. Such statements seem to reproduce the game of identity search as opposed to what previous generations have been able to elaborate (Drescher, 2021).

Our intervision group discussed the two cases presented in the Tiresias paper within different workgroups linked to seminars, conferences, and supervisions. We have kept the pronouns the patients used about themselves at different stages of their lives. Every reference that is not indispensable for understanding the case has been changed for deontological reasons and the patient's privacy.

Alex (LB)

In the first case, the analyst described the delicate trials of the five-year-long analysis of Alex, an adolescent who was brought to therapy by his parents for an initial problem characterised by inhibition and social phobia. The patient's search for himself went through the process of constructing a narrative of precocious marginalisation and violence he suffered, leaving space, through therapeutic progress, for the emergence of a vital desire that eventually led him to have his first sexual relations. In the last period, the patient's identity issues were presented in terms of gender. They declared to their psychoanalyst their will to be "neutral". The analyst found herself at crucial juncture points of their work, dealing with intense and complex countertransference feelings concerning her patient's communications of their identity issues, which changed within the discourse on gender.

Luca: in search of a possible connection (DB)

The second case was that of the psychoanalytic therapy of Luca, a 30-year-old patient who had undergone sexual reassignment surgery female-to-male, some time before his meeting with the therapist. We report here a brief vignette of this last case as an example and will try to show how the questions of identity posed confront all human beings, psychoanalysts included. Through the group discussion we explored the "live", intense unconscious movements that such a complex topic evokes.

I met Luca at an outpatient psychology service, where he had already been treated in the past. When he entered my office room, he sat and began telling me about a persistent anxiety and cannabis addiction. He told me he had come to Turin at eighteen, having dreamt about living in a city in northern Italy. After graduating at the classical high school with the highest grades, he had run away from his small town in southern Italy and his middleclass family. His mother was described as fatuous and "chronically depressed", while his father was often away for work and seemed particularly angry.

Before I met him, I read his medical records: his dead name as a girl had been erased to make it unreadable. Ten years prior to my session, the evaluation signalled nervous anorexia, for which she was admitted to the eating disorders ward. After the hospitalisation, she had been discharged as the psychological service did not have "the resources to treat eating disorders". The patient had returned to the service three years later, asking to be readmitted due to a sense of fragmented identity, a chronic feeling of emptiness, cannabis abuse and impulse control disorders, all of which had brought suicidal episodes – through drug ingestion and severe self-harm – where she had felt as if she were "crumbling to pieces". Her work curriculum was suspended with switches from one profession to another, for which she was progressively facing poverty and marginalisation. Likewise, she had trouble establishing stable emotional relationships for fear of disappointing herself and others. When, during her adolescence, she had revealed to her family that she was attracted to girls, she was literally kicked out, experiencing angry feelings of disappointment and guilt stemming from the rejection of her diversity by her family and socio-cultural context of her origin.

In her endless quest for acceptance, Luca by then had developed a more appropriate wording to convey her symptomatology, partly because of her nursing studies. This time around, when she returned to the service, she wasn't rejected but instead taken in and offered psychotherapeutic sessions along with a psychopharmacological therapy to lessen anxiety and inability to resist impulses. During the years of therapy, she met a university colleague with whom she began a relationship, in which, however, issues of rejection were repeated once again by the girlfriend's parents who disavowed their relationship. In a play where the backdrop was constant disconnections in her family and work, Luca was able to lean on the only continuity she had: psychotherapy at the service which, by now, had been going on for several years, and the emotional relationship with her companion. Thanks to the support, the patient autonomously decided to undergo sexual reassignment surgery, during which she stopped her usual sessions at the psychological service, followed by a gender identity service.

Luca returned to the service after years, during which he had managed to find stable employment as a nurse. The reason for his return stemmed from a state of profound demoralisation following his return to his small town for the funeral of his father, whom he had not seen since he was kicked out. The very brief return to his hometown put him in touch with ambivalence towards his father and with the rejection from family members who had never accepted his journey regarding his gender identity, to the point of not even wanting to hear about it.

Even though the clinical staff had assigned Luca's case to me knowing about my interest in anthropological studies on gender, I had at the time, very little practical experience with transgender individuals. During our first meeting, Luca did not tell me about his transition path, nor did he for a long time. Nevertheless, I immediately thought of which theories or experiences I could rely on to approach the case. Fundamentally, I was wondering if it wouldn't have been better for him to be assigned to another therapist, a phantasy which had to do with expulsive ideas towards a patient who didn't fit the "norm". Such a phantasy was uncanny: it didn't match with the idea my colleagues and I had of myself as a therapist who was curious and open-minded. My own professional identity was put into question through two openly opposing images. I was ashamed: I had always thought of myself as being free of prejudice, I had even fought for LGBTQ+ rights when I was younger; how could I consider Luca as an inconvenient case, inasmuch as to reject him?

After several months since the beginning of our therapy, Luca decided to tell me about his sex change: "It's easier this way" he said. I asked if he thought this could be a new beginning, a space where this subject could be avoided. He laconically answered: "It's not that, I just can't go telling everyone about my business". He then asked me, in detail, about borderline personality disorder, which was part of his first diagnosis and what my thoughts were on the matter, as if he had never received any explanation on that regard. I answered that if this diagnosis was true for him, then he was "in the right place", as if to tell him that maybe the desire he was trying to communicate was to have a place for himself in an environment usually marked by rejections. Through his request for my acknowledgment of this psychopathological diagnosis, wasn't Luca asking me to acknowledge his gender identity without me "kicking him out" as his family had done the first time that he had told them? Wasn't he asking me to give a fundamental recognition, having felt unrecognised and rejected, from a mother who couldn't take care of him and a violent and excessively work-driven father? These non-acknowledgments seemed to have been progressively amplifying one another, and constantly referring to other rejections, in a "disconnection" spiral. However, the patient's recognition could only come from my acknowledging the dynamics that were at play in my countertransference. Hadn't I too, during our first meeting, felt disoriented, missing a secure base I could lean on in terms of previous experience and theory on the issues presented? Hadn't I too, through projective identification, felt as if I were "put in a corner", and "disconnected" between two different images I had of myself professionally? I had to recognise within myself, the role prejudice played in considering an "un-usual" patient, on the cultural countertransference which links back to the compliance with an ideal and culturally determined model of the ego-ideal (Devereux, 1967; Glocer Fiorini, 2020)? Hadn't I felt ashamed, because of my life story, for the expulsive feelings towards my patient? As Drescher (2015) states, shame, which Luca himself must have felt on several occasions, is one of the feelings that are most strongly tied to the social control of sexuality, sexual orientation and gender identity.

Only through these steps was it possible to create a place within me to welcome Luca, which he was asking me for. This new space created was not already given in a pre-established way, it was neither against nor collusive ("if this diagnosis is true"); it was an open-minded place where the two of us could finally meet. The main theme brought by the patient seemed to have to do with the primary rejection and with the dilemma of recognition and continuity of psychic and bodily aspects. From a certain point of view, could it not perhaps be said that Luca not only proposed, in his compulsion to repeat the caesuras that characterised his life, to fill again an experiential void through compulsive repetition, but that he also desperately desired a welcome and greater continuity and correspondence between the parts of his psychic self and bodily self, perceived *ab ovo* as excessively fragmented and incongruent?

Opening minds, finding intersections: group discussion of clinical material

Luca's therapist, just like Alex's one, discussed the case first with the intervision group, then in seminars and conferences. Both analysts found themselves, at crucial juncture points of their work, dealing with intense and disturbing countertransference feelings. These concerned the patient's communications of their identity issues, declined within the discourse on gender. The category of gender, which falls within cultural productions, is subject more than others to phenomena of social control, exercised through value judgements that pass, in our Western societies, through a heteronormative and dichotomous vision which, like a stage backdrop, supports the play of possible identifications, roles which are played by different actors who find themselves playing their specific part. Within this dichotomous vision, not only the characters of the patient's intrapsychic world but patient and therapist themselves are at risk of being "crushed" into a two-dimensional perspective, which corresponds to the law of excluded middle: *tertium non datur*. The discourse on gender is "good to think", according to a famous phrase by Lévi-Strauss, because it puts this construct in crisis, forcing the therapist to deal with their own theories of reference and putting back into play the affiliations of the analytic couple, as well as social belonging.

In Luca's case for example, the therapist felt a discrepancy between two different self-images: one of an "open-minded" therapist and the other, generated instead by a phenomenon of internalised transphobia, which reproduced the societal discourse on gender through enculturation processes. The awareness of the emergence of these two different mismatched images reflected the patient's experience, allowing the therapist to get in touch with it and not reproduce the dynamics of rejection the patient had previously experienced. The work of the intervision group allowed the therapist to acknowledge the feeling of shame due to his own expectations towards a patient who did not fit within the "norm". Recognising the possible reproduction of social prejudices within the therapeutic relationship made it possible to break the chain of shame that the patient felt for his sexual orientation and gender nonconformity, which was also expressed in attacking his body with a restrictive diet and self-harm. Probably like every patient in psychotherapy and in analysis, Luca needed "a respectful listening" (Nissim Momigliano, 2001).

At the end of the therapy, years later, Luca showed a more cohesive self, certainly from a long therapy but one could hypothesise that the gender reassignment course at a specialised centre may have contributed to this outcome: it certainly allowed the gender discourse to enter Luca's therapy and become "playable". A positive outcome of a gender reassignment – where it accompanied a restoration of mutuality between mental and bodily experience – shows us how it may be necessary to alter the physical body to promote a change, even on the internal level (Suchet, 2011). The subject could finally begin to feel like themselves in the body in which they lived: overturning another corroborated psychoanalytic rhetoric that contrasts thought with action. In short, it may be necessary to act in order to symbolise (Roussillon, 2008). Conversely, with these patients especially but ultimately with all our patients, it is up to us, as psychoanalysts, to accept that perhaps only a *posteriori* can we understand which of many efforts are in the direction of becoming an authentic subject.

The choice to present the same clinical material in different group settings could be compared to the situation described by Bollas (2009) in which, if the analyst were to ask the patient to present the same dream at every new session, evoking each time the associations that the dream elicits, he would realise that that single dream leads to new meanings each time and constantly opens up new ways of thought. This group experience stimulated further reflection in the original intervision group. We generally observed that from initially polarised positions, we usually reached positions of greater dialogue and integration. This primarily concerned the original workgroup itself, where we initially witnessed a violent dichotomous opposition of positions. The group seemed to be split into two parts. One of those used a more "classic" psychoanalytic theory that was felt, however, by the other side of the group as an imposition, sometimes stigmatising, regarding the experience of the patients, bringing to mind the cornerstone concept of medical education *"primum non nocere"*. On the other side, acceptance and welcoming were perceived as a "prejudice" and an ideological position ("disease of acceptance") that ultimately led to the prohibition of thinking critically (against fashion). On the other hand, perhaps even thinking about the coincidence between biological sex and gender can be considered an ideology, moreover, not subject to criticism as such.

Another defence mechanism that was put into play in the work and discussion groups was the denial/refusal of the existence of a specific issue around gender, reducing it to existential and more familiar categories in psychoanalytic theory (e.g., unnamed terror and narcissistic pathology). This caused extreme confusion amongst the presenters. Discussing our emotional response to the groups' prompts, however, led us to think that the denial of the trans issue as specific may reproduce the broader social phenomenon of denying trans identity with the opposing movement of the renegade group's angry assertion. This phenomenon, which at its extremes can manifest in censorious or even violent interventions by the authority of "silencing" unacceptable or "annoying" content, probably originates from the same unconscious movements that elicited the initial reaction of rejection that both therapists experienced towards their trans patients (Balottin et al., 2022).

Criticism within the psychoanalytic movement itself is emerging, thanks in part to the IPA's Committee on Sexual and Gender Differences Studies. This criticism draws on interdisciplinary contributions concerning the history of psychoanalysis, gender studies, cultural anthropology, and the feminist movement. In this regard, on 29 June 2022, the Finnish Psychoanalytic Association issued a public apology:

> … for all views expressed within its sphere of influence, which have contributed to individuals belonging to sexual and gender minorities being stigmatised as diseased, disturbed, developmentally challenged or in any other way abnormal, based on their sexual orientation or gender diversity. This apology is addressed to all those individuals for whom these views have caused suffering and harm. It is especially justified to apologise for harmful treatments based on these pathologizing theories.

This statement as reported by the President during the 2022 European Federation of Psychoanalysis conference in Vienna arose after a long period of research and reflection in the field.

The complexity of the themes presented by patients regarding gender suggests the need to open the therapeutic space to multiple interpretations, which can allow the patient to understand and appropriate their own narrative. To this end, the creation of a third space that opens the field to dialogue and allows the overcoming of narcissistic barriers appears fundamental. The disturbing questions about identity posed by transgender patients resonate in therapists not only regarding issues related to their own personal identity but also regarding their professional identity: Could the fear of stigmatising patients also manifest in the therapist as a fear of not being considered sufficiently "orthodox" regarding reference theories? The work of the psychoanalyst deals with what is not yet known and emerges gradually, while not exempt from the emergence of a certain anxiety (Bion, 1967): in this sense, these occasions of open and non-judgemental dialogue amongst colleagues appear fundamental in trying to access new and creative thinking.

References

Balottin, L., Bruno, D., Caslini, E., Pistarino, D. J. (2022). Ripensare il genere insieme ai pazienti gender-fluid. Due casi riletti a partire dalla discussione in gruppo. *Report presented at XX S.P.I. Congress*, Naples, 26–29 May 2022.

Bergler, E. (1959). *One thousand homosexuals: Conspiracy of silence, or curing and deglamorizing homosexuals?* Paterson, NJ: Pageant Books.

Bergler, E. (1944). Eight prerequisites for the psychoanalytic treatment of homosexuality. *Psychoanalytic Review*, 31:253–286.

Bollas, C. (2009). The wisdom of the dream, psychoanalysis in Europe. *EPF Bulletin*, 63:24–34.

Bion, W. (1967). Notes on memory and desire. *The Psychoanalytic Forum*, 2(3):272–273, 279–280.

Davis, L. D. (1998). The sexual and gender identity disorders. *Transcultural Psychiatry*, 35(3):401–412.

Devereux, G. (1967). *De l'angoisse à la méthode dans les sciences du comportement*. Paris: Flammarion, 1980.

Drescher, J. (2015). Gender policing in the clinical setting. Discussion of Sandra Silverman's "The colonized mind: Gender, trauma and mentalization". *Psychoanalytic Dialogues*, 25(1):67–76.

Drescher, J. (3 December 2021). *IPA Webinar*: Rainbow Families. www.ipa.world

Fiorini, L. G. (2020). *Psicosessualità e genere: intersezioni. É possibile una prospettiva di genere nella psicoanalisi?* [*Psychosexuality and gender: Is a gender perspective possible in psychoanalysis*]. Tr. ita by Maria Teresa Martin Laguna. *Rivista di Psicoanalisi*, 1:193–207.

Greenson, R. R. (1966). A transvestite boy and a hypothesis. *International Journal of Psycho-Analysis*, 47(2–3):396–403.

Grotstein, J. S. (2007). *A Beam of Intense darkness. Wilfred Bion's Legacy to Psychoanalysis*. London: Karnac Books.

Levin, B. (23 April 2018). The Best-Kept Psychotherapy Secrets. How to Get Help with Today'S "Problems of Living". *Psychology Today*. https://www.psychologytoday.com/au/blog/psychoanalysis-unplugged/201804/the-best-kept-psychotherapy-secrets

Nissim Momigliano L. (2001). *L'ascolto rispettoso. Scritti psicoanalitici*. Milano: Raffaello Cortina Editore.

Petrella, F. (1993). *Turbamenti Affettivi e alterazioni dell'esperienza*. Milano: Raffaello Cortina Editore.

Roussillon, R. (2008). *La réorganisation de la symbolisation à l'adolescence*. In: R. Roussillon, *Le transitionnel, le sexuel et la réflexivité*. Paris, Dunod.

Saketopoulou, A. (2020). Thinking psychoanalytically, thinking better: reflections on transgender. *International Journal of Psycho-Analysis*, 101(5):1019–1030.

Stoller, R. J. (1968). A further contribution to the study of gender identity. *International Journal of Psycho-Analysis*, 49:364–368.

Suchet, M. (2011). Crossing over. *Psychoanalytic Dialogues*, 21:172–191.

Index

Note: Page numbers followed by "n" refer to end notes.

For Product Safety Concerns and Information please contact our EU
representative GPSR@taylorandfrancis.com
Taylor & Francis Verlag GmbH, Kaufingerstraße 24, 80331 München, Germany

www.ingramcontent.com/pod-product-compliance
Lightning Source LLC
Chambersburg PA
CBHW070341270326
41926CB00017B/3934